The Secret of the Century

A novel by

Roger Levine

ISBN: 0-7596-6219-3 (e-book)
ISBN: 0-7596-6220-7 (Paperback)
ISBN: 0-7596-6221-5 (RocketBook)

This book is printed on acid free paper.

1stBooks - rev. 07/03/02

This book is lovingly dedicated to my mother, Miriam, who gave me her love of history and to my father, Emanuel, who passed on his skills with language and logic; to the memory of my grandfather, Jacob Levine, who first told me the tales of the "U-Krayeen" and to the memory of John F. Kennedy and what might have been.

I.

The Setting

I wasn't always in the government witness protection program. Certainly not on that sunny Dallas morning in November of '63 when my grandfather took me down to Dealey Plaza to see the President. Poppa stood on an elevated step to boost his tiny frame and braced himself against his secretary Marilyn to steady the movie camera. I held Marilyn's hand and clutched a little Instamatic camera in my other hand. The crowd started buzzing as the head of the motorcade turned off Main Street and onto Houston. I caught a glimpse of pink as I recognized the familiar form of Jackie Kennedy waving in the distance, and then disappearing from view. The motorcade slowed for the wide turn that would bring the President down Elm Street past the School Book Depository Building where Poppa and I were waiting to see him.

The crowd started clapping wildly as the limousine emerged from the turn. *There he was!* Bronzed, handsome, like a god. My heart beat madly, adrenaline pumping on all cylinders. Poppa braced his movie camera as the President rolled down Elm and waved in our direction. I thought I was going to pee my pants.

Pop! Pop! A firecracker went off and then another. The President clutched his throat and rolled toward Jackie. Poppa jerked with each blast as he kept his finger on the Bell & Howell. I turned as I heard a crack to my right. I saw a man poke a gun over the top of a fence and blow the head off the President of the United States.

The velvety tongue slid lovingly down the shaft, the soft blond curls moving slowly in rhythmical splendor. *Oh, that shaft. That famous elongated quiver of delight. How many women had there been? Two thousand? Twenty-five hundred?* He had lost count somewhere over 1500, but for sure there must have been over 500 since then. The constraints of marriage had slowed things considerably, but the rigors of political travel insured that the shaft would be exercised religiously. A vigorous workout three times a week. Isn't that what the doctor had said? Yes, great *vigor*, indeed.

The warm sucking lips had completely engulfed the golden prod, the soft hanging orbs dangling pendulously in slow motion from above, brushing lightly against his aching loins, now perched on the edge of sweet release. It should have been a moment of uninterrupted, unmitigated bliss. After all, how often did one get nominated to be the presidential candidate of a major American political party? The nimble tongue continued working its moist wonderful magic, spreading paroxysms of delight in its wake. The moaning grew louder. "And so, my fellow Americans (Ooh, God!), ask not what your President can do for you, but (OOOOH, slurp, slurp) what you can do for your President."

The grainy film danced majestically against the hotel wall, but the nominee had seen enough.

"I think, ah, Edgar, we get the point."

The stolid Director ambled slowly to the projection machine and switched off the motor, sparing the exhausted brothers the anti-climax of the climax.

"This is OUTRAGEOUS! It's nothing but blackmail, that's all it is," screeched the shorter one.

"Calm down, Bobby. I think, ah, gentlemen, we are all in agreement as to what it is. The only thing we are negotiating is the price. Am I not right, Mr. Hoover?"

The impassive figure stared blankly back at the Golden Boy and savored this moment of clandestine triumph. It would not be the last.

"It's not money that I seek, Mr. Kennedy."

Not money? Impossible! What could the crusty old fuck want? Women? Did he want the keys to the Augean stable of sensual delights that lay in the grasp of the Senator's beck and call? *I thought the old cocksucker was gay. Surely he doesn't think I can be of any use to him there. What does he mean not money?* The candidate's bewildered gaze was brought back from the ceiling by the riveted icy stare of his antagonist.

"Then what is it, might I ask, Mr. Director, that you do want?"

"I want you to nominate Lyndon Johnson as your vice president."

"IMPOSSIBLE!," bellowed the younger brother, as he moved menacingly toward the rock-like presence and then swiftly brushed by, continuing on to a corner of the room, as if to protect himself from his own anger. He wheeled back on his heels and began shaking his fist at the monolith across the room.

"Who the fuck are you to dictate to us who we can and can't nominate for anything we goddamn please? Where the hell do you get off telling the NEXT PRESIDENT OF THE UNITED STATES what to do? Huh?" A silence. The anger rippled under Bobby's boiling red skin, the veins in both temples visibly pounding. "Well, answer me, you fucking pervert!"

The block of ice stared back at the slumping candidate and rolled his eyeballs as if to say, "Can't you control this untoward youth?" The Senator half-grinned back.

"Bobby, let's not be too quick in our judgment. Let's see if we can give Mr. Hoover the benefit of the doubt. I must say though, Edgar, it does seem a rather strange request. Would you mind if I inquired as to why?"

The master of the monotone shifted slowly on his haunches. "That, Mr. Kennedy, is for me to know and you to find out."

Bobby lost it. "I can't believe you're going to let him get away with this horseshit, Jack. I mean, is this what we worked so hard for?"

The nominee drew a slash across his mouth with his left hand and indicated with his waggling right index finger that he had had enough of his emotional sibling's outbursts.

"But, Jesus, Jack, it's just that..."

"Can it Bobby, NOW." He then turned his frosty blue-gray eyes back to Hoover.

"And suppose we do as you ask. What then?"

"Then, Mr. Kennedy, you have to win the election or the whole thing is moot. But if you should be so fortunate to prevail, then you would be assured of my complete cooperation and discretion during the course of your presidency."

"How generous of you," snorted the nominee. The Director bristled at the Senator's sarcasm.

"And if we should not choose to follow your sage advice?"

"That, Senator," shot back the sawed-off stump of a man, as he started packing up the projector, "is your decision. Which, if you could let me know in the next six hours, would be appreciated." With that, the shadowy presence moved slowly toward the door, and opening it a crack, looked back at the newly compliant duo.

"I bid you *adieu*, gentlemen," he whispered, as he slithered out into the hallway. The brothers fixed their discomfited gazes upon the shutting door.

"He can't get away with this," yelled a seething Bobby, as he crossed back through the room and over to the window. Jack sat at the edge of the bed, chin resting on clenched fist.

"Oh, he can, and he will; I can assure you of that."

The crestfallen Robert slunk back to the bed where his brother was sitting, and pulling a chair across from it, slumped down like a decompressing bean-bag. Jack just shook his head, which was now nestled in his cupped hands.

"But all we've worked for, Jack. *Lyndon Johnson? That snake-in-the-grass?* I'd sooner nominate Mamie Eisenhower."

The candidate chuckled. He was quickly adapting to his newly compromised position.

"Think about it, Bobby. Maybe it won't be so bad. After all, it'll balance the ticket geographically and ideologically."

"Ideologically? Johnson has no ideology!"

"Yes, but neither do we." Hmm. Good point.

A knock on the door. UPI was by for an earlier promised picture. The two brothers hung their heads low in mulled silence, as the photographer snapped away and caught the hauntingly eerie scene of the practically touching foreheads, for eternity. If only the public could know what was currently transpiring in those weighted-down frontal lobes. The cameraman thanked them for their time and made a quick exit. The soon-to-be President mused.

"You know Bobby, I could make you Attorney General. You'd be the old slimeball's boss." Jack chuckled to himself.

"You can't do a thing like that. Congress would have a shit fit."

"I know," mumbled the candidate. "Just a thought." He could never pull it off. But it would sure be nice to have somebody he could trust in the Cabinet. Of course, he'd have to get elected first.

The Senator lay back on the bed and felt the full pounding of his eternally aching spine pulsing through his entire upper torso. He was exhausted. *"Lyndon Fucking Johnson,"* he kept mumbling to himself. *Of all people, why Johnson? What did Hoover have to gain from it?*

"Maybe he thinks he can control Johnson and through that, can control us," speculated a now calming Bobby.

"And maybe," responded the pondering political master, "he isn't wrong about that." He smiled to himself. The eyes of Texas are upon you.

Texas. I hate fucking Texas. If I never have to go to Texas again, it'll be all too soon. The goddamned place is cursed. And now its favorite son was to be thrust upon them, festooned like a fatted pig to their steamrollering express, to be dragged across the political landscape of America like a festering boil, to be tolerated and endured. Ominous, thought the future progenitor of Camelot, but also equally necessary. Of that he was certain.

Bobby sat dour in the chair in front of him.

"So Jack?"

"What now, Bobby?," winced the candidate. He was too tired to sit through another outburst, his younger brother's alter ego status notwithstanding.

"How was she?"

Jack stared calmly up at the ceiling and smiled.

"She was great, Bobby. Just great."

The cigarette burned low in his fingers. From a distance he could hear the noise of the crowd picking up, a sure sign that the motorcade was right on schedule. A few more quick turns and they'd be upon him. He crouched lower behind the picket fence.

What was it that the Organization had told him? *Not to worry*, that was it. Everything had been taken care of. A patsy in an overlooking building was all lined up, a rifle had been planted, and even photos had been doctored, incriminating the unsuspecting foil. Not to worry. Just be there and shoot, one shot, maybe two, at point blank range; then duck into the getaway car parked five feet behind, and be gone. The lookout beside him would scoop the shells and quickly follow him into the idling vehicle. By the time anybody knew what happened, they'd be on their way. *Not to worry*, he told his pounding heart.

It wasn't as if he hadn't killed before. Many times, in fact. Coolly, methodically, scientifically, with *panache*. He loved the danger, the excitement, the living on the edge. Which was why they had chosen him to begin with. He was the best. But this was beyond danger. If gunning down the president of the country in broad daylight, downtown in one of the nation's largest cities wasn't living on the edge, then he wasn't sure what was. Yes, he was the best and that's why he was there. He softly cradled the stock of the leveled rifle and rolled the barrel gently to and fro between two beveled edges of the upright posts. He would engage the picket fence in a little foreplay while waiting for the approaching motorcade, presaging the orgasm of the blast.

And, oh, the money! The contract of a lifetime. Two hundred and fifty thousand dollars for one well-placed bullet, for an eighteenth-second of work. What did that figure per hour? The thought made him giddy.

But there were so many questions. *What about security? What about the Secret Service?* It would be light, he was assured. Ever since the President's trip to the South had been announced several months earlier, details had been meticulously monitored. The motorcade route had been gone over with a fine toothcomb. Security, at this stretch, would not be a problem.

The direction of the bullets? An autopsy report? Details, strictly details. Besides, as the Organization had pointed out, that's our problem, not yours. Let us worry about it. You just be there and shoot, that's all. We'll take care of the logistics. *Okay, fine. That's my specialty, after all. But it's usually pimps and pushers, not presidents.* The rifle started shaking in his tightly gripping hands.

The motorcade came into view and the noise from the crowd ricocheted off the surrounding buildings as the long procession negotiated its final turn. It was just a job, he reminded himself. A very big job, but still a job, just the same. The big limo started the slow descent that would bring it to within fifty feet of the impending blast.

He caught his first glance of the stately, tall President, seated next to his wife, the feel of monarchy expansively emanating from the confining borders of the open-topped vehicle. What a life of achievement this man had had! From war hero to president. Too bad it would have to end so soon, so suddenly. *Just a job, it's just a job.* The dying cigarette hit the ground.

He turned for one last look at the get-away driver. A half grin and thumbs up, the same that he got from the lookout. The President was twenty-five yards from the kill zone. The motorcade was moving at a snail's pace.

He caught the erect bearing in the cross hairs. Right temple, lock on; fifteen, ten, five, NOW! A flick of the index finger.

Click! What the hell? NOTHING; SILENCE. THE GOD DAMN GUN HAD JAMMED! Get the hell out of here, now! A mad scramble to the car, and tear ass out. The getaway was perfect, just like they had planned. Only they forgot to kill the President.

Down on the road below, a beaming Charles DeGaulle moved peacefully by. Now basking in the triumph of his Marseille reception, he would never know how he had come to within a whisper of his death. That twit Kennedy thought the people loved him? *Voila, pretty boy, you are no match for the icy titan!* Visions of Charlemagne filled his surprisingly still-attached head.

Speeding to the distance and safety of the countryside, the failed assassin beat his fists in fury upon the back of the driver's seat. The little Renault bounced rhythmically in response. He had checked the rifle just the day before, and the day before that, as well. No problem. Hair trigger response. Why now of all times? Was it fate? Why would fate want to spare DeGaulle? It was inexplicable, just one of those things. An exceedingly big just one of those things.

The contract of a lifetime, lost in the bat of an eye, a jam of a chamber. Two hundred and fifty thousand dollars, down the tubes, just like that. Would he get a second chance? Not likely. It would be too risky. The Organization would lose trust. No, you only get one shot at the big time. Literally.

But he had done what he could. Hadn't he? He was the best. They had told him so themselves. The driver, the lookout, they knew, they saw it all. They'd defend him. And yet, in spite of the pep talk, the mental bravado, he had failed, plain and simple. It didn't really matter why. Failure was failure.

He would plead for redemption. But with all the months of planning, just for this one brief encounter, what were the odds of it happening again? Pretty damned slim. Well, maybe a different victim, another big shot that the Organization needed to take care of. But who could be bigger than DeGaulle, leader of one of the most powerful nations on earth? There would never be anything as big as this, and even if there was, would the Organization give it to him? Highly unlikely.

He slumped back in his seat, a gray gloom cloud of depression engulfing him. The driver and the lookout tried to cheer him, to no avail. He was inconsolable.

He had pictured the headlines: DEGAULLE SHOT DEAD; WAREHOUSE CLERK HELD. His own private little triumph, a secret of incredible magnitude, to be basked in along with the comforts of 250K. Gone in a heartbeat.

As the crowded Renault bumped along the winding country road, the soft misting rain cleared and a bright powerful rainbow spread in the valley before them. The driver turned and smiled. "It is a sign of fortune, of good things to come; you shall see."

Rainbows? Fortune? I don't think so. One crack at the big time, one shot at the show. Right? The darkness quickly descended.

Everything about Lyndon Johnson was larger than life. His ears, his nose, his ego, his energy, his ambition. No question about it, he was larger-than-life Lyndon.

Johnson had taken that energy and used it to bounce out of the hills of southwest Texas into the U.S. Congress. He hitched his star to the New Deal of FDR who had taken a liking to this exceptional young man. After several years in the House, Lyndon ran for the Senate in 1940 against savvy Texas Governor, Coke Stevenson. Despite having won a solid and published victory, Lyndon watched the election mysteriously snatched away from him in a major heist, outrageous even by Texas standards. Licking his wounds, Lyndon prepared for the 1948 race, and this time he was not a man to be fucked with. Recruiting the tombstones of scores of departed Mexicans, he won a smashing victory of 87 votes, earning him the sobriquet "Landslide Lyndon."

Ole Landslide took the Senate by storm and under the guidance of fellow Texan and House Speaker, Sam Rayburn, forged connections and alliances that would take him to Majority Leader.

Lyndon ate, breathed and slept politics. Armed with a phone in each hand, cartons of cigarettes and cases of Cutty Sark, he was a whirlwind of activity. Wheedling, cajoling, entreating, Lyndon was a horse trader nonpareil. Politics was his mistress and Lyndon would smear his oversized body with oil and roll around naked on the Senate floor with her, immersing and consuming this passionate lady through every pore in his being.

Lyndon loved the Senate, loved every little thing about it. Except for The Boy. The Boy stuck in his craw.

The Boy had an easy grace about him that Lyndon, with all his furious energy, could never match. The Boy got laid. Regularly. With different women. Scores of them. The Boy was a nonentity, but somehow, he managed to stay above the fray. The Boy was usually absent, and when he was there, he might as well not have been.

Lyndon didn't understand why The Boy existed, and much less, what he was doing in the Senate. The Boy had national aspirations, or at least his father did, and Lyndon decided that The Boy must be a test of God's will on earth for him. Yes, indeed, that must be why The Boy existed, and Ole Landslide was never one to walk away from a challenge.

But Lyndon was no match for The Boy's charm or his daddy's money, and slowed by a heart attack, Johnson was forced to concede ignominious defeat at the 1960 convention. Things looked pretty bleak for Lyndon, what with The Boy ascending and all, and his own future uncertain. It wasn't that The Boy didn't like Lyndon; it was just that the two were totally different and The Boy had never had any need for him. Until now.

In a strange twist of fate, The Boy had decided that Ole Lyndon would be the perfect man to balance the ticket, philosophically and geographically. Despite knowing his ancient fellow Texan, John Nance Garner's maxim, that the vice presidency wasn't worth "a warm pitcher of spit," Lyndon said he would consider the offer; he just needed time to think about it. After three or four minutes, longer than the introspective Johnson usually took on such matters, he accepted. Lyndon figured that one in every four presidents had died in office, and even though The Boy was only 43, you never knew. He'd take the odds.

The deal was done. Lyndon sat in his hotel outside the convention and relaxed, for the first time in ages. He loosened his tie, took off his shoes, put his feet up on the table and sipped his Cutty Sark. No phone was attached to his ear. Perhaps there was something to this acceptance of fate, after all.

Lyndon had started slipping into a blissful dream when he heard a loud rapping at the door. *What could this rude interruption be at such a moment of peace?* He got up, slowly walked across the room, and opened the door a crack. There he was. The Boy's little brother. The Infant. The Infant was full of fury as he pushed his way into the room. *Who did this impudent little bastard think he was?*

The Infant paced back and forth and without warning blurted out, "My brother wants you off the ticket, now!" Lyndon could hardly believe his gargantuan ears. Wasn't it less than twenty-four hours ago that The Boy had asked him on to the ticket, invited him of his own free will? No, this would not do. The Infant just did not compute.

The Infant demanded, The Infant bellowed, The Infant threatened, The Infant was inconsolable. Lyndon watched in amazement, and though repulsed by him, decided that The Infant was more of a kindred soul than The Boy would ever be. But Lyndon had not gotten to be where he was by being bullied by petty tyrants or their self-appointed emissaries. If The Boy wanted him off the ticket, then The Boy would have to tell him himself. Lyndon made this quite clear to The Infant as the latter stomped out of the room. The call never came.

And so it was that Lyndon, The Boy and The Infant joined forces in the summer of 1960 for a bumpy voyage that would change the course of history.

The first time I heard the name John Kennedy, I was flipping the AM band, searching for the Cardinal game. It was a hot night in the summer of 1960 as I sat in the screened porch of our Levittown style house on the outskirts of Dallas. Levitt, the postwar builder, had made a fortune turning out cookie-cutter homes across America's big cities for the returning GI's.

My Cardinals would not win the race against the Pirates that summer; they were still half a decade away from their glory days. Though the Cards were two states over from us and not nearly as close as the Kansas City Athletics, no self-respecting baseball fan could root for that Yankee farm club. Who would have thought that the A's, those floundering bozos, would win three consecutive World Series barely a decade later, although it took an escape to Oakland to do it. Dad loved the Cardinals and baseball in that order and I had inherited those loves from him.

But something about this thing I found on the radio made me abandon the nightly search for my heroes. There was noise and cheering, the pounding of a gavel and some man yelling over and over again, "Mr. Chairman!, Mr. Chairman!" They were trying to quiet the crowd to take something called a roll call.

I heard the names Lyndon Johnson and Hubert Humphrey, names I had never heard before. I heard the name Adlai Stevenson. Him I had heard of. But mostly I heard the name John Kennedy over and over again, with booming cheers following every mention of it.

As "Mr. Chairman" spoke, each state would proudly cast its votes for the next President of the United States. I didn't understand how all four men could be the next President of the United States, but being only ten at the time, I figured they knew something that I didn't. And yet there was something riveting and electric about this unfolding radio drama and it sucked me right in. I later found out it was something called the Democratic National Convention and it came from someplace called Los Angeles, which I had heard of because the Dodgers had moved there recently.

Along with baseball, Dad liked birds. In fact, Dad loved birds. Every Sunday morning, he and his nutball group of friends would go to some park or lake and hide in the bushes with their binoculars to catch a glimpse of the latest yellow-bellied sapsucker or red-tailed kook-a-joob or whatever. Dad wore a *pith* helmet that was covered with black and white missiles dropped high from above by his winged friends. He dragged me along two or three times until I made it clear to him that I had no intention of going through life like some Central Park statue with pigeon stuff for shoulder pads. Baseball was great and I loved Dad for that, but this bird stuff was, well, strictly for the birds. Besides, my friends laughed at me.

Now Poppa, he was something different altogether. Poppa was a gentle man, much gentler than Dad, and I never understood how one begat the other, though Mom assured me that's just what happened. Poppa would tell me about the Cossacks and some place called the "U-Kray-een," where he had come from many years before. I loved it when Poppa told me stories.

And Poppa loved politics. Old politics anyway; it was his passion. I knew from my social studies book that his heroes had never become presidents, but the names of Eugene V. Debs and Norman Thomas became the most familiar duo to me this side of Mantle and Maris. Poppa had spent every Sunday as a young man organizing socialist rallies on the Coney Island boardwalk. I often thought that one of the reasons he had come to Dallas was that he was blackballed from every factory in New York.

As Jews, we were supposed to be Democrats, and we were. Mom had taken me into the voting booth during the 1956 election where she let me pull the lever for Stevenson. It was the first of a long line of unsuccessful presidential choices for me. Dad didn't seem to care much for politics, certainly not as much as birds, although he had a particular loathing for someone named Richard Nixon, who seemed to be connected with it somehow. Poppa didn't follow recent politics too much, having lost interest somewhere after Franklin Roosevelt, who he thought was no Norman Thomas, but not bad as far as presidents went.

But in the summer of 1960, I inherited Poppa's lost interest in politics. As I listened to the crackling radio that summer night, the name John Kennedy was imprinted on my brain. I think I was not alone. The teeming hordes of fellow baby-boomers were just coming into consciousness when this man appeared upon the scene. The timing couldn't have been better.

And what a man he was! Handsome, physically graceful, witty and reserved at the same time, he had a charm and appeal I had never seen before or since. Mom swooned. Moms across America swooned. Dad was more reserved but seemed to like him okay. Poppa didn't comment, Norman Thomas lying long dormant.

I knew John Kennedy was going to win the election. John Kennedy had to win the election! All of Mom and Dad's friends and all my schoolmates' parents were going to vote for him. That strange person Dad didn't like, named Nixon, was running against Kennedy, and I didn't know of one person, not one, who was going to vote for him.

There were the debates on TV. Mom couldn't take her eyes off John Kennedy and I wasn't too far behind. Poppa snored in the rocker. Kennedy drew a crowd of 750,000 people on Broadway in New York and the momentum continued to grow. John Kennedy was not only going to win the election; he was going to be coroneted!

On November 8, 1960, John Kennedy won the election, but with a whimper, not a bang. At age ten I couldn't have known that we lived in an "unrepresentative district," and that there was such a thing as Catholicism. I knew that I was Jewish and that most people belonged to one other very large group that wasn't.

If the country's passion for John Kennedy was moderate during the campaign, it turned into a veritable love affair with him and his wife Jackie, after the election. Although there was no coronation that January, there developed a gradual and ongoing one throughout his term of office. He energized the country, especially the young people, drawn by his youth, beauty, and "vigor." There was a cult of personality and I, along with millions of others, was drawn to that cult. If you were there, you know. If you weren't, ask somebody. Anybody.

Interesting things were happening in the world, important things. The Bay of Pigs. The Berlin Wall. The marches in the South. I didn't fully understand what they meant, although I do remember sitting terrified in seventh grade English as the deadline for the Cuban Missile Crisis came and went and the world was still there. I went back to staring at Miss Davidoff's large breasts. A new interest had arisen the previous year.

But what I mostly remember was John Kennedy and how he towered over the era. I didn't know that there were thousands, maybe millions, who hated him as passionately as we loved him. That was pretty hard to do, especially living in Dallas, but believe me, it was true. And few people knew that he was human, all too human, as we sadly found out later. By 1963, John F. Kennedy was a living god.

One night in October, Poppa announced at dinner that the President was going to visit Dallas sometime the following month. I squealed with delight and begged Poppa to take me to see him. Dad shot me a dirty look and said not if it was a school day. I pleaded with Poppa in secret conferences for a week until I finally wore him down. He told me if it was a school day, we'd figure out some scheme to fool Dad. He wasn't going to let me miss the President. Sometimes I wish he had. He also told me to be sure to bring the camera he had given me for my *Bar Mitzvah* that spring.

Among the many situations John Kennedy inherited upon assuming the Oval Office, none was quite so confounding as the boiling cauldron known as Cuba. The prior year, Fidel Castro and his rag-tag band of followers had tromped out of the backwoods and sugarcane fields to lay claim to what had been America's playground in the Caribbean. Upon seizing power, the bearded rebel leader decided that socialism might not be such a bad thing after all and proceeded to set up a mini-Moscow 90 miles from the American mainland. In response, the island's entire middle class closed shop and floated toward Miami. Castro also boarded up the lucrative Mafia-owned casinos and booted the local Sicilian Captains of Industry out of his tropical domain. Neither the departing merchants nor the displaced *Dons* was pleased with what they perceived was going to be a temporary inconvenience and neither reacted passively in dealing with the situation.

For the select function of resting its former home from the clutching hands of Fidel Castro, each group turned to the aid of its erstwhile business partner, the CIA. This rogue elephant of American government, always itching for a little mischief, was more than happy to oblige. Deep in the bowels of the CIA's Virginia headquarters, diligent little spooks hatched such items as revolvers hidden in movie cameras and poison cigars; both built with the express purpose of dispatching his *bearded-ness* to the great beyond. No expense was spared, no scheme was too ludicrous, outrageous or bizarre to be considered.

The plot to assassinate Castro and retake Cuba was well under way when it was rudely interrupted by the election of John Kennedy. But the boys from the CIA-Mafia-Cuban trinity were not to be deterred by such an unfortunate occurrence. Not when there were dictators to be assassinated and gambling casinos to be reclaimed. Under the aegis of the Joint Chiefs of Staff, they prevailed upon the young, inexperienced and malleable Chief Executive and he reluctantly agreed to their earnest entreaties.

Recapturing Cuba would be a snap. Just land a few thousand exiled Cubans on the lush shoreline and the local populace would rise up *en masse* against Castro. What could go wrong?

As it turned out, just about everything. The landing was botched. It took place in an inaccessible area requiring a 150-mile march across the mountains to reach the objective. Needless to say, it was not reached and over 1000 "freedom fighters" were captured and imprisoned, while scores of others were left dead. This fiasco was later to become known as The Bay of Pigs. From Miami, the Cubans blamed Kennedy for being slow to provide air cover, but in reality it was an ill-conceived plan from start to finish, with Kennedy's basic function becoming that of scapegoat. Not only did the population not rise up *en masse*, it did not even rise up *en solo*.

Kennedy took the heat and the blame, but vowed never again to be flummoxed by the CIA, which he swore he would "smash into a thousand pieces." CIA Director Allen Dulles and Director of Operations, General Charles Cabell, received their walking papers. How curious that less than three years later, one of these men would sit on the Warren Commission, investigating the President's murder, while the other man just happened to be the Mayor of Dallas' brother. But I digress.

The Cubans and the Mafia left the venture with a deep distrust of Kennedy and an equally deep commitment to pursue their earlier goals. The CIA had made itself a formidable enemy, one who had inflicted substantial losses, losses that would not go unavenged.

As for Kennedy, he stiffened his resolve to keep his own counsel. Although it would not be his last venture in dealing with Cuba, he decided that political assassination would not be on the agenda of the United States Government. Others lurking in the murky depths of Washington's corridors did not share this conviction. Chief among them was one William Harvey, head of the "Cuba desk" for the CIA. This (pearl handled) revolver-toting maniac had modeled himself after the clown prince of jingoistic buffoons, General George Patton. In the late fifties, Harvey had set up, at taxpayers' expense, the "executive action committee," an unholy alliance with the Mafia. The express purpose of this "committee" was to secure the assassinations of heads of state who displeased its governing body. It had been started for the specific task of eliminating Fidel Castro but was mobile enough to adjust its target to fit the prevailing sentiment. The Mafia would supply the hitmen and the CIA would provide the means of entrance and egress, as well as the necessary cover-up. It worked well in principle, with assassination teams practicing crossfires in the muddy swamps and outbacks of Florida and Louisiana.

Castro was a natural target since both the mob and the CIA had a direct interest in Cuba that the hirsute socialist had so rudely derailed. The "committee's" domain however, was not restricted to the Caribbean, as later actions in Central America and Southeast Asia would demonstrate. But The Bay of Pigs had taken its toll with the Director, the Deputy Director, and even the illustrious Harvey himself, jettisoned from the Agency by the newly elected President.

Castro retained his grip on power as Dulles *et al* cooled their heels in the dusty anterooms of the shadow government. The "executive action committee" was in place. They could wait. There were bigger fish to fry.

New Orleans of 1920 was a bawdy riverfront town famed for its voodoo, Cajuns and houses of ill repute, not necessarily in that order. It was into that world that Carlos Marcello came as a boy of ten.

Burdened with old world parents, Carlos was quickly drawn into the rough and tumble life the Mississippi waterfront offered. New Orleans was the home of the oldest Mafia enclave in America and the resourceful Carlos quickly worked his way into its good graces. Although not physically imposing, the short, stocky Carlos was blessed with a fearless temperament that made him particularly useful to his new employers. Not encumbered with the usual restraints of conscience, Carlos employed the tools of physical violence like the ambitious apprentice he was in this guild of butchery. *La Cosa Nostra,* they called it, and Carlos was proud to be a part of it. Damned proud.

As he entered his late teens, the entrepreneurial bug bit Carlos. He got his hands wet in the vending machine business under the tutelage of crime boss and J. Edgar Hoover confidant, Frank Costello. He went on to operate a string of saloons catering to the "Colored," whom Marcello, like the rest of his Mafia brethren, despised, but who were easy and lucrative pickings for the venues of liquor, dope, and women that Carlos was offering. All of these cash-rich businesses strengthened his network and elevated his status as a rising star in the New Orleans Mafia.

As time passed, Carlos cemented his position as the local Godfather of the area and moved his operations out to the back bayou of Jefferson Parish. He presided over his rural fiefdom, idyllically and inappropriately named Churchill Farms, with an iron hand, holding Sunday afternoon dinners to transact and conclude the week's business. Occasionally, a displeased Carlos would find and confront a rogue operator who might be holding out on him. Carlos employed a tub of lye for such occurrences and the bleached bones of the errant charge would soon be floating in the brackish backwaters of his swampy kingdom. Always a great stickler for privacy and secrecy, he displayed his office motto proudly above his desk: "If three people know, two can't talk if they're dead." The message was not lost on his faithful flock.

Except for the occasional blip, Carlos' business grew and prospered throughout the '40s and '50s. The war had ended and the hordes of returning GI's populated his gambling, narcotics and prostitution interests. For all intents and purposes, by the time 1950 rolled around, Carlos controlled the state of Louisiana as well as the adjacent areas of East Texas and the lower Delta.

In the late '50s, the Federal Government, much to the annoyance of J. Edgar Hoover, decided to investigate organized crime in America. The Director had formerly opted for a peaceful coexistence with the Syndicate, which often proved to be an effective low-level informant to the Bureau. Consumed as he was with massive paranoia about the all-pervading communist menace, as far as Hoover was concerned, if nobody brought it up, the Mafia didn't exist.

The chief protagonist selected for this Federal investigation was one Robert Kennedy, younger brother of the junior Senator from Massachusetts. The younger Kennedy, cocky little bastard that he was, proved to be most tenacious at this task, to the great displeasure of the collective bosses dispersed around the country.

Bobby had discovered that an effective tool of prosecution was deportation, real or threatened. No self-respecting Godfather could run an efficient operation in a large American city from the back of an olive press overlooking the Sicilian hillside. Since Carlos was one of his primary targets, Bobby pursued this tack with hound-dog like perseverance which caused the New Orleans Don no end of grief, taxing him legally, financially, and emotionally. Carlos was not amused.

The crime boss looked forward to the election of 1960 with great trepidation. If Nixon was elected, Carlos figured the heat would be off, at least temporarily, with the *red menace* recapturing the Government's limited attention. But if the nomination of John Kennedy caused him concern, the thought of Kennedy's election was downright frightening. He figured his

Bermuda shorts and tourist maps of Sardinia might be useful after all.

Kennedy squeaked by in a highly debated election, some say with the help of the Chicago Mafia. Carlos, perplexed by this apparent irony, was not disappointed in his fears. The attack dog, in an unparalleled dose of nepotism, had become attorney general and quickly flashed his gleaming pincers Carlos' way.

Bobby had a brilliant plan. It involved kidnapping Carlos and jettisoning him out of a biplane over the jungles of Central America. With government agents swooping down on the unsuspecting Carlos as he dutifully visited the local INS, the plan worked to perfection. Two days later, the New Orleans Don found himself tramping without a road map through the lush Guatemalan undergrowth. Let it never be said that the new attorney general was confined by the surly bonds of law.

But Bobby had made one key mistake. Never expecting to see the New Orleans boss again, he had greatly underestimated Carlos' resourcefulness. This mistake was to cost him dearly in the not too distant future.

When John Kennedy inherited the White House, he was the glowing picture of good health. This wasn't always the case. In fact, it wasn't even the case then.

Who was this white knight arrived to charm and entrance a nation? A tough, forceful leader, elegant and witty? Or an insensitive, miserly philanderer who referred to his sex organ as JJ? As it turns out, a little bit of both.

John Kennedy started out in life as the sickly second son of a rising Boston political dynasty. His father, Joe, a fireball of energy and ambition, had married the daughter of one "Honey Fitz," the first Irish mayor of Boston. Even though Joe had gone to Harvard, he always felt the sting of WASP condescension to his Irish heritage and spent his life perpetually pissed off and railing against it. If they wouldn't accept him, he would beat these bloodless dilettantes at their own game and then rub their faces in it. Fuck 'em all.

Joe was a man on the move, literally and figuratively. His nomadic lifestyle played into his philandering spirit as he started the Kennedy tradition of "hosting" Hollywood starlets. His wife, Rose, dignified and prudish, reacted to these wanderings by becoming deeply religious and taking extended trips abroad, staying home only long enough to pump out another Kennedy.

It was into this world that John Kennedy was born on May 29, 1917. From the start Jack was a frail child, with one leg shorter than the other. Although shy by nature, he was thrust into his father's world of fierce physical action and competition. Unfortunately for Jack, his older brother Joe was more adept at all of this activity and Jack suffered the results of that advantage.

Despite his ill health, Jack was blessed with unusually good looks and a sparkling wit. He was a mediocre and slovenly student, but fortunately for him, his father had banked most of his hopes on Joe, the swifter, stronger brother.

After consolidating his fortunes in banking, bootleg whiskey and Hollywood productions, Joe Sr. turned his eye toward politics. By 1932, he was the wealthiest man of Irish heritage on the planet. Mostly to get Joe Kennedy out of his hair, Franklin

Roosevelt appointed him ambassador to England (how ironic for this Anglophobe), where Joe proceeded to publicly sympathize with Hitler and denounce democracy. So much for his political ambitions. These he transferred to his oldest son, Joe Jr., by now a Harvard graduate, fighter pilot, and white-knight-in-waiting.

Jack figured he had it made. Free of his father's ambition, he decided he would take his looks and his father's money and live the life of a carefree playboy. He had inherited his father's respect for women, which was none, and he was monstrously successful with them. Hordes of them. Jack was priapic and that's how he liked them, in hordes.

He penned a thesis in the late '30s, *Why England Slept*, which was turned into a book. This literary venture was followed by war hero status as a PT boat commander, a status of dubious origin. But mostly there were women and occasional hospitalizations for various ailments. All in all, it was a pretty good life.

Tragedy struck the Kennedy family in 1944 when Joe Jr. volunteered for a particularly risky mission over Europe and did not return. This event turned out to be a double tragedy for Jack, who not only suffered the loss of a brother he genuinely loved, but also forced him to accept the yoke of his father's political ambitions, which were considerable. So much for the carefree life of a playboy.

Joe Kennedy was a stern taskmaster. After the war in Europe ended, he pushed and prodded his reluctant son to run for Congress in 1946. Though the candidate was shy and wooden in public, his father called the shots (and spent the money) and Jack responded compliantly with long days at factory gates and evenings at tea parties sponsored by his mother. Jack's election had become a cottage industry for the family. Largely unknown going in, he outspent (at least his father did) and outworked a large field, and won going away. These tactics were to become Kennedy trademarks.

After young Jack spent six undistinguished years in the House of Representatives, Joe decided it was time for his son to move on. With vigorous campaigning and bushels of money, Kennedy captured his state's Democratic nomination for senator. The fall campaign pitted him against the powerful Massachusetts incumbent, Henry Cabot Lodge. Joe relished this race. Oh, to vanquish a Cabot and a Lodge, the two quintessential Brahmin clans in one sitting, was almost too good to be true. No amount of money would be spared for this contest, and no amount was. Jack had to work harder than ever, campaigning tirelessly and endlessly. He earned a 70,000 vote victory and an extended stay in the hospital. But he had arrived.

Jack's senatorial victory set the scene for Joe's national ambitions. The elder Kennedy informed his son that this stage of development would require a wife. Such an arrangement would not necessarily restrict his proclivity for sexual variety and adventure, the father said, but the Senator-Elect would need to be more discreet about his meanderings. All things considered, the benefits of marriage outweighed the liabilities. Selected for the spousal slot was one Jacqueline Bouvier, a dark eyed beauty who had the right family ties, debutante credentials, and was Catholic to boot. Besides, Jack seemed to like her okay, and the father had found a kindred spirit in this tough little cookie. The couple's fate was sealed with the "wedding of the decade" at a ritzy Newport, Rhode Island mansion in September, 1953.

Jack went on to have the same distinguished career in the Senate as he did in the House, marked by absences, hospitalizations, and a total lack of ideological focus. Viewing this awe-inspiring record, Joe decided on the national strategy. The presidential election of 1956 would be a hopeless one for the Democrats, with that intellectual boob, Adlai Stevenson, facing a virtually unbeatable Eisenhower. But the vice presidential nomination might make a nice springboard to a more winnable year, as it had been for FDR in 1920. The stampede for Kennedy at the convention fell short of the mark, but his gracious concession to Estes Kefauver, seen on national TV, marked the beginning of the rise of his star. He was to have no equal on this blooming and omnipresent medium, which both loved and was loved by him. The campaign for the presidency began November 7, 1956, the day after the second Eisenhower landslide.

The quest for the presidency had not tempered Kennedy's derelict ways even though the birth of his first child, Caroline, had brought a semblance of responsibility and commitment to the rambunctious Senator. Jackie was proving to be troublesome, with less patience than Rose for tolerating the roving Kennedy libido. But the presidency was too great a prize to be squandered by some domestic turbulence and Poppa Joe insured that Jackie's every want and need would be satisfied until that precious portal had been crossed.

Although Ike had presided over eight years of peace and prosperity, the country was tiring of the Eisenhower golf game and the Democrats actually had a legitimate shot at the White House in 1960. After two losing efforts, Stevenson was through in all but name only. Kennedy's chief rivals for the nomination were the Senate majority leader, Lyndon Johnson, and the garrulous pharmacist (and Senator), Hubert Humphrey.

Kennedy had one major asset over his competition, unlimited money, and one major liability, unpredictable Catholicism. Money versus Catholicism, an old equation Joe was used to dealing with. He would make sure the former outweighed the latter.

But 1960 saw the emergence of something else in the candidate that transcended these variables. Somehow, somewhere, John Kennedy had become a man of substance. Whether it was his baby daughter, the national spotlight, or just time and age, a new component appeared in Kennedy that simply hadn't existed before. And though Joe spent freely on the nomination, Kennedy addressed the Catholicism issue in a straightforward and firm way, steamrollering his opponents on the way to a first ballot victory at the Democratic convention in Los Angeles.

His antagonist for the 1960 general election was one Richard Nixon, reigning vice president, and therefore heir-apparent to the aging General. Eisenhower had endorsed his veep with all the warmth and conviction that one lavishes on a discarded dish towel. Still, after eight years of the vice presidency, the Protestant Nixon, despite his all too apparent flaws, was much better known and connected than his opponent. Through these factors alone, Nixon started with a substantial lead.

Though Kennedy's age (43) was to be used against him, he was only four years younger than Nixon. And despite the campaign degenerating into the usual vitriol, Nixon, in fact, was one of Kennedy's best friends in Congress, and their views on issues were virtually identical. They had come in as representatives together in 1946 and shared office space, camaraderie and household visits, along with another pal, Senator Joe McCarthy of Wisconsin. Kennedy liked Nixon and vice-versa, but politics was politics.

Although TV had been around for some 15 years, it had mostly dispensed variety shows, sitcoms, and cartoons. Much to his credit, Kennedy was the first major politician to realize the power of this fledgling media, with which many Americans were spending up to half of their waking hours. Kennedy realized that his cool demeanor and photogenic looks would give him a distinct advantage over Nixon on TV, and the debates proved him correct in that assessment. Although their words could have been interchangeable, only one of the men displayed sweating lips, darting eyeballs, and stubble laden jowls; and that man was not Kennedy. The camera loved the charismatic Democrat and that love negated Nixon's eight-year head start.

Throughout September and October, the race, infused with Kennedy energy, charm and money, remained a dead heat. The election looked like it would be extremely close. As it turned out, it was unbelievably close, not being decided till the next day. Out of more than 68 million ballots cast, Kennedy won by slightly over 100,000 votes, a margin of less than one-fifth of one percent. There were dubious returns from Cook County, Illinois, where it was said that Joe Kennedy prevailed upon the reigning warlord, Mayor Richard Daley, as well as the local

Mafiosi. This charge remained unsubstantiated, but then again, such charges, by their nature, tend to defy substantiation.

Although not the mandate that the Kennedys had wanted, a victory was a victory. Surprisingly, the combative Nixon chose not to contest the election, though he was well within his right to do so. Having absorbed the combined abuse of the media, the Kennedys and Eisenhower himself, Nixon figured that this TKO constituted a moral victory in and of itself. He went back to California to lick his wounds and plan bigger and better things, like losing the governorship of his home state two years later. Little did anyone suspect at the time, that long after Kennedy had ceased to be, Nixon would go on ticking like a faithful Timex, year after year.

And so it was that Jack Kennedy became the thirty-fifth President of the United States. He was his own man, with his own money, an adoring public and no agenda other than winning the election. But that could come later. Right now he had a free hand at guiding the nation's destiny as he wished. Little did he know that he would meet a sinister and deadly opposition at every turn.

The Director was an institution. He was gruff, egotistical, humorless, paranoid, vainglorious, petty, spiteful, and unforgiving. He was, however, an institution. And like an institution, he was as solid as a granite edifice, ensconced as a fixture at the Bureau. In fact, he was the Bureau. The two were joined at the hip like Siamese twins.

Everything about this man spelled menace. From the firm set of the jaw, the bulldog face, the slicked-back hair, the tie stick-pin and matching cuff links, he was measured, precise, ominous and there. Most of all, there.

It hadn't always been that way. Once upon a time, the Director had been useful, even valuable. Back in the 1920's he had come in to a corrupt, slothful bureau and whipped it into fighting shape. This hard-nosed young lawyer had implemented innovative measures like the National Crime Lab and the FBI Training Center, which vastly increased the agency's effectiveness. He amassed the largest collection of fingerprints on earth and gone after crime figures with blinding fury. The G-Man became a fixture on the American consciousness.

Through the '30s, his agency tracked and ran down the notorious gangsters of the era. Al Capone. Baby Face Nelson. John Dillinger. Ah yes, the glory years. J. Edgar Hoover had become a hero. Even into the '40s, with the world in the throes of global chaos, the FBI continued its usefulness by successfully smashing several international spy rings.

But like most good things, J. Edgar had stayed too long. And though his pre-war activities were a means to the end of maintaining law and order, his post-war actions were basically ends in themselves: preserving, protecting and enhancing his power. The methods he employed for these ends were the collection of dirt on politicos who were in a position to disrupt his comfortable reign and the use of the international specter of communist domination. From the '30s on, Saint Edgar led the holy crusade against Godless communism.

As Stalin took the brunt of Nazi aggression unaided in the dark days of World War II, Comrade Joe decided to keep what he had marched over in the process of driving the Germans back to Berlin. What the hell, he had earned it. Hadn't the Allies delayed any meaningful landing into Europe until the Red Army had sucked up the power and the wrath of the German war machine to the tune of twenty million dead comrades? Why, that was almost more than old Joe had *offed* himself. The hell with these Western dilettantes. Joe was there, and Joe wasn't leaving. Besides, you never knew with these Krauts. You could drive a stake through their hearts and twenty years later their ugly mugs would be pressed across the foggy glass of your border, demanding *lebensraum*, or some such crap. Better to buffer yourself with a nice wide corridor against these Huns, even if that corridor happened to be somebody else's country. Them's the breaks. Things hadn't changed since Ivan the Terrible and Joe doubted they ever would.

America was seized with the *red menace*. Communists were turning up under rocks, coming out of baseboards, materializing from the ether. Poland today, Arkansas tomorrow. What a period of creation. The House Un-American Activities Committee. Richard Nixon and clandestine film stuffed into pumpkins. Alger Hiss. And finally, the ultimate product, hard drinking Senator Joe McCarthy, risen to fight the evil, contain the plague. Never mind that it never made it past the French border. Stalin thought he had a corridor? Try the Atlantic Ocean, and even that wasn't safe.

Of all the "patriots" communism brought out of the woodwork, none reacted more violently than J. Edgar. Whether it was the visceral response of his general paranoia or the opportunism this alleged menace presented, the Director immersed himself in its smarmy tentacles and snuggled up to its breast. No person, communication, event or situation was above suspicion; no circumstance, innuendo or remark beyond investigation. J. Edgar had massive powers at his disposal and he used them. Maliciously. And continuously.

Harry Truman was a communist, of this the Director was certain. Democrats in general were suspect, and this accidental

President for sure was pinko. And though his *Bulldogness* could not get anything on this straight-living man, Hoover was sure Truman wouldn't last long, and he didn't. The Republican Eisenhower was a man the Director could deal with. The thrust of this new administration was inactivity and that was something J. Edgar admired in what he considered a competing entity.

The other tactic at the Director's disposal was the assembling and dispersal of confidential information on matters relating to the protection of national security. In other words, digging up dirt on politicos in a position to challenge, oppose or unseat him. J. Edgar had gotten very good at this, having started during the Roosevelt era. And after all, was not Congress ripe for the plucking? Philanderers, bribe takers, alcoholics, child molesters; Hoover had seen it all, and better still, recorded it. A vineyard full of pimps. The Director could make his toes purple stomping on them.

J. Edgar had made his peace with the Mafia. They were too much trouble, too messy, and they controlled too many things that he enjoyed, like racetracks. There was even talk that they had blackmailed Hoover in sexually compromising positions. Besides, the Mafia made good informants and what with the communists coming out of the floorboards, there was never a shortage of good informants. They hated the *red tide*, and as Hoover told his buddy, New York boss Frank Costello, "The enemy of my enemy, is my friend."

Of course, the Director was harboring the biggest secret of all. Fortunately, no kindred soul at some competing agency was monitoring him. For this man of steel, this man of action, this moral pillar of rectitude, was gay. This was not the best kept secret in Washington; it was just the best kept unspoken secret. Everybody knew about Clyde. First there was Bonnie and Clyde. Then J. Edgar and Clyde.

Clyde Tolson was a quiet, discreet, hardworking agent, who joined the Agency soon after J. Edgar did. Somehow, somewhere, in the course of their endeavors, their paths crossed and intermingled, as it turned out, forever. Clyde and J. Edgar became inseparable. They ate lunch together every day. They dined together most nights. They went to the horse races almost every Sunday. And they traveled together, extensively. Constant companions.

As J. Edgar's star rose, so did Clyde's. He was made assistant director of the Agency, but more importantly, he was the one and only confidant of the man considered by many to be the most powerful person in Washington. What J. Edgar knew, Clyde knew. And J. Edgar knew a lot.

The Director snoozed through the '50s. After the McCarthy business ran its course, the country settled into the quietude known as the Eisenhower administration. Life was good. J. Edgar could tend his rose garden, travel with Clyde as he liked, and throw the fear of God into anybody who crossed his path. Yes, life was good indeed.

In 1957, extreme inconvenience was thrust on the Director's mid-century nap when the Senate decided to set up the Anti-Racketeering Committee. Since the Mafia didn't exist, at least in the mind of our moral crusader, what was there to investigate? Apparently, quite a bit.

Selected to head this committee was some snot-assed kid brother of that moral degenerate from Massachusetts, John Kennedy. This did not bode well. Not only was the Senator a potential presidential nominee, but family money kept the Kennedys beyond corruptibility and therefore, of limited blackmail potential. Although Hoover had a complete file of John Kennedy's failure to keep his privates in his pants, he thought this would be of limited value for the upcoming hearings.

Bobby Kennedy was bad news from the word go. His tenacity, his pugnaciousness, his fervor, all reminded Hoover of a younger version of himself. Jimmy Hoffa was on the ropes, gasping for air. The Director thought that his non-existent friends might come to him for help, thus putting him in the unenviable position of having to choose between his government and his loyalties.

There was a possible light at the end of the tunnel, however. His name was Richard Nixon. He was an ardent anti-communist and Hoover's soulmate in paranoia. He was the vice president and most probably the Republican nominee for president. Hoover relaxed. Richard Nixon, representing the forces of good (who would have thunk it?) was way ahead in the polls and was going to triumph. Wasn't he? The alternative was unthinkable.

When somebody asked John Kennedy why he was seeking the presidency, he answered with the simple, straightforward, "Because that's where the action is." In the spring of 1961, there was no shortage of action around the country and in the world.

Kennedy sought to shake up the entrenched bureaucracy, still slumbering from the Eisenhower years, with his call to the country for a commitment to action. There was much work to be done and he intended to do it. Young people responded to his New Frontier program and especially to the Peace Corps. There was a new energy in the country and a new optimism, unmatched since the end of World War II. The Kennedys brought glamour and youth to the White House and the country responded in kind. Most of it, anyway.

There were large factions unhappy with the election of Kennedy and these factions were to become unhappier as time went on. The Military feared that the new President would interfere with their little ventures around the globe, run under the guise of stemming the *red tide*. The exiled Cubans worried that Kennedy was not committed to undermining Castro and returning their island to them. The business community fretted that he would fiddle with their perks, such as the oil depletion allowance. The considerable right-wing faction worried that Kennedy would be soft on communism and also would coddle the demanding hordes of niggers, spics and other undesirables. None of these groups were to be disappointed in their concerns.

The new President inherited a number of works in progress. The Eisenhower Administration was sending a steady trickle of "advisors" into Vietnam and the Joint Chiefs of Staff had no intention of stopping just because their beloved Ike had departed, his military-industrial complex warning notwithstanding. Plans to assassinate Castro were well in the works, cooked up by a weird amalgam of exiled Cubans, the CIA and the Mafia. The young President would be an impediment in implementing these plans, but his youth, indecisiveness and inexperience would assure that they would happen. The groups were right in their assumptions, for a while. But as Kennedy settled into the job, he started feeling his oats and was less inclined to be shoved around by the vested interests he had inherited, as demonstrated by his actions in Cuba and Vietnam, and his dealings with the CIA.

The big events dominating the news were Berlin, internationally, and civil rights, domestically, along with Cuba, which was a little bit of each. Kennedy's instinct was to go slow on civil rights, accommodating the groups and leaders where possible and advocating patience where not. The NAACP, SNCC, CORE and other sundry groups were frustrated by JFK's deliberate pace but knew that when it came to their concerns, Kennedy's heart was in the right place.

After stumbling initially, the President's stature as a world leader started to grow, so much so, that by the time of his death, he was an international leader of unparalleled magnitude. After living down the Bay of Pigs fiasco, he successfully confronted Khrushchev and the USSR during the Cuban Missile Crisis and immortalized himself with the "Ich Bin Ein Berliner" zinger, spoken in front of the infamous Berlin Wall. That day, delivering one of the greatest taunts of all time, he harangued Khrushchev as follows: "Democracy may be imperfect, it may have its flaws, but at least we don't have to build a wall to keep our people in!" In your face, white man, or red man, as the case may be. Had it been delivered in the 1990's, there would have been high-fives all around. Oh, could that man speak! Crisp, precise, delivered in the cadence of Winston Churchill, filtered through that marvelous, distinctive Boston accent.

Kennedy had a love affair with the media and they with him. He played them with precision, using wit, accessibility and cooperation. The camera loved him, and he made sure it was snapping at all the right times.

The media was not the only thing he had a love affair with, as a steady stream of female visitors flowed in and out of the White House. Or Kennedy would visit them in his off hours, like some high-tech tom cat, helicoptering in for assignations with the likes of Marilyn Monroe, as the mood hit him. Talk about the Teflon presidency. If Reagan had mastered it,

Kennedy invented it. Despite his numerous peccadilloes, he always rose above the fray, the media turning a blind eye. Women and open motorcades. Kennedy, the cool patrician, definitely had a reckless streak in him.

But of all the presidential goings-on, there were two men and one organization that his actions and persona threatened the most. The men were FBI Director J. Edgar Hoover and Kennedy's own hapless vice president, Lyndon Johnson. The organization was the Mafia.

Hoover hated everything Kennedy was and stood for. To the Director, Kennedy was hopelessly soft on communism, ridiculously liberal on social and civil rights issues and morally degenerate, to boot. This perceived moral degeneracy, in Hoover's twisted mind, equated to the moral degeneracy that he saw in America. Of course, this consisted of anything Hoover didn't like or approve of, which was most everything.

But more than anything, Hoover hated Kennedy for the very real control the Chief Executive had over him. Hoover was used to having direct access to the president, but Kennedy made him go through channels. In this case, channels meant the attorney general, who just happened to be the President's younger brother himself, that worm, Bobby Kennedy. If Hoover hated John, he loathed everything about Bobby. Especially the little bell that Bobby had installed on his desk. The express function of this tinkling signal was for J. Edgar to pop up and run down the hall, like one of Pavlov's dogs, when the A.G. beckoned. Somebody had finally correctly identified Edgar's genus and species, and Edgar was not pleased about this, not pleased at all, as little flecks of spittle started appearing around his choke collar.

But worse even than Bobby was the President's very real ability to put Hoover out to pasture when the Director reached the mandatory retirement age of seventy, which would happen on the first day of 1965. Whether re-elected or not, Kennedy would still be president on this date, and he fully intended to use this power. He felt that Hoover had long outlived his usefulness and was nothing more than a paranoid relic clinging to an ancient past and blocking the flow of progress. Hoover had hoped to use the ample opportunities the President gave him to blackmail the Chief Executive, but Kennedy was proving to be too popular and this threatened exposure would probably only expedite the Director's departure. Despite the G-man's direct requests for re-appointment, the President was adamant and Hoover was facing the certain loss of his long running power base and everything that had meant anything to him.

For Lyndon Johnson, the vice presidency was turning out to be the ninth circle of hell. An active and vigorous man, Johnson had run the Senate floor with the speed of a greyhound and the ferocity of a doberman. Every minute of every day was jammed with people to cajole, projects to advance, phones to cradle. Then Lyndon took the step up to the national ticket because Kennedy needed Texas' electoral votes, and *peter-principled* himself out of existence. When he wasn't busy attending third world funerals or being shit on by the Kennedys, Lyndon had time on his hands, lots of time. Time to get into trouble. Which Lyndon managed to do in a big way.

With his beloved Senate at a distance, Lyndon concentrated on making himself rich through oil & gas connections, hotel and casino ventures, and television interests. This he did with the help of his friends, Billy Sol Estes and Bobby Baker, and their many unsavory associates. They became Lyndon's own *Billy-Bob*, and as their shady ventures unraveled, so did the Vice President's political future.

Things looked bleak for Lyndon. Kennedy had not had the good sense to die and didn't look like he was going to do so any time soon. Johnson had dropped out of sight and become inaccessible to the press. When he was available, he was subject to their incessant inquiries about his dubious partners' dubious dealings. Lyndon was rapidly becoming a large stone chained around the President's neck, who with his increasing popularity, didn't need the Veep's help to secure any of the country's regions in his reelection bid. Surely Kennedy would cut this chain and Lyndon would sink to the bottom of the pool of political oblivion. With any luck, he would avoid jail.

As for the Mafia, they had correctly predicted that what Robert Kennedy had demonstrated starting in 1957 would escalate and get out of control when the new administration took over. It did. The Kennedys attacked organized crime with a fury heretofore unknown. Every day there were new bills, acts, orders and trials, designed to eradicate the Mob and its activities, to wipe it off the face of America, with unparalleled haste. The brothers Kennedy seemed to be on a personal mission of shutting down the gambling, prostitution and narcotics ventures of the Syndicate and of repopulating the island of Sicily. Gangsters were hauled into court for tax evasion, racketeering, jury tampering, obstruction of justice. You name it, they were there for it. It was getting to be expensive, worrisome and goddamned inconvenient.

Who in the hell did these Kennedys think they were, these Irish putzes, holier than goddamned thou, who didn't have to worry about making a living in this rough and tumble world because their goddamned father had done it for them? How in the hell did they think the old man had gotten his money? Manufacturing ladies' undergarments?

And so with the unholy triumvirate of the Director, the Vice President and the Cosa Nostra nipping at his heels, John Kennedy guided the nation through the choppy waters of domestic and international entanglement. Or attempted to guide it. For the ankle biters and their allies could not locate the Achilles heel of this rising titan, and decided that the jugular might make a better target, after all.

Lee just couldn't seem to get it together. God knows he tried, but no matter how hard he tried, he just couldn't seem to get it together. It wasn't that he was dumb. His Marine IQ test had measured him at 120, which put him thirty points above most recruits and some twenty beyond his superior officers. It just seemed he had been born under a bad star.

And in fact, he had. He never knew his father. Mom was a space shot from the word go. Uncle Dutch was cool, though, as he let Lee run errands in his backroom numbers business. Lee liked the intrigue.

School was barely tolerable and not nearly as much fun as Uncle Dutch's biddings. Lee was a good student, but he kept to himself. As soon as the opportunity presented itself, he leapt at becoming a Marine, lying about his age to get in. Who knew what intrigue old *semper fi* might lead to?

Lee was dangerous around weapons. If he was on the range, self-preservation demanded a position a minimum of three stations away and even that was precarious. Maybe it was a hand-eye thing or a suspected inner ear defect, but safety demanded great caution. Like the time his bunk mates clambered for cover as the loaded pistol Lee had dropped exploded below their feet, breaking the Sunday morning reverie. Lee was a crack shot all right; it just depended on which crack you'd have to crawl into or out of when the well meaning holy terror walked into view.

Lee was not without merit, however. He worked the radar like a charm and seemed to possess an astonishing capacity for languages. Such men were of value. Great value. Would Lee like to learn Russian? Russian was the greatest value of all. Yes, Lee would like to learn Russian, so Lee learned Russian. Well, very well. Would Lee like to go to the Soviet Union? Boy, spying on enemy aircraft was fun, but this was some serious intrigue. You bet Lee would like to go to the Soviet Union. So Lee went to the Soviet Union. With his honorable discharge.

But the boys at the CIA thought about it and decided that anyone with a modicum of suspicion might quickly assess that an honorable discharge and a newly arrived defector just didn't add up. And the drones at the KGB had more than a modicum of suspicion; they had a boatload. So the boys at the Agency asked Lee if they could change it to dishonorable. Could he change it back at a later date? No problem. Well Lee didn't really like falling on his own sword, but if this was the price of intrigue, so be it.

Only Lee didn't find much intrigue. He was collecting "facts" on Soviet life, whatever that was supposed to be, which required the guise of long hours in Russian factories. Unfortunately, Lee had to be there to work those hours. He started wondering if maybe this Agency stuff wasn't all it was cracked up to be.

Always a loner, the late blooming Lee found the isolation of the Soviet Union almost more than even he could bear. He went to a dance the Agency had found for him. They were worried about Lee.

The ungainly stud, Lee scanned the wall of heavily scarfed *babushkas*. Anything that was less than two hundred pounds with a full set of teeth might do, at least to talk to. Some stereotypes lived up to their billing; this one might be worse, he thought.

And then, there in the back corner, clinging to a stairway, she was. *Who was she?* Somebody's niece, the adjunct told him. What was this vision of loveliness doing in the Soviet Union, he pondered. With leaden legs and thumping heart, he started his long journey across the room.

She saw him coming and froze like a deer in the headlights. Short, emaciated, balding, a sight to throw terror into the heart of the boldest maiden, which Marina, braced precariously against the wall, was not. She waited for his vodka laden breath to envelope her, for his muted inarticulate grunts to bounce off her ears like crushed beer cans. She'd been there before.

But this one could make a complete sentence. He spoke with an unusual accent she had never heard before. His diction was perfect. She wondered what part of the Motherland he came from.

Americanski! You are Americanski? Marina could not believe it, not this man with the funny accent and the perfect Russian. Yes, indeed, Lee reassured her, he was in fact, Americanski. And the Americanski would very much like to dance with her. Would Marina be interested? You bet Marina would be interested. So they danced. Lee gazed into Marina's beautiful blue-green eyes and saw love. Marina gazed back and saw her big American passport. Just like her uncle said she would. So Lee and Marina courted, and then Lee and Marina wed.

The Agency's concern for Lee's companionship worked too well. Lee was happy, but Marina now had the credentials to make a beeline for the closest border, which she quickly proceeded to do. What could the Agency do? Certainly Lee could be of some use in America.

"New Orleans? Go see Mr. Bannister, he'll set you up with something." So Lee went to see Mr. Bannister. *"Sorry kid, nothing right now, but we'll keep you on the payroll. Stay in touch."*

Lee thought about Uncle Dutch. Maybe he would have something. "No, better not," thought Lee. "Now that I'm working for the official clandestine organization, it wouldn't make sense to work for the unofficial one. Conflict of interest." Or so it seemed to Lee, not realizing that such double dipping represented a long standing tradition.

Mom was in Dallas. Lee was all she had, and Lee had a little baby girl now. So Lee, Marina, and the baby went to Dallas. He took a series of menial jobs and collected his Agency paycheck. Survival was tough, and Marina started demanding things, like washing machines. Life in America had not proved to be the gold paved streets she had heard about. She and Lee quarreled constantly. The economic stress was too great, and they separated. But Lee loved his little girl and vowed to provide, somehow. Besides, Marina was pregnant again.

After he had been back a year, Mr. Bannister called, sometime in May of '63. Could Lee come to New Orleans? There was work available. If there was one thing Lee needed, it was work. His prospects had been limited because he had the same capacity to drive a car as he did to fire a weapon. Somehow, the concept was beyond his grasp. In addition, he suspected that the FBI, given his recorded dishonorable discharge, his alleged defection, and his Russian wife, was somehow responsible for his inability to maintain stable employment. Couldn't these two agencies get their signals straight? *Yes, Mr. Bannister, of course I can come to New Orleans to work.*

Mr. Bannister asked Lee about politics. Did he hate the President? Did he want to see Castro die? Lee was indifferent. He wanted to feed his baby and win Marina back. He would do what was necessary.

What was necessary, Mr. Bannister said, was to publicly portray a leftist Marxist, advocating "fair play" for Cuba. This would include passing out leaflets backing Castro's rule and speaking to whatever media possible to further this alleged cause. Mr. Bannister said something about his purpose also being the infiltration of pro-Castro groups, but Lee found no pro-Castro groups to infiltrate. He *was* the pro-Castro group in New Orleans.

Mr. Bannister wanted Lee to mail order a rifle and a pistol to make it look like he had revolutionary credentials and intent. Strange request, but with the Agency feeding his family, Lee was in no position to quarrel. Marina and his soon-to-be two offspring meant too much to him.

Of all the things Mr. Bannister asked Lee to do, the strangest one was to meet David Ferrie. This was one bizarre individual. Racing around in a polyester wig and penciled-on eyebrows, Ferrie was a frenzy of rabid right wing activity. He stated that Kennedy was soft on communism and responsible for keeping

Castro in power and ruining the Western Hemisphere. They both needed to be dead. Now. For this purpose, at least the Castro portion of it, Ferrie had organized a military outpost and training center on Lake Ponchitrain. This base was established, at taxpayers' expense, for exiled Cubans, adventure seeking mercenaries and other assorted whackos, to participate in the retaking of Cuba. Sort of a Bay of Pigs Two, only this time with a happy ending. Kennedy could be taken care of later.

Only Kennedy had closed down Ferrie's little paramilitary operation first and left him a commander without troops. Lee was now Ferrie's troops. And so the Fair Play for Cuba Committee and the troopless General, with their combined forces of two, banded together to fight the forces of evil in the summer of '63.

Lee just didn't get Ferrie. David really seemed to believe all this right wing crap. He was an ex-commercial pilot who had gotten grounded somehow, a current homosexual of voracious and frenzied appetites, and he knew Lee's Uncle Dutch. Was he involved with the Mafia somehow? And what was with the hair thing? Bannister had told Lee it was some kind of disease, but somehow the look seemed to work for Ferrie. This bizarre creature was matched only by his equally bizarre appearance.

Despite all this, David was the General, and Lee was at his bidding. David wanted Lee to take a bus to Mexico City to try to get a Russian passport at the Cuban Embassy there.

"Make a scene if necessary," barked the hairless wonder. "Go to the Russian Embassy as well, if possible."

"Why?," asked Lee.

"Because the Agency is paying you handsomely to do so," replied Ferrie. "And report back to Dallas by October 15th where Bannister will line up a job for you."

So Lee went to Mexico City and did as requested, raising not just one, but two scenes, and making himself a general nuisance. "Well done," said Ferrie.

The second part of the request, Lee liked. He was growing tired of his strange summer of '63. He didn't wait for Bannister.

Through a friend of Marina's, he had gotten a job at the Texas School Book Depository. As soon as he got himself on his feet, he would rid himself of the Agency. He would forget about Ferrie; he would forget about Bannister. Marina had just given birth to another daughter and there were fewer arguments. Lee had two little girls to play with now. Maybe things would work out okay, after all.

II.

The Plot

Carlos had come to a decision. By the fall of '62 his situation had become hopeless. His world was crumbling around him and he was almost powerless to stop it. Almost.

After surviving his adventure in the Guatemalan jungle, Carlos, spirited back into the country in the dead of night, returned a bitter man. Nothing the Kennedy brothers were now doing would lessen that bitterness. He was under indictment for tax evasion and his organization was besieged on all sides by government investigations. Anti-racketeering laws were being passed, it seemed almost daily. The Syndicate was in danger of losing the right to take the Fifth Amendment. Imagine that, the Mafia without the Fifth. It would be like Bartles without James. Even a special audience with the President by Frank Sinatra, at the behest of the besieged organization, had fallen on deaf ears. It only served to sever that relationship.

Chicago boss Sam Giancana and Miami Don Santos Traficante, were still fiddling with the stooges at the CIA, trying to assassinate Fidel Castro. Hoffa was talking about blowing up Robert Kennedy with dynamite. Carlos rolled his eyeballs. "Great," he thought, "exploding attorney generals, just what we need." Faced with certain jail or deportation, he knew they were gunning for the wrong man. With the imminent loss of all he ever had and worked for, Carlos had come to a decision: John F. Kennedy must die. It was the only way out. Carlos had nothing left to lose.

He would call a council. Being the head of the oldest and most independent Mafia family in the country, a meeting wasn't really necessary, permission wise. But etiquette demanded it, and Carlos figured he might get a good idea or two in the process. "Mafia etiquette, what a concept," he mused.

Since it was the middle of winter, the boys would be more than happy to come down to Traficante's place in Miami. Even though Santos had become obsessed with the elimination of Castro after he had been jailed and booted out of his beloved Havana, Carlos still considered Santos a trusted friend as well as his closest business partner. Between them they controlled whatever was worth controlling below the Mason-Dixon line. It would be good to see Santos again.

Santos welcomed his Sicilian cohorts to his lush Key Biscayne resort. The boys sampled the waters of the Bay and the pleasures of Traficante's imported hostesses. Santos knew how to do it right. But now it was time to get down to business. So they adjourned to one of the dark back rooms of Santos' villa.

Seated around the large oak table was the Mafia Hall of Fame. Frank Costello and Carlos Gambino from New York. Sam Giancana from Chicago. Angelo Bruno from Philadelphia. Raymond Patriarca from New England. And making a special guest appearance, Jimmy Hoffa. He was almost like family, anyhow. Along with Carlos, Bruno and Costello were in imminent danger of deportation.

Santos, ever the efficient host, called the meeting to order and softly started speaking. "Gentlemen, as always it is good to see you again. I assure you that the security of this meeting is complete. There is important business to discuss and this will be no Appalachian Two." Several of the members nodded, remembering the disastrous invasion of that prior meeting of Mafia chieftains in upstate New York in 1957. Security would be paramount this time.

"The reason that I have called you here is that Mr. Marcello has an interesting idea that will effect all of us and our concerns. As Mr. Marcello explained it to me, I saw it as an idea of great merit and I think it deserves your undivided attention. Mr. Marcello, please." Santos gave him a nod, indicating the floor was his.

They waited. They all knew what the idea was. The elimination of the Attorney General. Messy. Dangerous. And probably necessary.

Carlos pushed his chair closer to the table and rested his stocky torso on his elbows. He scanned the assembled brethren and slowly began. "Gentlemen, as I'm sure you know, the last three years have not been the best of times. Not only have we lost Havana, but our families are all facing continuous and unceasing harassment from our brothers up in Washington. We are facing the loss of everything we have worked so hard to achieve. Several of us are facing deportation. And gentlemen, this is not going to stop by itself. We must act. We must act decisively, and we must act now." Carlos stopped, letting the words hang in the air. There were grunts and grumbles of agreement around the table. Carlos was saying nothing new. He was just acknowledging something that everyone had been collectively putting off. The Attorney General must die. But how?

Jimmy Hoffa was a man of strong emotions. "Carlos, we been talking about *offing* Bobby for over a year now. We just ain't been able to get close. It's just a matter of time. We got a munitions guy on it."

Oh Christ, Carlos thought to himself. *Here we go again with exploding attorney generals.* "Mr. Hoffa, with all due respect, I don't think your plan is without merit, but it misses the point. As you all know, our beloved Bobby had me recently UPS'd to Guatemala, so I have no love lost for the man. We will take care of him in time, but imploding him will not solve our current situation."

The crowd grew quiet. Carlos had something unexpected up his sleeve.

"I know that Santos and Mr. Giancana have been working with our cooperative allies in Washington to eliminate Mr. Castro, to return the lucrative resorts to our domain. A good and necessary idea. And I have been apprised, Mr. Hoffa, of your attempts to disembowel our Attorney General. Also a good and necessary idea. But gentlemen, I submit to you this. When you cut off the tail of a dog, he keeps on running around. But when you cut off the head...and I submit to you, the Attorney General is just the tail."

The group went white with fear. This was different, exciting and dangerous. Hoffa looked perplexed. Why was Carlos talking about dogs?

Raymond Patriarca blurted out, "Are you proposing we attempt to kill the President, Carlos?" Whether it was regional pride or whatever, Patriarca seemed genuinely put off by this attack on his fellow New Englander. Some things were just incomprehensible, and the assassination of the President was one of them.

Carlos stared ahead at Patriarca. *These East Coast bosses had undue fear of the federal authority in Washington,* he thought to himself. *Maybe I shouldn't have called the council.*

"No Mr. Patriarca, I don't propose we attempt to kill the President. I propose that I fully intend to have the President killed, hopefully with all of your consent."

A general murmur broke out once the group absorbed the shock of this idea. Angelo Bruno of Philadelphia, who practically faced the next departing boat for Palermo, voiced the unspoken concerns.

"Carlos, with all due respect, this is a man who it is very difficult to get close to. He must have fifty Secret Service men climbing in and out of his ass at all times. And, if we somehow were able to get at him, how would we ever get away with it? The Feds would be all over us like a pig on shit. This is *the President of the United States* we are talking about."

Carlos had anticipated this reaction. "Gentlemen, I did not say it would not be dangerous. I did not say it would be easy or that it would not involve the risk of getting caught. But, gentlemen, it can be done. And it must be done. There is no alternative. Open your eyes."

Carlos was wound up now. "This cocksucker Kennedy is going to be reelected, no question about it. Do you think he's going to call off his little vendetta that is threatening to ruin all our lives? No way. I hate that little asshole of a brother of his as much as you all do, but he is just a tool. Suppose we explode the little twerp? Do you think the Government will just go away? Talk about being all over something like a pig on shit, gentlemen, we would be hounded, squashed, trampled. The full resources of the Federal Government, which as you know, are substantial, would be thrown at us. It's not like they wouldn't know who to look for. No, gentlemen, that is not the way to go."

"As for Mr. Castro, he is a side issue. Granted, losing Havana was a big blow, but it is not central to our existence. This is. There will be no *us* to worry about Castro, if we don't take care of this first. We can deal with that asshole later."

Giancana had been quiet and Marcello worried about that. Carlos knew that the Chicago boss shared or used to share a girlfriend with Kennedy and that Giancana, through his association with Joe Kennedy, had given money, lots of it, to the Kennedy campaign. But Carlos also knew that Giancana had felt double crossed by the President and was facing the same pressures as everybody else in the group. Besides, next to Traficante, Giancana had been Carlos' closest associate. He had always come through.

Giancana looked worried, but broke his silence. "Carlos, I'm sure none of us disagree with what you want to do, but how are you going to get at him? This is the most heavily guarded man in the world."

Carlos had anticipated this question as well. "Sam, as you know, Kennedy's got a bit of a reckless streak in him." The group chuckled. Everybody knew about the President and Giancana's shared mistress, Judith Campbell. "But women aren't his only weakness. This motherfucker loves the adulation of a crowd. I've been watching him. He likes riding in motorcades in his big open Lincoln. He does it all the time. I think he can be hit from a tall building."

Carlos Gambino, who had also been quiet, brought up the next concern. "Carlos, suppose we could do all this, how would we get away with it? I mean, just like you said about Bobby, everybody would know who did it. And, besides, how would the man get in and out of the building?"

"That's two questions, Mr. Gambino, and both good ones. First of all, they won't necessarily know who did it, not like they would with Bobby. Look, everybody, except the voters, hates this guy. The CIA hates him for Cuba. He sacked Dulles and is attempting to dismantle the friggin' agency. The Cubans here in Miami hate him for the Bay of Pigs. They'd probably offer to kill him, just for target practice. Everybody in the South hates him for trying to shove the niggers down our throats. The Joint Chiefs hate him for the Bay of Pigs and now for this missile business. I understand he calls his own shots. The word is he's making the Joint Chiefs get out of Vietnam and they're pissed. So you see, we wouldn't be the only ones they would suspect. In fact, any of these groups would probably be more than happy to help us. But that may not be necessary."

"You know the last two presidents that got killed, McKinley and Garfield, were assassinated by some screwball acting by himself. So if we set it up that way, they may not even be looking for a group."

The plan was taking on the proportions of brilliance. Carlos' historical perspective had fascinated the crowd. The audience was rapt at attention.

"So we get this nut up in a building and he shoots the President, and then what happens? What if they catch him?" Frank Costello had spoken for the first time.

"Frank, the nut doesn't do anything. We just have the nut in the area for the cops to conveniently track down while our killers get away. And I mean killers. I got this fella who works for me, David Ferric, flew me back into the country, who's into this sort of thing. Been talking about a crossfire, to make sure the job gets done."

"Well how do you keep the nut from talking, at least about who recruited him?," Bruno offered.

"Well here's how I figure it," Carlos continued. "You find somebody, a patsy. You tell him he's working for the FBI, the CIA, or something. You get him to do things that make no sense, which will incriminate him at a later date. He doesn't ask questions, because as far as he knows, he's working for the Government and they're paying him. You kill the President, you must be sure that the nut is in the area. In the meantime, you've planted all kinds of evidence implicating the nut. Then before the nut can talk, you kill him, maybe for fleeing the scene of a crime."

It was too easy. Simple. And brilliant.

"Suppose we do all this with the nut and we kill him. What about the President's autopsy? What if they see bullets coming from different directions?"

"Good questions, good questions. Once we kill the President and kill the nut, it gets beyond our control. If we plant enough evidence and the Government doesn't want to know, they'll do whatever is necessary to implicate the nut. It'll be easier that way."

"Then how do they know we won't do it again?"

"Because the people in the Government who will benefit from Kennedy's death will know that they don't need to know and they'll know that if they leave us alone, they won't need to worry. Look at Lyndon Johnson. Kennedy's about to cut his balls off in '64, so you think he doesn't want him out of the way? Do you think he's going to investigate? Hell no! Johnson's up to his ass with his Texas buddies, and our friends, Mr. Sol Estes and Mr. Murchison. Johnson don't give a fuck about the Syndicate, he just wants to be president. This happens or he's gone. He'll probably send us a thank you note."

Chuckles all around. "And gentlemen, may I remind you, when you have them by the balls, their hearts and minds will follow." More chuckles, as he spouted biblical text from the Mafia scriptures. Carlos was on a roll.

"Now, as for our investigative body, who's going to be controlling this but Frank's good buddy, Hoover." Carlos nodded in Costello's direction. "And who in Washington hates Kennedy even more than Johnson, but Hoover? Hoover is dead meat if the pretty boy stays. Kennedy is going to boot his ass out after the election. Hoover knows this. Hoover, good American that he is, sees Kennedy as a moral degenerate. Hates him, absolutely hates him. You know Bobby put a buzzer on his desk to ring him like a dog? You don't think he wants Junior dead, too? Hoover may be strange, gentlemen, but he's not stupid. Hoover could work with Johnson; Johnson would keep him on. They walk their goddamned dogs together, for Christ's sake."

Carlos was getting into the soliloquy. "So would Hoover kill himself to find out the truth? I don't think so. Could he squash the investigation? I think he could and I think he would. Can he control Johnson? He should know about Lyndon's Texas buddies already, and if he doesn't, we can make sure that he does. Hoover likes things like that."

"Will he leave us alone? You know, gentlemen, that Hoover made his peace with us many years ago and only when the Senate and then the Kennedys forced his hand did he have to act, and even then, with no conviction. Soon as the Kennedys are gone, Hoover will be very happy to go back to fucking Clyde and leave us alone. Trust me on this one."

The plan was simple. It made sense. It was easy. But it was outrageous, fraught with danger and almost impossible to comprehend in its magnitude. But then again, as Carlos pointed out, what choice did they have? If they didn't act, they would all certainly be imprisoned or deported, their lives and businesses ruined. If they did act, it might work; they might pull it off. Some chance was better than no chance. They'd take their chances.

Somebody asked about logistics. Where would they do it and who would do it? Carlos talked about the South, Miami, New Orleans, maybe Texas. Lots of people hated Kennedy down there and it would be easier to set up a plant or spread the blame, if necessary. As for who would do it, Santos had given him an idea. Better somebody outside the country, not known to the police, harder to trace. Somebody with a code of silence, which meant certain death if there was a hint of talking. Somebody nerveless and experienced. Santos had some connections with the Corsican mob, which operated out of Marseille in France. They met all the requirements. It would cost a couple of million, but this was peanuts compared to the alternative.

Gambino's ears perked up when he heard Corsican. He had used somebody there. He was good, very good. Bold, reckless, fearless. He was the superstar of hitmen. His name was Lucien Sartee.

Lucien stared up at the paint-chipped ceiling. He attempted to spread his slit-like eyelids to no avail. He shifted to his right. The sun was peeking through the half closed Venetian blinds, but a glimpse in that direction brought a stabbing pain to his throbbing head. *Oh Christ,* thought Lucien. *Another world class hangover.*

He peered left and saw a mass of crumbled blankets topped by an outcropping of tangled black hair. The blanket above it was rhythmically swaying up and down. *Who was she*, Lucien wondered, not recalling a moment of last night's antics. The girl and the headache were connected, of that he was sure. *Gotta stop doing this*, Lucien chided himself, knowing he had made that promise before. *This time I mean it.* Right. He had made that claim before, too.

Lucien contemplated the ceiling again, trying to collect his thoughts. There was a message, he remembered, from Gavinet, said it was important. Important? What low-life back alley pimp or Third World tribal lord did Gavinet want him to dispatch to the great beyond now? Important meant nothing; Gavinet wanted a job done, so Lucien would do it. The leader of the Corsican mob always paid his bills and Lucien could use the cash. The excitement would have to wait.

Lucien stirred slowly. He didn't want to wake the sleeping mass of hair lying beside him. With any luck, he could make a clean getaway. *God*, Lucien thought to himself, *I really have to stop doing this*. He rummaged through the wad of clothes piled next to the bed and assembled his crumpled wardrobe in silent haste. Five cat like steps and he'd be out the door. *Slow, steady, yes*. He had made it! He breathed in the cool morning air and felt the warmth of the overhead sun striking his bronzed skin. His green eyes flashed in the blinding sunlight. If only he could get rid of the pounding in his head.

Lucien had done all right for himself. He had never known his parents. The earliest memories were of the orphanage on the Italian hillside and the kindly Sisters there. There was enough to eat and a view of the beautiful coast, but the snail's pace of the sun-drenched village life was more than Lucien's restless soul could bear.

Lucien was a boy who needed Ritalin before it existed. He had energy to spare and the soporific pace of the school and the orphanage allowed no place to unload it. These holding pens were quickly dispatched of so Lucien could give his full attention to the street. He drifted off, arriving in Marseille at the ripe old age of thirteen, ready for adventure. The Corsican mob was there to provide it for him.

There was an apprenticeship. Clandestine deliveries, secret pick-ups, pre-arranged drop-offs. Stuff to keep busy with, stuff to earn pocket change with. The war in Europe was in full throttle and Lucien was blossoming. The black market meant adventure, excitement and profits.

By the time he reached sixteen, the war had ended and Lucien was getting tired of this penny-ante stuff. He needed a man's work. He was cool of demeanor. He was efficient. His proficiency was not unnoticed. Lucien was ready for the big time.

The big time was narcotics, run ruthlessly and efficiently by the Corsican mob out of Marseille. Known first as the French Connection, it later branched out with its trade into South and Central America, to become the Latin Connection. The kingpin in Marseille was one Antoine Gavinet, who ran a no-nonsense operation, which included the Code of Silence. The Code of Silence was certain death for anyone who talked about anything going on inside the organization. It was enforced and it worked.

The key man in these operations was the drug runner. This position required nerves of steel, fearlessness, and total disregard for human life. The drug runner was a trained killer. Good ones became contract hit men, where the killing was an end in itself.

Gavinet had followed Lucien's apprenticeship with interest, knowing he had a young prodigy on the rise. Lucien was given some grade-B jobs and handled them with *panache*. No hesitation here. Lucien could kill at a moment's notice and walk away to a good night's sleep. He rose through the ranks swiftly and by the summer of 1963 was one of Gavinet's top men. Lucien was bold and reckless and took enormous risks, but that was precisely what made him the well-oiled killing machine he was. Lucien liked to drink to relieve the tensions of the day, and when he drank, he liked to whore. But hey, nobody's perfect, not even well-oiled killing machines.

The spring of '63 had been slow and by the time June rolled around, Lucien was getting antsy. Gavinet recently had some small stuff for him, which Lucien quickly disposed of. When the Corsican leader called him in early June, Lucien figured it was more of the same. But work was work and Gavinet paid. Lucien would go see him.

Lucien arrived early on the evening of June 9th at the *Mediterenee*, Gavinet's waterfront club. He strolled up to the bar and was about to order his *Chivas Regal* when he thought better of it. Gavinet always came straight to the point and the night would still be young after their meeting. Better to be clear-headed.

Lucien ascended the narrow winding staircase leading to Gavinet's second floor office. He knocked. A gentle voice beckoned him and Lucien stepped inside.

Gavinet sat reading behind his cluttered desk. He glanced up at Lucien and told him to be seated. *How bizarre*, thought Lucien, looking down at the small Corsican leader. Lucien, with his wiry frame, close-cropped hair and laser emitting eyes looked like the killer he was. The man in front of him, with his soft smile, curly locks and rounded features, looked like a librarian. The gentle voice began to speak.

"Good of you to come, Lucien. Sorry I couldn't give you more notice."

"That's all right Mr. Gavinet," replied Lucien. "It's always good to see you." The pleasantries were sufficient.

"Let me get right to the point, Lucien," Gavinet continued, as if Lucien expected anything else from this precise little man. *An accountant, that's it,* Lucien thought, *the man should be an accountant.* In fact, he was an accountant, balancing human lives along with dollars.

"Paul Montoloni stopped by the other day. He's got a contract for us, a big contract, an important contract." Lucien listened intently. Maybe this would be worthwhile after all. Montoloni was Gavinet's link to the American Mafia. Montoloni had worked in Havana at Traficante's resorts and when the entire harem had been booted out of Cuba, he fled to Montreal to establish the Latin Connection there. Lucien liked hearing from the American Syndicate. They paid well and the work was usually interesting.

"The contract is on an American politician, a very high politician." Lucien sat forward in his chair. This was definitely getting interesting.

Lucien inquired, "a senator or congressman?"

Gavinet shot him a stern glance. "Lucien, we are talking about the highest vegetable, the President of the United States."

Lucien thought he was going to fall off the chair. *My God,* thought Lucien, *the President of the United States, the most powerful man in the world. Talk about your contracts.* Lucien got giddy. The blood drained from his upper torso.

Gavinet continued. "The contract was given to Montoloni by Santos Traficante on behalf of his friend Carlos Marcello of New Orleans." Yes, Lucien knew of Traficante and also Marcello and that strange French place he was from. *Louisiana* was it? "The contract, our portion of it, that is, is for two million dollars." The remaining blood drained from Lucien's lower body.

"Now Lucien," Gavinet continued, as if he were reading a parking summons, "this as you can imagine, is going to be a very dangerous job. They would like it carried out somewhere in the American South, before the first of the year. Mr. Kennedy is supposed to take a trip to that region sometime in the late fall. I come to you because you are the best. I would understand completely if you were to refuse. Also, they are looking for three to four men. They would like to arrange a crossfire."

Lucien sat silently as the words filtered through his numbing consciousness, stinging him like little BBs. *Dangerous*, Lucien thought, that's the understatement of the century, especially inside the United States. *Crossfire?* Yes, that was a good idea. Lucien had participated before in crossfires and a well planned one could work like a charm. To assassinate the President of the United States, they would need a very well planned one. There would have to be a point man; there always was. It was the position of greatest risk. Lucien knew who would be taking that post.

Who could he get? Christian David, maybe? He was the best. Giancarlo? His young friend, Robert? A powerful quartet. Lucien's mind raced.

"Lucien, are you interested?" Gavinet's soft query startled Lucien out of his reverie.

"Yes, Mr. Gavinet, how could I not be interested in such a thing? It's the opportunity of a lifetime. I was just thinking how and with who." Gavinet nodded. He understood. Apparently the messy business with DeGaulle had been swept under the rug.

"Christian David?," Lucien offered.

Gavinet shook his head. "I asked him already. He thinks it's too dangerous; he won't do it." Lucien was momentarily insulted that he hadn't been asked first. If David was too chicken-shit to do it, well, Lucien would show him otherwise. Nobody would walk away from two million dollars, even if it meant his life. Which it very well might, in this case. Besides, we're not talking about some Colombian jungle pimp. This was excitement. This was the contract of a lifetime.

"Are they good for it?," Lucien asked.

A look of great insult crossed Gavinet's rubbery features. "Lucien, this is Antoine Gavinet talking. When have I ever lied to you?"

Lucien felt a stab of remorse. "Mr. Gavinet, it's not you that I doubt, but it's such a big job and so much money. You understand my concern."

Gavinet softened. “Lucien, I know these men; you can trust me. Money exists on a much larger scale in America than in Europe. This is not that much for them and they are very anxious to have it done. Will you consider? Gambino in New York remembers you. Montoloni told me he asked for you.”

Ah yes, Gambino, Lucien remembered. He had done some work for him. Lucien was flattered.

“Mr. Gavinet, as a courtesy to you, of course I will consider it. I just need some time. There are some people I have in mind.”

“Who?”

“Giancarlo and my friend Robert.” Gavinet nodded his head. Giancarlo Mercier was a little older, but competent and fearless. Robert DeMoupoissant was less familiar to the Corsican leader, but if Lucien recommended him, that was good enough for Gavinet.

Lucien pondered a moment. “How are we going to get in and out? If we do it, how are we going to cover our tracks?” As the magnitude of the possible event started to sink in, real concerns came up.

Gavinet sucked his pen. “Lucien, our American friends will provide all the logistics. You will be whisked in and out. A patsy is being prepared. All you have to do is be there and shoot. Trust me. Our associates have as much incentive as we do to make sure this goes right. Two million dollars, Lucien.” Gavinet let the carrot dangle in the air.

If Gavinet thought he painted pictures of yachts and villas in Lucien’s mind, he was wrong. Money didn’t motivate Lucien, danger and excitement did. This was some serious danger and excitement.

“I must talk to Giancarlo and Robert. Can you give me till Friday?”

Gavinet was gracious. “Do what you need to do, Lucien, but I need an answer soon. Our American friends are anxious.” Gavinet knew he would do it.

Lucien cornered Giancarlo and Robert the next day. The three of them sat on a wooden bench overlooking the harbor, staring out at the boats and the seagulls. Giancarlo sat in contemplative silence as Robert skipped stones on the water's surface. Lucien's animated hands pumped up and down. To an outsider, they might have been discussing the dog races or the latest porno film.

Robert was excited. At 25, he was a more animated and lighter version of Lucien. And like Lucien, danger was his *métier*. Giancarlo was reluctant at first, but the two million dollars, at least his portion of it, plucked at his heart strings. If Gavinet's yachts and mansions were wasted on Lucien, they were not on Giancarlo. At 42, he was ancient by hitmen's standards, and one more good score could bring him retirement and comfort. Sort of a gangster's pension. Giancarlo would take the safest post. Lucien would agree to that, for sure.

In the summer of 1963, Lucien Sartee was 33 years old, the age he knew that Jesus had died. And like his savior, Lucien now had a mission, too. He gave Gavinet the okay the next day and asked him for some earnest money in advance. Gavinet peeled off a quarter of a million dollars and handed it to Lucien. He smiled. The superstar of hitmen was coming to America.

When Lyndon Johnson answered the phone, the Director was curt. When, he wanted to know, was the earliest possible time that the Vice President would be available for a top secret meeting? His curiosity aroused, the Veep inquired as to the nature of the meeting. "Can't tell, top secret," shot back J. Edgar in that staccato monotone of his.

"Does the President know about this?"

"This doesn't concern him," was the abrupt reply from the Director.

This is getting very interesting, Lyndon thought to himself. He glanced down at his afternoon schedule. A few marginal appointments, job seekers, mostly Texas politics. He could blow them off.

"How's about three o'clock this afternoon, Mr. Director?"

"That'll be fine. Three o'clock. And Mr. Vice President, not a word to anybody." With that, the Director hung up and left Lyndon with the phone buzzing in his ear.

When Lyndon entered the Director's office, he nearly fell through the floor. Seated in front of him was the strangest collaboration of powerful individuals he had ever seen. Lyndon turned white with anticipation.

"Afternoon, gentlemen," he offered to the assembled group. There were a few grunts and nods in return. The Director pointed him toward a chair and Lyndon ambled over to it and plopped down. In addition to the Director, sitting around the table were H. L. Hunt and Clint Murchison, Texas zillionaires and private businessmen; Leon L. Lennon, recently dispatched Chairman, Joint Chiefs of Staff; Clyde Tolson, Hoover's paramour and aide-de-camp; Allen Dulles, recently fired Director of the CIA, and another gentleman dressed in a military uniform, whom Lyndon didn't recognize.

"Mr. Vice President, I think you know Mr. Hunt, Mr. Murchison, General Lennon, Mr. Dulles and Mr. Tolson." Know them. Lyndon had practically slept with them. Hunt and Murchison were fellow Texans who Lyndon had dealt with for years, and though they were both rabid right wingers, Lyndon had managed to accommodate each of them over time, in return for healthy contributions.

Dulles, younger brother of the former Secretary of State for Eisenhower, John Foster Dulles, was a long-time power broker in Washington and a fixture at the CIA. His long career in intelligence started in the Balkans during World War I and continued with the OSS, predecessor to the CIA, during the Second World War. Up until his firing by Kennedy after The Bay of Pigs, he had been Director of the CIA for the prior ten years, capping a fifty year career in intelligence. A professional spook here. In fact, the consummate professional spook.

Lennon was head of the Joint Chiefs of Staff of the Armed Forces, or more accurately, recently dispatched Chief of Staff, relieved by Kennedy over philosophical differences regarding the assorted ventures of the military around the globe and specifically, The Bay of Pigs. And of course, Clyde was Clyde.

"And this," continued Hoover, "is General Charles Cabell, Mr. Dulles' associate." Lyndon stood to shake his hand and vaguely recognized something familiar about the face. "General Cabell is Earl Cabell's brother."

"Oh, Earl, fine man," Johnson chimed in. "Thought you looked familiar, General, pleased to meet you." Earl was Earl Cabell, Mayor of Dallas.

"Pleased to meet you sir," the General offered back.

"Gentlemen, let's all be seated," the Director, reassuming his hosting duties, continued. "The matter before us today is of the utmost urgency and secrecy." With that, the Director turned toward Lyndon and continued to speak.

"Mr. Vice President, there is a matter of highest priority that concerns us all, including you. Especially you. There is no delicate way to broach this subject, but it must be handled before the fact so that it can be dealt with effectively after its occurrence. It is something that must be done for the sake of the country and not, incidentally, for our own concerns as well." Hoover paused. The others peered over at Johnson, looking for a reaction. There was none.

Go ahead, pit-bull face, Johnson mused to himself. *Hit me with your best shot.* Johnson, more than usual, was all ears. He nodded at the Director to continue.

"Mr. Vice President, The President is going to be liquidated. We're going to need your cooperation." With that J. Edgar stopped.

With the blood draining quickly from his face and his large nose and ears dangling in the hushed silence, Lyndon looked like a miniature white elephant. J. Edgar's best shot was more powerful than Lyndon had anticipated. He began to shake. The others caught this and concern swept across their faces. Hoover remained calm.

Johnson desperately tried to compose himself. It was not that he didn't want it to happen. Nothing would please him more. He often dreamed of Kennedy's unfortunate demise either through accident or illness. But Kennedy, barely 46 years old, was unlikely to meet such a fate. The thought of precipitating the event was almost beyond the Veep's ability to comprehend, much less conceive of. As the thought sunk into his quickly numbing brain, his immediate reaction was that it was not "do-able." And even if it was, it would be impossible to cover up. Lyndon was into the do-able. This one simply was not.

Johnson stammered. "Mr. Director, are you referring to the killing of President Kennedy?"

Worried looks flashed around the table. They all thought Johnson would be more receptive to the idea. What they didn't know was that Johnson was not being unreceptive, he was just stunned.

"We prefer to think of it as the neutralization of the President, but, yes, Mr. Vice President, the killing of the President would also be accurate."

Spook talk, thought Lyndon. *Liquidation. Neutralization.* Where had he heard that before. *Auschwitz?* How hygienic for such an ungodly function. Sort of took the sting out of it.

"And who is going to be doing the liquidating? The Mafia?" Johnson was not unaware of the feud going on between that esteemed organization and the Brothers Kennedy.

"Well since you ask, Mr. Vice President, that is the general area of genesis. Several of the families..."

Johnson abruptly cut the Director off. "Edgar, the less I know about the specifics, the better."

"Fair enough, Mr. Vice President. But be assured that this will happen; we are powerless to prevent it. And if you give it some careful thought, I think you will agree that it is only for the good of the country. And when it does happen, you, as the new president, will need the most accurate and precise information to guide the nation through a time of fragility."

Translation: It is going to happen because we have no intention of attempting to stop it. In fact, we're glad that somebody else is going to do it for us so we don't have to do it ourselves. It is good for the country because we will be able to preserve our jobs and our power base, which we would otherwise be losing shortly. You're in the same boat as we are, Lyndon, so it is best that you go along. If you think about your own personal interests, you will clearly see this. And if for some bizarre reason you don't, we will ensure your complete cooperation. So why not do it on your terms instead of ours?

Lyndon was starting to thaw. *Lyndon Johnson, President of the United States.* Boy, did that have a nice ring to it. *But how were they going to pull it off and get away with it?* Lyndon was having trouble accepting this.

"Mr. Director, suppose it is as you say. My concern is how are you, or, excuse me, they, going to get at the man and how is an investigation going to be avoided?" Lyndon had thawed to the point where the potential murder didn't really matter; it was just the process that was troubling him.

"These are legitimate concerns, Mr. Vice President. In answer to your first question, we are going to indulge the President in his habit of riding in open motorcades. The President will be traveling to several cities in the South in the next couple of months and the neutralization is scheduled to take place there, probably in Florida or Texas. As far as the investigation is concerned, be advised that this is a well thought out and researched plan and that the investigation should be minimal. What there is of one, if any, can be contained by the agencies assembled here."

Lyndon didn't know whether to be honored or insulted at the choice of Texas, and said so. "Why Texas?" Lyndon blurted this out with a look of genuine hurt crossing his fleshy countenance.

"Because," continued the Director, "that is where Mr. Kennedy is vulnerable. General Cabell is coordinating the project for us, and he can update you on the details."

Sounds like these boys are involved in more than just the cover up part, Ole Lyndon thought to himself.

Hoover nodded to the General, giving him the floor. The General peered deferentially toward Johnson. "Please be advised, Mr. Vice President, this is an unpleasant but necessary business. We do it only in furtherance of our country's goals, which are threatened to be derailed if the country stays on its present course."

Blow it out your dick, you military horse's ass, mused Johnson to himself. *You do it because Kennedy fried your balls and now it's payback time.*

Cabell continued speaking as Johnson drifted. "There will be a motorcade. We would like you to ride in it. Credibility is of utmost importance." Johnson liked that part. Nobody would willingly place himself in jeopardy with foreknowledge. Nice touch.

"And what do I have to do, General Cabell?"

"Duck," was the one word answer. Laughter all around. This assassination business could be fun after all.

"Seriously, Mr. Vice President, all you need to do is be aware of the forthcoming events and be prepared to assume the stewardship of the country afterward. We are looking forward to your leadership."

I'll bet you are, penis breath, Johnson chuckled to himself. *Imagine this,* Lyndon started to fantasize. For years he had knocked himself out in search of the elusive presidency and now it was being handed to him on a silver platter. All he had to do was...nothing. Sit on a murder, but outside of that, nothing. *Ain't life bizarre. Damn,* thought Lyndon.

At this point, Hoover dismissed everybody else from the room, indicating he wanted to spend some time alone with Johnson. Lyndon correctly suspected that the others had been there mainly to gauge his reaction, and that the real business of the meeting would be transacted now.

Hoover nudged his chair up to Johnson's. *Not so close, gaybo*, Johnson breathed to himself.

"Lyndon, I speak to you as an old friend. Believe me, nobody wants to avoid what is about to happen more than I do, but it is absolutely necessary for the country's sake." Lyndon nodded. He was getting tired of this patriotic bullshit.

"But," continued his *pitbull-ness*, "there are practical reasons for it to transpire as well." Great, thought Lyndon. Thirty-five minutes into the meeting and the flame boy was finally getting around to the truth.

"Lyndon, as you know, neither of us has any love lost for the Kennedys, nor they for us." The understatement of the century. Maybe the millennium.

"I have worked for forty years to build this agency to what it is today and I'll be damned if I'm going to let it be ruined by a pair of horses' ass rich boys." Thirty years, Johnson thought, and he had never heard the Director swear. *Let it all hang out, J. Edgar. Lay it on me, Bro.*

"Now as you know, I am scheduled for mandatory retirement, the first of January, 1965. Only the President can waive that retirement. And Kennedy has given me no indication that he will exercise that option, despite my direct requests. You know as well as I that the pretty boy will be reelected in 1964, so you know where that leaves me. But more importantly, do you know where that leaves you?" Lyndon gave a quizzical look, indicating he was more than happy to let the Director continue his soliloquy. "Lyndon, do you know the President will not renominate you to the ticket in 1964?" Lyndon had considered this possibility despite Kennedy's reassurances to the contrary. He thought he would quiz J. Edgar on this one.

"How can you be so sure, Mr. Director?"

Hoover couldn't believe that Johnson was being so obtuse. Either he really was blind or he was playing dumb. The Director was always amazed at how someone could be so clouded about something that was so obvious to everyone else.

"Mr. Vice President, in all due respect, the President doesn't need you to be reelected. And since he doesn't need you, he will select someone with whom he is more politically and personally compatible. And someone with no political baggage."

Lyndon's antennae were up. J. Edgar was about to hit him with the haymaker and Johnson knew it.

"Political Baggage?"

"Look Lyndon, I know you know full well about what I am speaking, but just so there is no misunderstanding, I will delineate it clearly for you. We have complete knowledge about your friends, Mr. Baker and Mr. Sol Estes, and your involvement with them. We can bring down an indictment at any time."

Lyndon began to boil. *Why you motherfucking, fudge packing, blackmailing slimeball. Who are you to threaten me?* But Lyndon did not dare give voice to this line of thought because he knew Hoover could and would do it. *Got to* marvel at the old cocksucker's wiliness. Jail or the Presidency. Interesting choice the Director was presenting him with.

"Look Lyndon, let's sit down and reason together. Bottom line is, if Kennedy is reelected, we're both through. You know that that's true." In his heart Lyndon did, though he couldn't bring himself to admit it. Perhaps Hoover had a function, after all.

"Through no effort of our own, we have been given a second chance. This is not a coincidence, Lyndon; this was meant to be. Everything about the Kennedys is wrong and reeks of moral degeneracy. We were not responsible for generating this idea, nor are we responsible for putting it into effect. We just need to manage the outcome. Believe me Lyndon, if we both cooperate, it is quite do-able."

Hoover had touched on Johnson's favorite word, *do-able*. The normally garrulous Vice President sat there in a contemplative stupor, mulling the Director's words. Everything about them rang true. Unlike Johnson, whose only guiding principle was opportunism, Hoover seemed to have a genuine disdain for the Kennedys' libertine lifestyle and concern for the country's moral rectitude, as he saw it. The fact that it conveniently tied in to his own personal and political agenda was a matter of fortuitous coincidence.

Johnson looked up, and tired by the Director's harangue, shrugged his shoulders at J. Edgar, as if to say, "All right, I am a beaten man. It is a *fait accompli*. I accept your nomination for co-conspirator." J. Edgar smiled. He knew Lyndon would come to his senses.

So Lyndon Johnson was going to the South, probably Texas. To ride in a motorcade. Lyndon Johnson was going to be President of the United States. And all he had to do was remember to duck.

Things had not been going well for Jack when the phone rang one early May morning. It was Nofio Pecora from New Orleans. There was some work available. Might involve big money. Could Jack come down?

If there was one thing Jack needed, it was money. His whole world was coming apart and the only thing that could save it was money. Quick money.

Jack's whole world consisted of his two striptease joints, which he was in imminent danger of losing to the IRS, to the tune of forty-two thousand dollars in back taxes. Jack was nothing without his clubs. They provided him an outlet for his ego as the hamming *emcee* and a front for his illegal activities and ventures. But most of all, they gave him a forum to indulge his passion for mingling with Dallas' finest. Every Tuesday was Policemen's Night at the *Carousel* and Jack bobbed among the sea of blue like the glad-handing *maitre d'* he was. With his buddies from the force, Jack was in his glory. It was pure joy. He belonged to that strange breed of individual found in most every town that is *with* the police, but not *of* the police. And now he was in danger of losing it all.

He had been born one Jack Rubenstein, in Chicago, and grew up a tough street kid. He had served his apprenticeship as a numbers runner for Al Capone in the '30s. With the post-war expansion of Dallas, Jack became one of the charter members of the Mob to filter down from Chicago, for the express purpose of expanding their business to the booming Texas market. He evolved into a run-of-the-mill small time hood, dabbling in the big three: gambling, narcotics, and prostitution.

But there was a soft side about Rubinstein, who now called himself Ruby, that differentiated him from the standard John Q. Gangster. For one thing, he was a fitness freak and health food nut, oddities for those of the ilk. For another, he had a sense of compassion that caused him to take in the downtrodden. His clubs served as his own private little Salvation Army to facilitate his philanthropic activities. And finally, he was gay. All in all, a strange little hoodlum, this Rubenstein.

Despite living in the murky shadows of the underworld, or perhaps because of it, Jack was consumed with police work, police activities and policemen. He was their gracious host as well as their humble parasite. The station house was his second home, the same function his clubs served for the men in blue. There was nothing that went on in Dallas Police Headquarters, or no one associated with it, that Jack did not know. And because of his proclivity for the police, his association with the underworld, and his residency in Dallas, he was the right man in the right place at the right time. That is if your viewpoint coincided with Carlos Marcello and his brethren.

Nofio Pecora was as dark, sinister and large as his name implied. He was Marcello's own private merchant of death and the one personally chosen to handle sensitive issues. Ruby knew that a phone call from Pecora had to be something important and he was soon on the next bus to New Orleans. When Jack dutifully reported to the backroom of Pecora's Bourbon Street bar, the burly Sicilian was in an animated phone conversation with some recalcitrant lieutenant, in what appeared to be a disagreement of principles. Life spans for recalcitrant lieutenants with divergent principles were known to be precariously short and this one didn't seem that it was going to be considerably different. Pecora motioned Jack to come in and sit down; he would be with him in a minute.

Pecora slammed the phone down. He ran his fingers through his thick tuft of brushed back hair. He was searching for a cigarette.

"That fucking Dago intellectual," Pecora muttered, mostly to himself, "is fucking dogmeat. History." He found a cigarette and lit it. He offered one to Jack, who politely refused.

"Sorry, Jack to have to burden you with this,..." Jack put up his hand, cutting Nofio off, as if to say, "Mr. Pecora, I understand you are a very busy man with many important things to do. I'll wait here for you like the toady I am till you wrap them up."

Nofio gave a little smile. "Thanks, Jack, for understanding." Jack nodded back. Pecora composed himself, went behind the large oak desk and plunked himself down in the overstuffed swivel chair. He turned the full force of his laser black eyes in Jack's direction.

"Jack, it's been a while. What was it, '60, '61, you handled those shipments for us going out of the country?" Jack nodded again. It was '60 and the shipments had been guns headed for Cuba. Sufficient pleasantries had been exchanged.

"Jack, the reason I asked you here today is we know the problems you are having with the IRS concerning your clubs and we know how much your clubs mean to you. We are in a position to help." Ruby remained smiling despite the little alarm bells going off inside his head. The Mafia was not a something for nothing organization, and something about Pecora's tone indicated a very large something was expected in return from Ruby. But Pecora was right on the first part. Jack was having trouble with the IRS and was about to lose control of the central core of his life. Jack would listen.

"Jack, I'm sure you are aware that there is a contract out on President Kennedy's life." Jack nodded. He had heard such a thing, but then again, he heard many things. This was the first confirmation of it that had come his way.

"In fact, Jack," Nofio continued, "we are behind it and we intend to carry it out shortly." *Fine*, thought Jack, *but what has this got to do with me? I'm strictly small potatoes. What do I know from political assassinations*?

Pecora continued. "We intend to carry it out in Florida. Or Dallas." All of a sudden Jack knew what it had to do with him. The little alarm bells had become a ten alarm fire.

"Jack, we are in a position to clear up your debt completely. What we need in return is some help with a few minor details of the plan. *Kapish?*" Jack *kapished* all right. God only knew what a few minor details meant to the likes of Pecora. An ax murder maybe, or having Kennedy drawn and quartered on the Stemmons Freeway, perhaps.

"What details are you referring to, Nofio?"

"Jack, we need your help in two key areas. First, we need somebody with good contacts within the Dallas Police force. We know you're that man." Ruby couldn't deny that one, nor anyone else's knowledge of it. He was flattered.

"Secondly, we are preparing a patsy and we need some help in that area. Nothing major." Okay, thought Jack, so far so good. All depends on what you consider major. Unlike the mainstream of the Mafia, Ruby had no personal vendetta against Kennedy. In fact, he sort of liked him. A life long Democrat, Jack had voted for him in '60 and would do so again in '64. But if an assassination was going to happen, it would happen with or without him. This could be some big money they were offering.

"Nofio, what are the particular details you are asking me to help you with?"

Pecora eyeballed him. Ruby was being particularly reticent, but then again, Nofio figured that Jack was entitled to the details before deciding. If he gave him that option.

Nofio hunched forward in his chair. "Jack, I'm going to bring in someone to go over the details with you. He's a little eccentric, but bear with him; he's very efficient and he's coordinating the plan for us." Nofio punched a little box on his desk. "Carla, can you ask Mr. Ferrie to join us."

A little eccentric! W.C. Fields was a little eccentric. This guy was a walking circus. Ruby gazed at the hyperkinetic piece of work busy bouncing off walls in front of him. He was embarrassed for his kind. *Didn't these young queens have any sense of shame, any dignity? And what was with the hair and eyebrows?* Great, thought Ruby. Now the Mafia is in the freak business as well.

Ferrie came to a gradual halt, or at least to a momentary cessation of hyperactivity. He was pleased to meet Ruby. Always liked Dallas. Good clubs there. Ruby owned the *Carousel?* No kidding!

"David, Jack is considering helping with the plan," Pecora offered, as if this was the first time Ferrie had heard of it. "He needs you to catch him up on the particulars."

"Fine," replied Ferrie, and started to pace again. Ruby was getting vertigo.

"Mr. Ruby, I know that Mr. Pecora has informed you of the gist of what we are looking to do. Did you tell him about the patsy?" Pecora nodded.

"We are preparing a patsy by the name of Lee Oswald. We have had him purchase a rifle which we have told him to keep in his garage. We will subsequently steal it, unbeknownst to him, and plant it at the scene of the crime." Ruby was beginning to like Ferrie. At least he could call a spade a spade.

"If we can successfully shoot the President, they will rush him to the nearest hospital, which will be Parkland. We need somebody familiar to the police who can get past a police blockade to plant a bullet from Oswald's rifle on or near the car or stretcher carrying Kennedy."

"Where's the scene of the crime?"

"Dealey Plaza."

Ruby turned to Pecora. "And how much do want to pay me for this, Nofio?"

"We are prepared to settle your debts of fifty thousand dollars and offer you a springboard of another fifty as well."

Not bad, thought Jack. One hundred thousand dollars to drop a bullet at the emergency entrance of Parkland Hospital. Dangerous, considering the circumstances, but do-able. "Okay," said Jack. "Consider it done."

"There's more," barked Ferrie. There always was.

"Once we have planted the evidence against the patsy, it is imperative that he be implicated, but not fall into the hands of the police. He must be killed immediately after the assassination."

Jack started turning red. "You want me to kill this guy? Nofio, that's not my line of work!" Ruby was on his feet.

"Calm down Jack, please, relax. We're not asking you to kill anybody. Please, just let David continue." Jack sat back down and mopped his brow. Ferrie started to pace again.

"We are setting up the patsy to leave the crime scene on another mission altogether. This can be construed as attempting to flee the crime. While he is in the process of doing this, he will be shot and killed by real policemen, who will later be vindicated for cutting down the President's assassin, an obviously dangerous man." The plan was starting to assume the proportions of brilliance.

"See Jack, we don't want you to kill nobody," Nofio smiled. "What we need is two policemen willing to take down the patsy at fifty thousand apiece. Be fuckin' heroes for shooting this cocksucker and bag 50K to boot. Not bad for a day's work. Know anybody who might be interested?"

Yeah, Jack knew people. About half the Dallas Police force. Most of them were so right wing, that if they knew it involved Kennedy, they'd do it for free. But this was risky business. Talking about killing somebody was easy, actually doing it was something else altogether. Especially in the confusion and frenzy following a presidential assassination. Or maybe this would make it easier; Jack didn't know. Sure, he knew people. Two names bounced right to the front of his brain. Benton and White. Rabid to the bone. Good old boys disguised in fancy blue uniforms. He would talk to them.

"I think I can find some people for you, Nofio. I may need a little time. How long do I have?"

"It's May now, the President's coming in October or November. How about by July 4th?"

Jack smiled. "Very patriotic. That's fine."

"What if he gets away?," Jack queried.

"Who?"

"The patsy."

"He won't. And if he does, we'll deal with it then." Little could Ruby know the dire consequences of those words.

"How did you pick this guy, this Oswald?"

"Because," Pecora pontificated like the intellectual sage he wasn't, "he was at hand." Ferrie liked that one. He let out a howl.

"Anything else?" said Jack.

"A few minor details." *Oh, God, here it comes,* thought Jack. *Here's where I jump out of the Mr. Softy van and shoot Vice President Johnson and the staff of the New York Times.*

"We will need you to monitor and inform us of all the details of the motorcade as the police coordinate them with the Secret Service."

"Nofio, those are the first minor details you've hit me with today that are actually minor details." They all laughed. The meeting was ending on a high note, a consensus. Ruby might be able to bail his ass out after all.

The Texas gangster got up to go. Nofio pulled open his top drawer and took out a wad of bills. "Jack, just to show you we are dealing in good faith, I am giving you ten thousand dollars now. We will pay you forty thousand more on the completion of the job and fifty thousand a week later, when the furor dies down. Try to stall the IRS till then, and if you can't, let me know. I am also giving you another ten thousand dollars for the policemen. We want two, just to be sure. Five thousand in advance, for each man. If they don't accept, let them keep the 5K, to keep their mouths shut. If they accept, they get 45K each after the completion of the job, regardless of who does the shooting. If they accept and welsh out, they're history; they bought the big *manaña.* And Jack, choose wisely. We don't want to go spreading our money around like horse manure." They laughed again. Jack told Pecora he would see him in a month, bid goodbye to Ferrie, and was on his way.

"Whaddaya think?" Pecora was querying Ferrie.

"He'll be okay. He just better hope to hell his boys get Oswald."

Officers J.D. Benton and Roscoe White came down the stairs at the usual time and sat at the usual table, had the usual scotches and watched the usual naked bodies prance across the stage. "Dang, God bless Jack Ruby, showing the boys a good time like this and all at no charge."

Ruby watched the dynamic duo gently get soused and quietly approached the table. He interrupted the usual conversation about niggers, Jews, communists and faggots, these intellectual titans never suspecting that Ruby might be a member of two of these groups.

"Evening, boys."

"Evening, Mr. Ruby, why don't you set a spell," offered White.

"Don't mind if I do, don't mind if I do." Ruby plunked himself down at the table.

"Fine scenery in here tonight, Jack, as usual," offered Benton. Jack looked over at the two men. The Nordic White was a vision of Teutonic loveliness. He looked like he just stepped out of the Waffen SS, with about the same sense of compassion. Benton was nondescript, but powerfully built, and by far the quieter of the two. Ruby leveled his gaze at them.

"Gentlemen, I am going to make an unusual offer to you. I will pay you five thousand dollars each just for listening to it, under the condition that if you choose not to accept, you say nothing to anybody. Fair enough?" White looked over at Benton and Benton back at White. *Five thousand dollars for Mr. Ruby to flap his gums? No problem.*

Ruby was not one to beat around the bush. After taking a discreet look around, he pushed a wad of banded bills toward each officer. Benton and White sat up at complete attention. "This, gentlemen, is for your silence. Violation will be fatal. Do I make myself clear?" They both nodded. All of a sudden Fifi LaTush was not so interesting.

Jack hunched forward. "What do you think of Jack Kennedy?"

White's eyes flashed. "I'd kill that motherfucker in a heartbeat." Ruby had found a gold mine.

"You won't have to. Somebody's going to do it for you."

White had been joking. Ruby had not. Sensing this, the two policemen leaned closer.

"What are you talking about, Jack?," the quiet Benton chipped in.

"Kennedy's going to be hit, probably here in Dallas. Contract killing. Couple of months."

"You don't expect us to shoot the President of the United States for five thousand dollars, do you, Jack?" Ruby rolled his eyeballs. Rhodes Scholars, he was not dealing with here.

"Roscoe, I just told you, it's a contract killing. We don't expect you to kill the President for any amount of money."

"What is it you want us to do, Jack?," asked Benton.

"Well, there is a patsy being set up to take the fall. All kinds of evidence is being planted against him. We need to eliminate him before he falls into police custody. That's where you come in."

Benton stared at him. "You want us to kill an innocent man, Jack?" Ruby was beginning to worry about Benton. Maybe he wasn't so wise in his choice after all.

"He's not exactly innocent. He's a CIA operative."

"Is he dangerous?"

"Hardly. Strictly low level stuff. Deliveries and pick ups and the like. Lived in the Soviet Union, has a Russian wife."

"Fucking commie bastard. Probably Kennedy's brother-in-law," White laughed. Ruby had found a productive vein.

Benton hesitated. "No offense, Jack, but five thousand dollars is not a lot of money to shoot a man for."

Jack gave Benton an annoyed glance but realized he had left out a major detail. "Don't worry, Officer Benton, there's a lot more than that involved. I'll get to that in a minute. Fair enough?" Benton nodded.

"Okay, that's fair enough, but how are we going to get at him, Jack?" Benton was concerned with the practical side.

"That'll be easy. Roughly a half hour after the assassination, we have the patsy coming down to the club, thinking he's on a mission to drop something off. When he gets inside, you shoot him, no witnesses. Say you saw him run inside the club and when you asked him to halt, he pulled a gun on you. You had to shoot him in self defense. Once they start uncovering the plants, your asses will be off the fire. Obviously you're dealing with a very dangerous man who just killed the President. You'll be fucking heroes."

"Why do you need the police to do it?" Benton was starting to get on his nerves. He asked too many questions.

"Very simple, Officer Benton. Who but the police can kill a suspect and not have to go into a big song and dance about it? It gives us what they call credibility." Benton was satisfied. The plan made sense to him. White was excited. To be in on the killing of the nigger loving, pinko Pope boy was an honor, and to be paid for it was just icing on the cake.

"What about the money, Jack?"

"You each get fifty thousand dollars when the job is completed. Minus the 5K I just gave you." Benton whistled. White looked like he was going to fall out of his chair. Jack smiled. He had them.

"Do we both get paid the 50K or just the one who shoots him?" Benton wanted to make sure to cover all bases.

"It doesn't matter. You both get paid regardless if one or both of you shoot him. Just as long as he gets shot and killed. It's very important to the organization that this man be eliminated before he's captured; that's why they want two of you. Eliminates the rogue cop element as well. Remember, gentlemen, the patsy's death is imperative. No death, no money."

"What organization are you talking about, Jack?" Somewhere in the intervening months, Benton had turned into Socrates, unbeknownst to Ruby.

"Officer Benton, the cash is real now as it will be when the job is completed. What you don't know, won't hurt you."

Jack's stern glance indicated that no further questions would be in order.

Benton was satisfied. He had four kids to feed and fifty thousand dollars represented five years salary. Although inclined to the right, he was indifferent to Kennedy as a politician or an individual. But to get 50K as an innocent bystander and keep his mouth shut, would not be hard to do. White would shoot the patsy, of that he was sure. Benton was in. White could hardly contain his excitement. "Be itchin' to do it, Jack, itchin' to do it."

"Good, now you boys keep quiet about this and wait on me for details. If you're in, you're in, there's no backing out now. You in?" They both nodded.

Benton had another question. "How do we know we'll be in the area?" Ruby sighed, but had to acknowledge that this was a legitimate concern.

"Because with the presidential motorcade, most everybody will be in the area and once the President gets hit, all hell will break loose and you'll be able to free-lance without accountability at that point. Make sense?" Benton shook his head. It made sense.

"Any more questions?" No, Benton and White were satisfied, and Fifi LaTush beckoned. There was 10K to spend.

"Good," said Jack, getting up. "I'll be in touch with details. And remember..." Jack drew his hand in a slash across his throat and mouth indicating that talk was fatal. They understood.

Jack worried about Benton. He had been reticent. But Benton had a reputation of being a man of his word as well as a good soldier. Ruby figured he'd be okay. With White it was just a question of restraining him so he didn't take out half a dozen strippers along with the patsy. But nothing was perfect and Jack figured this was the best he was going to do.

Jack relaxed. He had finished the hard part. The clubs would remain his and consequently, everything else important in his life. Strange how fate had intervened in his favor. He was just one planted bullet and a few motorcade details away from one hundred thousand dollars.

Lucien gazed down on the wide expanse of Dealey Plaza. It was love at first sight, a thing of beauty. Ambush heaven. He drew up his collar as he braced himself against the late October winds and walked along the top of the overpass, Giancarlo and Robert in tow.

The plaza was a canvas for him and he studied it with a loving and steady eye. He gauged the angles, scoped the sight lines, perused the buildings and scanned the foliage. He bent, he twisted, he turned, he crouched, he flopped on his belly. He immersed himself in the Plaza and proceeded to make love to it. He was an artist deep in the middle of holy creation, the birth of his *magnum opus.* Here, in Dallas, Texas, of all places.

Lucien liked every little thing about this fruitful acre. If only it had a building on its southern rim, the place would be perfect, but outside of that, it was more than serviceable. More than serviceable. The Kennedy motorcade was due to ride straight down Main Street and dip into the bowl that was Dealey Plaza and then pass below the triple underpass on its way to the Trade Mart. Once it crossed Houston and headed into the Square, the President could be hit right in the middle, by shooters in buildings to the back and side, while Lucien delivered the *coup de grace* from the overpass in front. Lucien had been assured that the area would be clear of government interference and that he could get men into whatever building he wanted to.

They photographed the Square by day and studied it by night. Complete resources were at Lucien's disposal. Mock CIA operatives, fake policemen, bogus Secret Service agents. You name it, no expense would be spared. The Mafia wanted to insure success. The agreement was that the Government would not provide any agents to assist the event; they just wouldn't supply any to prevent it. That is, other than a few FBI agents assigned to confiscate any film they saw being taken during the shooting.

The only elements with the potential for interference were those members of the Dallas Police force and the Secret Service assigned to the motorcade, who were unaware of the plot. By the time they reacted, it would be too late. The Secret Service would be wined and dined till the wee hours the night before, Lucien was assured, and a key agent would give a halt order the second the shooting started. A few select Dallas policemen would jam the radio communiqué immediately prior to the shooting to confuse any uninformed officer who reacted immediately after it.

Lucien saw one small adjustment that he hoped could be made. If he could somehow get the motorcade to make a ninety degree right turn onto Houston and then an immediate left onto Elm, thus encompassing the dog leg of Dealey Plaza, he could slow it down considerably and make Kennedy a sitting duck. This move would also bolster the cover up by bringing it directly in front of the patsy's building and would provide Lucien with an excellent backup position as well. If for any reason the exposed overpass was guarded, Lucien could always dart down to behind the picket fence atop the grassy knoll area and have a clear protected shot from fifty feet away. Could Lucien get that change? Could the motorcade still reach its destination if it took this route? He waited. Four days before the event, on November 18th, he got the okay. The route had been altered. Much better, thought Lucien. Now it was time for final preparations.

Giancarlo and Robert would work in teams of three. Perched at a window in a building, each would need an assistant right next to him to scoop shells and disassemble the rifle, and another assistant to seal off the floor and act as lookout. One of the assistants would have a police type uniform and the other a business suit and CIA credentials. This would provide a potent combination for getting into a building, securing a floor, and accessing an exit, all necessary elements. Robert would work high and from the side, on the sixth floor of the patsy's building, the Texas School Book Depository. His team would plant three shells under the southeast corner window where Robert would be shooting from. They would also place the patsy's rifle in the northwest corner, just before the floor exit, to make it look like an escape down the opposite stairwell. The key radio man would also be with Robert's team, working from the southwest corner of the sixth floor of the Depository, from a position where he could see all three teams. Giancarlo would work low and from behind, the safest position, on the third floor of the Dallas County Records Building. A chauffeured getaway car for Giancarlo would be behind that building, directly east of the Square, and one for Robert would be at the corner of Houston, where the street looped around to the east, a block northeast of the Depository building.

Lucien, either on the overpass or behind the grassy knoll, would need the most protection. He would need an assistant next to him to work the radio, scoop the shells, and act as lookout. Since he would be working right next to the train track at either location, he had a brilliant idea of dressing a man as a railroad worker with a large tool box, to whom he could toss the rifle for immediate disassembling and stashing in the box. Who would question a calmly moving railroad worker in the immediate chaos surrounding the shooting?

He would also need several men with official credentials to keep the back of the picket fence and overpass clear, and to try to steer as many people as possible off the grassy knoll. He figured two phony CIA agents with suits to handle the real policemen and two fake policemen to detour civilians, for these functions. Lucien himself would wear a police uniform and have a getaway car parked near Robert's to the northeast of the Depository.

If all went well, shooting and pitching the rifle would take five seconds, at most, and by the time the crowd and the police started moving up the knoll, if they did, he would be halfway down Elm Street, in front of the Depository. He would be moving calmly in the opposite direction from the surging crowd, for a quick duck down Houston and the block and a half walk to the getaway car.

It was a good workable plan, requiring only half of the twenty five men at his disposal. Lucien wasn't so worried about the CIA suits, but having too many bogus cops around could get hairy. Best to limit the number.

He figured that Giancarlo and Robert should be able to get off three shots each and still make an easy getaway. As for himself, Lucien would have one point blank shot, possibly a second one as well, but two at most. That's seven to eight shots, one or two from fifty feet, any one of which could do the job by itself. Lucien knew that this number should be more than adequate. Mustn't get greedy. The getaway was as important as the shooting.

Lucien was set. He told Novello, owner of the safehouse where the three had been staying, to notify Ferrie that his plan was ready, and to procure the men and material needed to execute it. Marcello was pleased. Everything was running like clockwork and the plan had come in well under budget. Gambino had been right about this Lucien. He worked swiftly, efficiently, and intelligently. Now all he had to do was work successfully and Carlos could relax.

Marcello needn't have worried. Barring a major change in presidential plans, Lucien was sure he could pull it off. Despite the protests of Giancarlo and Robert, Lucien selected two exploding bullets, his *imprimatur*. They were too messy, they would give away the direction of the shots. Lucien didn't care. This was his masterpiece and he was damn well going to sign it.

November 17th was just an ordinary quiet fall Sunday across the heartland of the nation. The leaves had fallen and winter's ominous specter was poking its head around the distant corner. Americans went to church, visited relatives, watched football on TV and looked forward to Thanksgiving as they rested for the work week.

In Jefferson Parish, Louisiana, David Ferrie visited Churchill Farms, the estate of kingpin Carlos Marcello, to review the final details for the impending events of the coming Friday. Marcello was either about to unburden himself and his fellow Mafiosi, or seal their collective fate forever. He wanted to make sure he was doing everything to achieve the former and avoid the latter.

Was the team in place? Did they have the men and materials they needed? Was the getaway secure? Would all the incriminating evidence be planted and would the patsy be silenced before the authorities could get him? Yes, assured and reassured Ferrie, the plan had been solidified and the details had been looked after.

And what about *after the fact*, the part they couldn't really manipulate? Had they exercised as much control as possible? Yes, again, reassured Ferrie. Key people in the upper echelons of the different agencies were aware, stood to benefit, and would do their utmost to provide a cover up. Nothing was without risk, but for an event of this magnitude, they sure were getting a hell of a lot of cooperation. Carlos could relax, claimed Ferrie, but with the crime boss' own trial for income tax evasion expected to culminate shortly, it didn't look like a relaxing kind of week. Carlos would just have to wait.

Some five hundred miles to the northwest, Lee Oswald was spending a quiet Sunday watching football and playing with his two daughters. Ferrie had contacted him again, something about delivering a package somewhere on Friday. Lee would do it, but this would be the last hurrah. He was sick of these spooks with their weird requests and no longer would put up with their nonsense, even for the money. Some joker from the FBI had repeatedly tried to contact his wife for God-only knows what reason. In between the CIA and the FBI, Lee didn't know whether he was coming or going anymore. But that would all change soon. The birth of his second daughter had given him determination and direction, hitherto embryonic, but now fully blossoming. It was time for him to get serious and Lee was ready.

Halfway across the country, two lights blazed in the Oval Office, as the President stared into the gloaming and slipped off his shoes to put his feet up on a small ottoman. He was in a reflective mood as he readied for another week of action, crisis and intensity. If he wanted to be where the action was, he hadn't sold himself short, as the burdens of the office had aged him far more than the almost three years he had held it. But despite the worry, the pressure and the constant angst, Kennedy simply loved being president. He was good at it and the country loved him. He would be reelected in a heartbeat in '64; no one had any doubts about that. One of his biggest worries was what the hell he would do afterwards. After all, he would only be fifty one years old. What do you do for an encore?

As the President cradled his scotch and rocked back and forth in his chair, he was joined by the one person in the world he could trust, relax and let his hair down with: his brother Bobby. Bobby was not just brother or attorney general, but alter ego and soulmate, as well. Jack didn't know what he'd do without Bobby and hopefully he'd never have to find out. There was a magic, a chemistry between the two of them, an insoluble bond that existed on some spiritual plane. They could think each other's thoughts, complete each other's sentences. Jack was the Yin to Bobby's Yang.

Although physically larger, Jack was the softer, more reflective of the two. Bobby was a carbon copy of his father, tough, hyper, with bulldog like tenacity. He was John Kennedy's son of a bitch, a position he executed without peer. Arrogant, impulsive, condescending, the younger Kennedy collected enemies like bottle caps and had earned the sobriquet "most hated man in Washington," in a record six years. His brother was his God and he would walk through fire to serve and protect him, which he did. The team worked well together.

The President smiled wistfully as he gazed out at the White House lawn. "Did you ever think, Bobby, twenty years ago, that we'd be sitting here today?"

"I didn't, but I'm sure Dad did," came the reply, as they both chuckled.

"Well I sure as hell didn't," continued the President. "Figured Joe would do it for me. Just think, Bobby. Joe, then Kick, Rosemary, and now Dad. We've sure had our share." Bobby nodded. Growing up, Jack's two closest siblings had been his older brother Joe and sister Kathleen, or Kick, as she was known. Both had died in plane crashes. Joe's death had been on a high risk flight mission during World War II. Kathleen's demise in 1948, came after her marriage to a British royal, for which her mother disowned her. Rosemary, born retarded, had been lobotomized at the behest of Joe Sr., when sexual stirrings began to awaken in her. But the most recent tragedy had been to the patriarch himself, felled by a massive stroke in December '61. The former dynamo had been left paralyzed, in a wheel chair, and unable to speak. To see the diminished visage of their father had caused the sons great sorrow. Everything the progenitor had worked for his whole life had culminated in the ascendancy of his sons to president and attorney general, respectively, and he had less than a year to enjoy it. He seemed to be perceiving everything, but given his diminished state, it was hard to tell. Still, his dutiful sons visited him regularly at his Hyannisport and Palm Beach estates and the old man's life was not without its comforts.

"Did you ever think," began a surprisingly reflective Bobby, "when you were running, that we'd end up going through all we have in such a short time?"

The President laughed to himself. These were remarkable times. The Bay of Pigs. The Cuban Missile Crisis. The Berlin Wall. The marches in the South. The Space Race. So much had transpired and so much more was to come.

"Well, I would have preferred to put it in a more orderly agenda myself, but I guess we don't have that luxury; we'll have to take what comes."

"What do you think is going to happen in Berlin?" queried Bobby.

"Well, nothing for now, there or in Cuba. I know Nikita will wait to see what happens in the '64 elections before he offers any bold new initiatives. I think he feels he can work with us, especially if he knows that Goldwater is his alternative." The President paused and they both nodded. "On the other hand, I'm not half as scared of Khrushchev as I am of the goddamned CIA. God only knows what trouble those clowns will precipitate in Cuba or anywhere else for that matter. They're out of control." Kennedy shook his head. "If the people only knew."

Kennedy had been shocked to learn the extent of self perpetuating covert activity that he had inherited from the CIA and other governmental agencies. He called them the shadow government, and that's just what they were. Unelected, they worked under the guise of national security, using taxpayer dollars, to advance and maintain their own agendas, free from accountability, monitoring, or control. Kennedy was determined to smash the collective lot of them, but every time he brought the considerable weight of his office crashing down on them, they rose up like some hydra-headed beast, grinning, mocking, snapping at his heels. The CIA. The FBI. Naval Intelligence. The Joint Chiefs. All were out of control, all poking their grubby little fingers well beyond their original charters. *Fuck 'em.* After '64, they were history. Kennedy would have his mandate and send the squirrels packing. He would tolerate and coexist with them the best he could until then.

"But you know, Bobby, I think the thing I'll remember most about this time is what's happening with Martin. I never thought I would say that, but, damn, he really touched me in that last rally at the Mall. I just wish they weren't so goddamned impatient. We're talking about reversing three hundred years of history. You just don't do that overnight." The President was referring to the previous summer's march on Washington that had drawn a quarter of a million people and culminated with King's magnificent "I have a dream" speech. Both brothers had watched the event on TV and had been deeply moved. Kennedy thought he might have met his match on the oratorical front. According to Hoover's files, he had definitely met his match in the bedroom arena.

Kennedy laughed as he thought of this. Hoover, the paranoid nut, taping, monitoring, blackmailing. A communist behind every civil rights activity, every new idea, every Kennedy initiative. What an outrage that this man, this *thing*, was allowed to continue day after day, in his little world of intrigue, totally unaccountable to the American people, acting completely above and beyond the bounds of law, to the tune of his own agenda. All the while as head of the country's premier law enforcement agency.

Hoover would be seventy less than two months after the '64 elections and Kennedy looked forward with great anticipation to turning the old prick out on his ear. Hoover had repeatedly brought a presidential rescinding of the mandatory retirement to Kennedy's attention, amidst threats of blackmail for the latter's sexual proclivities. But the President wasn't buying it. *Bank your hopes on Goldwater, you primordial pimp, because once the election is over, you're dogmeat.* Bobby and Jack both relished the thought, although Bobby had to admit that he might miss antagonizing the old curmudgeon with his little bell of torture. God, was that fun! Well, there would always be Lyndon to torture. Or would there?

The President had thought about this one at length and still hadn't come to a decision. He figured events would eventually make one for him. Lyndon had spent his time being the *sub rosa* vice president, trading his visibility as former Senate majority leader for a clandestine world of quasi-legitimate activities. What the hell, as veep he had nothing but time on his hands. Time for Ole Lyndon to finally take care of himself. The President was apprised of his second-in-command's activities and figured Johnson could self implode without great damage to the administration or the ticket. Texas' electoral votes would be nice, but Kennedy figured he could win them without the erstwhile favorite son on the ticket. And even if he couldn't, election mathematics fell strongly in Kennedy's favor, even after writing off the South and the Lone Star Empire. No, the decision wasn't really over the election. It was more of, do you want him inside the tent pissing out, or outside the tent pissing in?, to quote the immortal Johnson himself. Either way, Kennedy wasn't concerned. Lyndon was peripheral, at best.

What was the agenda for the week, Bobby wanted to know. "Everything still on?" Everything was still on. Everything consisted of a quick trip to Florida, Miami and Tampa, a midweek birthday party for Bobby himself, and then a Thursday-Friday dash to Texas, before heading back to the White House. It was the beginning of the '64 campaign and Kennedy wanted to assess and shore up whatever strength he had in the South, a generally hostile region, especially Texas. But he was determined for a mandate and damn well wouldn't weasel out in the face of some potential opposition. The voters would have to reject him face to face.

Bobby was worried. Wasn't there some kind of assassination threat in Miami? Jack acknowledged there was and had canceled the motorcade, if not the appearance. The President pondered his mortality at such times, but the smell of the crowd was too much of an aphrodisiac. Kennedy liked to live on the edge, whether it be an open air motorcade or a woman. The Secret Service was good. They would protect him.

Besides, wasn't it Bobby's life that was threatened? Wasn't it Hoffa who was going to blow him up with dynamite? They both laughed. That crude behemoth would be behind bars within a year, of that they both were sure.

The war on organized crime had gone well. Local Godfathers were on the ropes, facing imprisonment, deportation, or both. The President figured it was because he didn't have to fight the CIA to achieve these successes. Nevertheless, a second term would see more of the same, a total smashing of this virulent pestilence. *Let them lie in the gutter with the fetid remains of the governmental reprobates. Good riddance to all these bloodsuckers.*

There was a gentle knock on the door. The Attorney General got up to answer it, as the President mulled his drink. The lovely form of Jackie Kennedy appeared, quickly followed by the mad rush that was Caroline and John-John.

Jackie smiled at the two brothers. She knew they were in deep reverie, sharing a bond that no one, even she, could hope to touch. She was happy for her beleaguered husband to have somebody he could share his burdens with. Marriage to this man had proven more bewildering than she had anticipated. After four years, she had been ready to chuck it, presidential ambitions and all notwithstanding. The philandering had been just too egregious and Jackie wasn't going to be held up to scorn, especially in the public eye. Poppa Joe had to lobby long and hard to quell her unhappiness, and only after trunkloads of money were promised did she decide to try to hang on till after the '60 election. Being First Lady might be interesting, she thought. Besides, she liked Poppa Joe, tough old bird that he was. If only she could like her husband half as much.

Maybe the presidency would change him. But after a ten minute assignation in a backroom closet at the Inaugural Ball, she decided it was hopeless. So she set off on a White House spending spree that would have made Mary Todd Lincoln green with envy. Wallpaper, carpets, dresses, you name it, Jackie was acquiring it. The President shook his head as he held a thick stack of mounting bills in front of him. He had seen it before, the price his straying *paterfamilias* paid to support Rose's mad dashes to Europe and other assorted ventures. At least Jackie had good taste.

She had to laugh when she thought about Camelot. "If only they knew," she smirked to herself. But being First Lady did have its benefits, apart from the gentle art of acquiring. Jackie was able to indulge her passion for the arts and hobnob with the creators, *cognoscenti* and intellectual movers and shakers she admired so much. *John Kennedy, patron of the arts, ha!* Jackie had to admit that the President did seem to enjoy "Hail to the Chief," and even a little bit of country music. But his overall attitude toward the arts was better exemplified when he refused to go backstage at a performance of the Bolshoi Ballet and be photographed with some "Russian fairies." But how could she fault the man if his only interests were politics and sex? He was good at them both, even if the latter was infrequently performed within the bounds of marriage.

As far as Jack was concerned, Jackie was turning out to be a pleasant surprise. Not only was she a good and doting mother, but more importantly, she was becoming a major political asset. After years of frozen potato ladies like Bess Truman and Mamie Eisenhower, the American public was hungry for the glamour, beauty and youth Jackie brought to the White House. More than anything, intentionally or not, she was the guiding light behind Camelot.

With her good looks, shy demeanor and ability at languages, she was becoming a player on the world stage as well. Kennedy had taken her to Latin America where she charmed the natives by speaking to them in Spanish. Using her expertise in French, she performed a similar feat and enthralled the icy DeGaulle, when she captured the hearts of Europe in the 1963 trip to France with the President. She didn't like the limelight, but when the President pushed her into it, she performed well. For the glory, the glamour, the access, the occasional spotlight was a small price to pay. She could stand being First Lady another five years. In the upcoming political year, the President would use Jackie extensively and the trip to Texas would be a testing ground for this strategy. It would be her first political trip of the campaign.

Her political assets notwithstanding, Jack did not mean to hurt Jackie. He just couldn't seem to break an old family tradition. When asked by a reporter friend if he wasn't concerned about his behavior effecting his presidential ambitions, he answered, "I just can't help myself." It was an honest answer. He couldn't help himself. This man, blessed with enormous charm, looks, and wealth, had women literally throwing themselves at him. He just didn't have the power to say no. It had cost him with Jackie, and at times, had almost cost him his political career.

Toward the beginning of his administration, JFK had become briefly entangled with Marilyn Monroe. He had not realized the unstable nature of the troubled starlet and was only to discover it later, much to his regret. As if being involved with someone who was also involved with a Mafia kingpin wasn't bad enough, this woman was a ticking time bomb. She besieged the White House, the hotels and the residences of JFK's travels with her calls. By the time of his now infamous Madison Square Garden birthday party, things were out of control. The President sent his brother, Bobby, to the starlet's Santa Monica home for the unseemly task of breaking off the affair. This action only exacerbated matters. Marilyn became hysterical and began the quick deterioration that would culminate in her untimely death barely two months later. A very bad business, this. Ugly rumors appeared about Robert Kennedy's alleged entanglement with the bombshell and later mushroomed into ungodly allegations about his involvement in her death. The brothers just shook their heads in amazement. J. Edgar Hoover had a basket full of material on this misadventure and Kennedy vowed to be more cautious in the future.

But despite his many failings on the home front, the President was turning out to be an exemplary father. Fatherhood seemed to have tempered his earlier carefree nature and given a new seriousness to his world view. Jackie could almost look past his peccadillocs because of it. Almost. Indeed, it had brought them closer in their three years in the White House.

Jackie asked the President to spend a little time with the children before she put them to bed and he was only too happy to oblige. Caroline wanted to play horsey, but the President's back was aching as usual, so it was up to Bobby to get down on his hands and knees to accommodate this desire. It wouldn't be the first time. John John was a fury of activity as he raced around the office, crawling under the President's desk and finally impaling himself on a lone standing chair in the corner. He went running to the President, who cradled him in his arms until the sobbing stopped. John John was losing it fast.

The Attorney General had lost his oat bag and was in mid gallop when the President beckoned Caroline over to him. She dismounted *pronto* and left the gasping A.G. to slow down to a restful canter. He paused to bray.

Caroline climbed into her daddy's lap next to the now slumbering John John. Her eyes wide, she wanted to know if Daddy could play with her after school tomorrow. No, Daddy couldn't; he had to go to Florida, but would be back Wednesday for Uncle Bobby's party. Was he going to visit Poppa Joe in Florida? No, not this time, but maybe in a few weeks they would all go.

"Daddy, how come you always go away?"

The President, uncharacteristically, was at a loss for words. "Well, sweetie, I have to travel a lot because of my job. I don't want to go away, but I have to. But someday soon, we'll all be able to spend more time together."

"When?"

"Well maybe next year, after the election. You can play with Uncle Bobby when I'm gone."

"But I want to play with you."

Uncle Bobby, currently dismantling his saddle, didn't know whether to be insulted or not.

"Uncle Bobby has all those other kids." Now he understood. He decided not to be insulted.

"Daddy, when can we ride the horses again, you know, the real horses?" Uncle Bobby was considering getting insulted after all.

"Can we do it next weekend?" The President gave a helpless glance in the direction of the Attorney General. "What say, Bob, anything on for next weekend?"

The Attorney General, now crouching on all fours, sauntered over to the couch and pulled out his schedule. "Doesn't appear to be anything. Maybe we should check with Mrs. Lincoln."

"No, don't worry about it, the hell with it. Barring Nikita going on the rag, I could probably use a day out at Hickory Hill."

He turned his gaze back at Caroline who was looking up at him with her blue gray cat's eyes. "Okay, sweetie, if Daddy doesn't get called away to any important meetings, we'll all go out to Uncle Bobby's house next Saturday and ride the horses."

"Do you promise?"

"Yes, I promise." John Kennedy had made many dates in his life, most of which he could break. This would not be one of them. Caroline seemed to be satisfied that she would have horseys next weekend and quickly faded into blissful dream, leaving the President with two sleeping bundles in his arms.

"Well, Mr. President, I see you are completely encumbered, so I shall take my leave. Have a good trip to Florida, I'll see you Wednesday." If tradition had permitted, they would have embraced, but the Attorney General settled for a quick mock salute which the President returned with a smile. *Soulmates.*

The President sat alone with his two sleeping charges. He went to rise and winced from the pain in his back. Cradling his progeny, he walked softly through the expanse of the Oval Office and tip-toed through the hallway to the living quarters. "Next Saturday," mused the President. "Horseys, for sure."

III.

The Assassination

"SHITTTT!"

Lucien peeled back the bedroom curtain and stared at the drizzling Dallas morning. Just when everything appeared to be going so well, he was about to be thwarted again, this time by the weather, of all things. First Chicago. Then Miami. Now Dallas. Lucien had been trailing around the presidential party for more than a month and still hadn't had a crack at them. *Waiting on go,* they called it. He was starting to get *assassination interruptus*, sort of hitman's blueballs.

The President's November 2nd trip to Chicago had been canceled at the last minute, which was all right with Lucien because he wasn't really satisfied with the setup there. The aborted presidential stop in the Windy City had given him plenty of time to scope Miami and Dallas for the motorcades which were scheduled there three weeks hence. Miami was better than Chicago, but Dallas was best of all. Any one would do, however. Even though the contract was open ended, Lucien was getting anxious to have it done with. He wouldn't get paid until it was, and he was starting to get homesick for Marseille.

There had been momentary concern when the Miami motorcade was canceled, also at the last minute, due to threats of an assassination. *Who had tipped them off*, wondered Lucien. Little could he know that there had been over four hundred assassination threats since the beginning of the year and this was just another one.

Would they cancel Dallas because of similar threats? No, it turned out, they would not. *This man Kennedy must want to die,* figured Lucien. He would be happy to oblige him.

The hired team's route had been circuitous at best. After flying into Mexico City, they had entered the U.S. at

Brownsville and been picked up by one of Giancana's men, who had driven them to Dallas. Lucien loved Dealey Plaza, but the President would be in Chicago in a week and there was no reason not to pursue him there. Except that he never came. So the fall of '63 Assassination Tour motored on to Miami.

Nice high rises, thought Lucien, scoping angles, calculating distances. And then off to the pleasures of Key Biscayne. Beats the hell out of the weather in Chicago, or Dallas for that matter. The gang of three partied, soaked up the rays and waited till Monday. And then, at the last minute, the motherfucker cancels the motorcade! More waiting, more driving. Oh what the hell, thought Lucien. Dallas was best anyway. Two unknowing patsies heaved sighs of relief in Chicago and Miami, respectively.

Lucien, Giancarlo and Robert loaded into the borrowed Mafia mobile and headed west with the rest of the caravan. Lucien was determined that Dallas would be it, but all this waiting and driving had made the boys restless. On Tuesday night they picked up a hooker and in their drunken revelry agreed to drive her to Dallas, where they were going. Driving through Louisiana on Wednesday, the trio, relaxed from their two day alcoholic binge, started telling the hooker how they were going from Miami to Dallas to shoot the President. This drunken euphoria lasted about an hour, when Robert, the *inebriato supreme*, decided it would be fun to push the hooker, one Rose Cheramie, from the car at forty miles per hour. This he proceeded to do. Lucien didn't think anything of it at the time, but when they got to Dallas and sobriety started to descend on them, he worried if they were impaling themselves on their own sword. Fuck it, they were back in Dallas, there was work to be done. Lucien was determined this time. He was tired of waiting on go.

What would the rain mean? No motorcade? A bubble top? Was it bullet proof? Lucien would just have to wait.

Over in the Oak Park section of town, Lee Oswald was rising for another day of work. He put the elongated package that Ferrie had given him under his arm and covered it with wrapping paper, as instructed, while he waited for his ride. Bizarre, thought Oswald, but he kept reminding himself that this was the last time. *Deliver the fucking package and be done with these jokers. Amen.*

Jack Ruby was in a state of agitation on rising, or more correctly, on continuing being awake after attempting to sleep, unsuccessfully, for the third night in a row. Today was the day and Jack's nerves were shot. *What's the big deal? Put a bullet on a stretcher at Parkland Hospital and collect 100K. What could be easier than that?* And yet, it was not in Jack's nature to relax about such things, and the impending events of the day were above and beyond any thing that Jack had ever known or experienced. All the tranquilizers in the world, half of which he thought he had already taken, would not help. Like Lucien, he would just have to wait.

Over in the high rent district of town, the visiting luminary rose after spending a restless night of sleep. His hard fought presidential campaign in the '60 election had been very much on his mind and he wondered how events had conspired to bring him to this Dallas hotel room. He thought about his strange dinner with J. Edgar Hoover and oil baron, Clint Murchison, at the latter's palatial estate, the night before. *What were these jokers up to?* He would talk to LBJ about it when he had a chance. But there was no time to tarry; there was a plane to catch over at Love Field. Richard Nixon was getting out of town while the getting was good.

Carlos had not slept much better. Today would be the day, he was sure, and despite Ferrie's reassurances, he was worried. He had been bankrolling what was turning out to be a very expensive operation and the two false alarms had put him on edge. On top of the potential assassination, his trial for income tax evasion would likely end today, with the verdict very much in question. A loss would trigger certain deportation proceedings, as well as set in motion the domino collapse of his empire, if the Kennedy administration stayed in power.

Carlos looked in the mirror as he dressed for court. November 22nd was going to be a very important day for him. By three o'clock, he would either be a free man, a co-conspirator in the murder of a president, a fallen gangster on the way to deportation, or any combination of the above. Boy, talk about just having to wait.

At about 11 A.M. the sun started peeking through the breaking clouds. Lucien smiled. Waiting on go wouldn't have to wait, after all.

Poppa and I had worked out an elaborate plan to slip the bonds of Sam Houston Junior High. As things turned out, it wasn't necessary. The school administration had decided that they would ferry us into town for this historical event. But after a lifetime of scouting positions for his 5' 3" frame, Poppa knew that the intended Main Street location proposed by the school would defeat the purpose. Since I was not tall for my age, Poppa was convinced that I would never see the President. He proposed that we go to a little elevated expanse of land just west of Main Street, where it would be less crowded and we would have a good, unobstructed view. I didn't care. I was so excited about seeing President Kennedy that I hadn't slept for two nights and would have followed Poppa to the moon to see him. Dealey Plaza, where Poppa had his office, would be fine.

Since my release was secured from the junior high school, Poppa decided to play hooky from work too, and take me out to breakfast. After all, it was his own dress manufacturing company, small though it be. Over eggs and waffles, Poppa regaled me with the adventures of Cossacks and Babushkas. Tales of the *U-Kray-een.* The conversation shifted to the President's visit. Poppa knew how much I loved Kennedy and conceded that he had developed a quiet admiration for him, despite some initial skepticism. Poppa felt that black people in America were treated much like the Jews were in Russia. In his empathy, he was very impressed with the Kennedy brothers' efforts to further the Negroes' cause.

After we finished breakfast, Poppa and I headed out to pick up his secretary, Marilyn. She had been with Poppa for many years and he knew she also wanted to see the President. Poppa was doing his civic duty. He would film it for all of us.

The morning had been gray and drizzly, but by the time we got to Marilyn's, the sky had cleared and the sun come out. We were all in good spirits, Marilyn and I because we were going to see the President, and Poppa, because Marilyn and I were happy. I graciously yielded the shotgun seat to Marilyn and off we went. The three musketeers were on their way to Dealey Plaza.

The President was up early, as usual. It was never hard to get out of bed when you were president of the United States. He reflected for a moment on what a charmed life he had led. Despite his chronic illnesses, he knew he had been a blessed man. Blessed with looks, wealth, humor, charm and intelligence. He flashed the million dollar smile into the mirror as he adjusted the handkerchief in his breast pocket. Vanity had not escaped John Kennedy, but it was vanity reinforced by the hundreds of adoring eyes he encountered every day. He didn't mind being a god; it was what the people seemed to want and he didn't really have to work at it.

The President had been encouraged by Texas. Yesterday's motorcades in Houston and San Antonio had produced large and excited crowds. The President was just starting to realize the magnitude of his presence. Today promised more of the same. The Dallas motorcade, lunch at the Trade Mart, Austin, and then off to the LBJ ranch for a big gala. If this was hostile terrain, bring on the election. Goldwater, if he was unfortunate enough to be nominated, would be dogmeat. Of this, the President was sure. The only question was whether Kennedy could pitch a shutout or not. Forty eight to two, minimum, he was sure, but a shutout, now that was unprecedented. FDR had gotten damn close in '36, winning everything but Maine and Vermont. Kennedy chuckled at his own arrogance. Alabama and Mississippi would be his Maine and Vermont, for sure. Probably quite a few others in the South, too. But a substantial victory, nonetheless.

Speaking of the '36 election, Kennedy had made a note to himself to phone John Nance Garner, the Texan who had served as FDR's vice president during Roosevelt's first two terms. This was a vice president from Texas who Kennedy could admire, a man who had the self respect to eschew the vice presidency over time, with his "warm pitcher of spit" assessment of the job.

Kennedy could hope for no such enlightenment from his own bumbling Texan, LBJ. Today was Garner's 95th birthday, hence the President's phone call. *Christ,* thought Kennedy, *this guy is more than twice as old as I am*, as he phoned the deeply honored old codger to congratulate him. If Kennedy was worried about what he was going to do at age fifty-one, he wondered what he would do if he ever got remotely close to ninety-five. *Maybe we can repeal the 22nd amendment after all,* idled the President, reminiscing back to FDR again, whose opponents had ramrodded that term limiting legislation through in response to the wily patrician's four terms. Never again, they vowed. Kennedy smiled to himself. *Just maybe...*

It was time to go down to the breakfast sponsored by the Fort Worth Chamber of Commerce. As usual, Jackie wasn't ready which annoyed the President, who should have been used to it by now. But she soon arrived in her pink outfit with matching pillbox hat and white gloves. She looked smashing and the President's anger softened. He flipped off the usual remarks in the short obligatory speech and, as feared, the mandatory Stetson hat was proffered. Oh, *Christ*, he thought to himself, *how do I get out of this one?* He quickly snatched it, raised it high and promised the audience that if they would come to the White House on Monday, he'd put it on there for them. The crowd chuckled. *Phew,* sighed Kennedy to himself, *that was close. Let's get the hell out of here.* Visions of Calvin Coolidge in Indian headdress flashed through his mind. He'd be damned if he would be seen wearing this oversized inverted toilet bowl on his head.

The party proceeded to Air Force One for the thirteen minute flight to Dallas. The President greeted a frozen LBJ who seemed strangely mechanical and remote. *Texas Mafia must have him by the balls,* Kennedy mused to himself, and didn't think about it again. Little could he know that Lyndon was going into the shock reserved for the rest of the country a few hours later.

On board the plane, the President had a chance to relax for a few minutes, and over coffee, started scanning the morning newspapers. He leafed through the *Dallas Morning News* and there he saw it. A "Wanted for Treason" poster, full page advertisement. With his pictures, front and profile, at the top. The President fumed and yelled out for Ken O'Donnell, chief lackey and bootlick, who was seated on a bench outside the cabin. "Kenny have you seen this? What kind of motherfucking asshole would print this in his newspaper?"

O'Donnell tried to calm the incensed Chief Executive, but to little avail. "Don't worry, Mr. President, *The Dallas Morning News* is a conservative newspaper in a conservative town. This doesn't mean anything." Suddenly Kennedy remembered who the motherfucking asshole was. Ted Dealey. That fool of a publisher who had made an ass of himself at the White House. *Figures,* thought the President, as the plane touched down.

A full flood of light bore down on the President as he poked his head outside of Air Force One and blinked to adjust to the brightness. *Terrific,* he thought to himself, as he descended the ramp. *Blue skies. Big crowds. Open motorcade, no bubbletop.* The earlier rain had worried him.

Big crowds all right, mostly friendly. As the President waited for the motorcade to form, he bounced over to the restraining fence to greet the assembled masses, with ten terrified Secret Service agents anxiously trailing in his wake. The crowd went wild. Pandemonium. Kennedy might as well have been a *bandanna'd* rock star throwing powerful riffs off his Les Paul guitar. The Beatles were still a couple of months away from happening, but the President's airport adulation presaged the mania in store for the sacred quartet. It could have been the Fab Five.

The motorcade moved slowly out of the airport and down a series of lightly populated connecting roads that would lead them to a twelve block stretch of Main Street, the heart of the motorcade. It was hot, very hot, and the occupants of the big open Lincoln began to roast. Jackie took out her sun glasses to try to get some relief. The President ordered her to put them away. The mandatory forty-five minute motorcade was a showcase to the voters and they were going to do it right. There would be plenty of time to rest later.

Much to the deep concern of the agents, Kennedy stopped the motorcade to greet a bunch of school kids from someplace called Sam Houston Junior High, who were holding up a sign beseeching the President to shake their hands. The students had found the thickly crowded Main Street impossible to negotiate and had wisely moved to the beginning of the parade route to catch a glimpse of the President. Randy Epstein couldn't believe his eyes, as the President stepped out of the car and started shaking hands with his classmates. *Wait till I tell Jake, he's going to die,* he laughed to himself, as he touched the President's hand. His friend and schoolmate, Jake Zuckerman, who absolutely adored Kennedy, had deserted his schoolmates to go see the motorcade with his grandfather at a place where they thought they'd have a better view. Randy, an amateur photographer who had his own darkroom, quickly snapped pictures of the President shaking hands with the squealing eighth graders. As the President stepped back into the car and the motorcade moved away, Randy gazed at the anointed hand that had touched the President's, and shook his head in disbelief. His classmates went into an orgy of delight, clutching hands and assorted body parts that had brushed against the President. *Wait till I tell Jake, the fool,* he muttered to himself again and again. The two boys had developed the bonding of young male friendship, based on mutual antagonism. This encounter with the President would drive Jake right through the wall. Randy would develop the pictures right after school, so he could torture Jake that night. That would have the maximum impact.

Jackie saw them first. *Oh God,* she thought, as if she wasn't frying already. A gaggle of nuns stood lined up along the sidewalk, like penguins waiting for the zookeeper to bring a bucket of minnows. Everybody who had spent any time around the President knew what this meant, as the motorcade came to a screeching halt. Kennedy stepped out of the limo and immersed himself in the bobbing sea of black and white. *More groupies,* mused Jackie, as the Sisters' large crosses swayed in time to the frenzied movements of their billowing habits. *At least these ones are safe,* she chuckled to herself. Agent Clint Hill in the trailing Secret Service car waited patiently for his charge to return. *If ever anybody wanted to shoot this guy,* he thought, *all they would have to do is dress up in a nun's outfit and whip out a pistol from beneath the flowing robes.* He laughed to himself at this bizarre thought.

What the Service was really worried about was the twelve blocks of uninterrupted high-rises and office buildings coming up on Main Street. Why did the President constantly subject himself to this dangerous and largely uncontrollable activity? Didn't he know what a sitting duck he was? Maybe he had a death wish. But seeing the adulation heaped on the man day after day, Agent Hill couldn't imagine anybody who would want to live more than John Kennedy. It just didn't make sense to him, but then again, he wasn't a politician in the vortex of power and celebrity. He was a highly schooled agent, conscientious and diligent. He was trained to maniacally focus on his task, which was protecting his President, laying down his life if necessary. It was beyond him how ten of his fellow agents, four of whom were riding on the follow-up car with him, could go out and drink till the wee hours when they had to protect the President the next morning. An unconscionable breach of protocol.

The motorcade entered the canyon of high-rises to an overflow of cheering crowds layered ten to twelve thick along the curb. The shade of the overhanging office buildings offered some relief from the blistering sun, but the noise echoing off the building facades was overwhelming. Kennedy smiled. Two cars back, Lyndon Johnson was amazed. Pure unadulterated adulation, right here, in his home state. They had never done this for him.

Clint Hill watched the buildings overhead with mounting anxiety. Too many open windows, too much confusion. He was not liking this at all, but his President sure seemed to be. Three more blocks and they would be through this god-awful hellhole and then Hill could relax. Kennedy was oblivious, soaking in the noise and excitement of the crowd. The day had been a triumph. If the Chief Executive could do it here, he could do it anywhere. *Well maybe not Alabama and Mississippi, his Vermont and Maine,* the President chuckled to himself. But, damn it, with a mandate like this, he could put a charge in his legislation and steamroll it through Congress, where it had been lying dormant. *Screw 'em.* Let those bloated, somnolent congressmen try to sit on his agenda in the face of this public ground swell. Not after '64, they wouldn't.

Peering down on the crowd were the hostile eyes of the Dallas elite. *How dare this Yankee pimp come strutting down Main Street and defile their turf right under their noses.* The malevolent stares of H. L. Hunt, Clint Murchison and Ted Dealey, as they glared down at the passing motorcade, said it all. This man was bad for business. Bad for the country. Bad for the vested interests of the power elite. And to have the unmitigated gall to parade his flash-in-the-pan pop-persona and ephemeral popularity in front of them, here in their city, beneath their footfalls! The Bastard would get his comeuppance, and damn soon. Damn soon.

The crowd had thinned out and the Bastard started to relax. As the motorcade reached the end of Main, Jackie spotted the Stemmons Freeway sign and the underpass. So close to speed, and with it, coolness. The President was parched and was looking forward to some acceleration as well. Nellie Connally turned around and mumbled something about Texas and the President nodded and smiled. *Whatever you say, Nellie, whatever you say,* he thought to himself.

The end of Main. Clint Hill relaxed. This little expanse of land and then the freeway. Thinning crowds. *Why this little dog leg turn? Why not steam straight through?* Something about catching the freeway entrance. *Okay. No need to panic, we're almost through now. We do the dog leg and then we're outta here.*

After a morning of loading books, Lee Oswald had gone down to the second floor cafeteria for lunch at 12:15. Ferrie had told him to wait for a phone call there and whether he got it or not, to proceed to the Carousel Club on Commerce Street for his one o'clock drop off. Lee would tell Mr. Truly, the Depository supervisor, that an emergency had arisen and that he would be back in a few hours. He knew this would be no problem. Lee had wanted to see the President pass and had poked his head out the front door to survey the crowd but decided that he had better go back to wait for the call. You never knew what to expect with Ferrie.

At 12:15 Lucien pulled into the railroad yard behind Dealey Plaza, right on schedule. The three cars in the caravan dropped off their charges and moved on to their respective waiting points. A man collapsed in a seizure in the middle of Dealey Plaza, drawing what little police attention there was away from the buildings in the Square. Robert and Giancarlo's teams quickly slipped inside each of their respective postings.

Robert's team scampered up to the sixth floor of the Depository building, swiftly planting Oswald's pilfered rifle in the northwest corner, next to the staircase. The central radioman was posted in the southwest window with a view of Lucien's team on the overpass or behind the knoll; Giancarlo's in the Records building; and, of course, Robert's, in the soon-to-be infamous "sniper's nest" in the southeast corner of the Depository. From this exclusive perch, the radioman would quarterback the operation.

Robert planted three empty shells from Oswald's rifle and got into position. Time to wait. The radioman looked over at Giancarlo, parked on the third floor of the Records building on the east side of the Square. The gunman's thumbs-up indicated that he was ready.

Lucien saw what he thought was a police guard up on the overpass and decided that the knoll would be safer. He signaled his team that this was going to be his position. Dressed in a blue police uniform, he stationed himself behind the picket fence at the edge of the parking lot, next to his own radioman, who could glance up to the Depository from that position. The location was not bad, thought Lucien. Although it didn't have the direct frontal access of the overpass, there were a couple of shielding trees in front of him and he would have at least two good, clean shots at the President. The first would be from about one hundred feet as the President approached and the second from only fifty feet as he passed. The security team was doing an efficient job of keeping stragglers from wandering behind the picket fence. Lucien figured if they could just momentarily delay the surging mob charging up the knoll after the confusion of the shooting, he would have more than enough time to get away.

Lucien checked his position about ten feet west of the juncture of the fence. The crowd was sparse, almost nonexistent on the knoll, although there were a number of people directly across from him on the other side of Elm Street. The trees would help with them. In front of him, near the top of the knoll, was some kind of soldier fiddling with a movie camera. Lucien signaled the security team to make sure to get any film this soldier might manage to take. There were a few stragglers on the steps below with no cameras, movie or otherwise, in sight. No major concern here. Finally, on the other side of the fence, to his left, standing on an elevated step, was an old man being supported upright by a woman, who in turn had a boy by her side. The man looked so tiny and frail that Lucien had no concern. He figured with the first shot the old man and his crew would fall off the abutment and be clutching the ground for dear life.

Lucien checked his watch. 12:25. The position wasn't perfect, but it was as good as he was going to get as he heard the first noise from the approaching motorcade. Lucien lit a cigarette and waited. He was ready.

We parked our car behind Poppa's office in the Dal-Tex building and walked out into the bright sunlight of Dealey Plaza. The clock on top of the Depository read 12:10. Poppa knew exactly where he wanted to go. We crossed over Houston Street and proceeded down Elm in front of the Depository building. The crowd was big there and getting bigger. Poppa grabbed my hand to move on. We passed the front door of the Depository and came to these white marble steps with this weird decoration behind them. Poppa pointed to a raised portion at the top of the steps and the three of us climbed on. Poppa was right. This was a great view, looking down on the motorcade, away from the big crowds but close enough so that the motorcade would still be going slowly. At least that's how Poppa explained it to me.

Poppa, afraid of falling off the stoop, asked Marilyn to hold him from behind while he played with his movie camera. As we waited, I saw three cars drive into the railroad yard on the other side of the wooden fence to my right. A number of men in different types of uniforms got out and the cars left. About six of the men, who were carrying a couple of cloth satchels and some hand-held radios, walked to the rear of the Depository building and disappeared from view. Two others, one wearing a police uniform and another with a white T-shirt and some kind of hard hat, started walking right toward us. Something about them scared me. They walked to the edge of the picket fence and looked over. The man with the white T-shirt and hard hat was talking into a radio and was looking up at the Depository building. Several people in suits and security uniforms came up to the other man in the police uniform and seemed to be asking him for directions. He pointed this way and that, and they went off as instructed. *He must be the Captain*, I thought. A railroad worker, carrying a large toolbox came up to the Captain, laid his toolbox on the ground and bent down to remove something. The Captain kneeled down with him and when he stood back up, he had a rifle in his hand. The railroad man closed up his toolbox and slowly walked back toward the railroad.

The Captain looked around like he was nervous. I could see where he would be nervous, what with having to protect the President and all. The Captain called over to one of the security people and pointed to a soldier who was playing with a movie camera in front of the fence. The security person nodded and went back to a position at the edge of the fence. The Captain looked over at Poppa and then at me and rolled his eyes and laughed. *Did he think we were funny?*

As the man with the hard hat and the radio jabbered away and looked up at the Depository, the Captain lit a cigarette. I had never seen a policeman smoke a cigarette before, at least not in uniform. *The Captain must be very nervous*, I thought.

Just then the noise picked up and I forgot all about the Captain. The motorcade was turning off Main Street and the President was going to pass right below me, just like Poppa said. *Just wait till I tell Randy Epstein and the kids at Sam Houston. They were probably lucky to have gotten a glimpse of the driver.*

Hot. That's all John Kennedy remembered thinking as the motorcade turned the corner of Main. Jackie must be pissed. But as he looked over toward her, she was smiling and waving to the left as instructed, like a good trooper. Kennedy looked at the strange white statuary moldings to his left and then he saw the sign. *Dealey Plaza.* He laughed to himself. He just couldn't get away from that fucker, Ted Dealey. *Wanted for treason. After '64, you're history, Dealey. Along with Edgar*. There were scores to settle.

The President looked up at the clock on the Hertz sign on top of the building in front of him. 12:29. Good, the luncheon was at 12:30, and they weren't too far behind schedule. The last turn onto Elm seemed awkward to the President, but a big crowd awaited there, and he waved and smiled. The crowd squealed with delight. The turn completed, the big Lincoln slowly headed down the incline of Elm Street. The crowd was thinning out. Kennedy saw the Stemmons Freeway sign. *Coolness. Water.* He could sneak a gulp once they were on the highway. *God, was the motorcade slow.*

He saw the tiny old man with the camera, who was being held up by a woman, who, in turn, was holding a boy's hand. He laughed to himself and waved. They looked like the picture of *Iwo Jima* to him, with a camera instead of a flag.

Then a loud popping noise. *What's that? AAARGH!* A sharp piercing pain exploded in his throat. He stared ahead. He saw a look of horror on the boy's face. *WHOOOAA!* A smashing stab of pain pounded into his back, pushing him forward as he caught a glimpse of the same horror on Jackie's face. A dull awareness of having been shot ascended on his quickly fading consciousness. *"Hail Mary, full of Grace, the Lord is*...then nothing. Blackness. Silence. A screaming bullet ripped into his skull driving him back into the limo seat and splattering his brain into the air above him. John F. Kennedy had ceased to be.

Robert saw him first. Moving slowly down Houston, coming straight at him, it took all the discipline Robert had to restrain himself from blasting away at the tantalizing target heading right at him at a snail's pace. He could have gotten off six shots in that stretch alone. Robert often wondered in the years to follow how anyone could believe Oswald would have waited to open fire till the motorcade was past him, and moving away, when he could have picked off the President like a tin can on a log, during the slow crawl down Houston Street.

Giancarlo watched the President's car pass below him and make the wide turn onto Elm. Fifty yards to the kill zone. He cocked his rifle.

Lucien stamped out his cigarette. The radioman took one last look up at the Depository and signaled a go. Lucien took up his position at the fence. The motorcade was turning onto Elm and starting its descent directly towards him. He got a full frontal look at the President and his wife, just over the boy's head. *God, what a beautiful couple*, he thought to himself, looking at the glow of health emanating from both Kennedys, highlighted by the bright Texas sun. They looked like royalty. Lucien was nervous, much more than he had expected to be, as he aimed his rifle at the descending god. The President had reached the kill zone.

FIRE! Robert got off the first shot and missed. The President looked startled. Lucien squeezed and the President clutched his throat. The assassins' adrenaline was pumping like mad. Giancarlo shot wide and hit the man in front of the President. Robert recocked and pumped a bullet into the President's back. The President started to pitch forward. He was almost directly in front of Lucien now, fifty feet away. The beautiful chestnut hair, the golden red skin, the wide ivory smile, now beset with confusion, reappeared in Lucien's sight. He aimed for the middle of it all and squeezed the trigger. Blood, brain, hair and skull flew up in a golden halo fifteen feet above Elm Street. The crowd gasped in horror.

Lucien heard the dull thud and stood watching for an instant. He had seen Kennedy's head explode and knew he had just killed the President. He trembled.

"Get the hell out of here!," the radioman screeched over at him, looking at the numb figure frozen with the gun. Lucien snapped to life as he came to his senses. He dashed twenty feet back along the fence toward the railroad and pitched the rifle to the railroad man waiting with an open toolbox. As the railroad worker quickly broke the rifle down, Lucien spun around, straightened his shirt and started walking calmly back to the

Depository. *Stay cool, walk slow,* he whispered to himself, his heart still exploding in his chest. By the time he got back to the eastern edge of the fence where the old man had been, a crowd, including police officers, was charging up the grassy knoll and being greeted by mock security agents, who were turning the stampeding mob away. The scene was fraught with confusion and horror. Lucien, now regaining his composure, would take advantage of this.

As Lucien passed the fence and headed for the Depository, he saw the boy point a camera at him. "Why you little bastard!," he screeched. Lucien took a step forward to snatch the camera, but thought better of it. There was no time to waste. He calmly continued walking down Elm, against the direction of the surging crowd, which was now headed for the overpass. He ducked left down Houston past the thinning crowd and continued another block past the Depository till he came to a little loop in the road where his station wagon was waiting for him. He saw Robert, half a block up, as he too stepped into a waiting car and flashed Lucien a thumbs up signal. *Getaway cabs*, Lucien thought to himself.

Lucien scampered up to the waiting car, opened the door and got in. The driver turned and smiled and without further ado, peeled out.

Lucien looked out the back window. *Nobody chasing them. No sirens.* He lit a cigarette with trembling hands and heaving a big sigh, eased back into the soft cushions of the rear seat. Lucien smiled to himself. He had just gotten away with the murder of the President of the United States.

"The President is coming! The President is coming!" I jumped up and down on our little stone step.

My grandfather turned and joked, "Listen, Marilyn, another Paul Revere we have here." Marilyn laughed. Poppa went back to playing with his camera. *Paul Revere?*

As the motorcade turned onto Houston, I caught a glimpse of pink. Could it be? Yes, in the distance, there was Jackie Kennedy, just like in the pictures. I couldn't make out the President, but I knew he must be there because the crowd was going wild. The motorcade came to the front of the Depository building and took this backward turn that seemed to take forever. The crowd in front of the building was yelling and screaming, cheering for the President. I didn't see him until his car had started coming down Elm Street, but when I did—WOW! My heart was beating madly. He looked just like all the pictures on TV and in the newspaper, except his hair seemed lighter, more red. He had this look, this glow. I can't explain it, but he seemed to have sunshine radiating from his face and smile. There was a golden aura about him. He was everything I thought he would be, and more. And now he was coming right toward me and Poppa, waving and smiling. Poppa put his camera to his face and started filming. I tried to lift my Instamatic but I was frozen, numb. I stood there and gawked at the oncoming god. He looked right at me and Poppa, smiled and sort of laughed to himself. With my joints thawing, I gave him a big wave back. He was so close I could almost touch him. Wait till I showed Randy Poppa's film. Oh, this was all too unbelievable!

The President disappeared behind a sign and I heard a firecracker go off. When he reappeared again, he was raising his hands to his throat. He had this funny look on his face. More firecrackers. The President looked at me again, with this confused gaze on his face, and started slumping forward. *What was going on here?* I heard a sharp noise over my right shoulder. I turned to look. The Captain was sticking the rifle over the fence and pointing it right at the President!

"*NOOOOO,*" I cried out. *This can't be happening! I can't believe what I'm seeing!* I wanted to run, to pull down his rifle, but my legs wouldn't move. Some primal instinct took me over and I raised my camera instead. The Captain squeezed and I clicked. There was a thud and the crowd let out a scream as the President's head blew up. It was all happening so fast. It was incredible. But it was really happening. It had really happened. *No, it can't be so.* But I knew it was. Panic and confusion broke out. Poppa kept on filming as Jackie Kennedy started crawling on the back of the car to pick up a piece of the President's head. A Secret Service man jumped on the car and pushed Mrs. Kennedy back inside. The President had disappeared from view. The Secret Service man spread himself on top of the trunk and in a flash, they were gone.

I looked over at the Captain, who stood watching this scene with his rifle by his side. The man with the radio gave him a shove and the Captain started running along the back of the fence till he saw the railroad man with the toolbox. He tossed the gun to the railroad man as I snapped a second picture. The railroad man broke down the rifle and stuck it in his box as the Captain turned on his heels and started walking back right toward us! The railroad man slowly walked away carrying his toolbox and moving along the railroad.

The Captain was moving toward the Depository building. He came to the end of the fence, no more than ten feet from me. I had always been a shy and timid boy, but some force had come over me. I pointed my camera right at the Captain, the same way he had pointed his gun at the President, and snapped a picture right in his face. The Captain, looking right at me, stepped toward me. The Captain was going to kill me, just like he did the President!

Then, all of a sudden, for no reason at all, he stopped and started walking away into the crowd that was moving toward us. I bounded down the step and started following the Captain, who was getting hard to find in the crowd. About twenty-five feet in front of me, I picked him up again, making a left turn at the other end of the Depository building. Far fewer people here; I would have to be very careful. I followed at half a block. The Captain was walking slowly, calmly, not looking back. I saw another man with blondish hair walking about a half block in front of the Captain, in the same casual way. The block was coming to an end and took some kind of loop, which headed east. The two men took the loop and the blond man sprinted up ahead and got into a car. He looked back at the Captain and gave him some kind of salute with his hand. The car took off. Closer to me there was another car, a rambler station wagon, with Illinois license plates, WE6-YEY. I hid behind a dumpster as the Captain got in. *Click.* My fourth and final picture. The car with the Captain sped off. I sat behind the dumpster and started to shiver. My whole body was trembling.

Poppa, I've got to find Poppa! He'll be worried about me. I tucked the camera into my coat pocket and dashed back to the Depository to find him. When I got back, there was a mass of confusion, hundreds of people running all over the place, yelling, screaming, in a panic. I looked at the Hertz sign atop the Depository. 12:33. Where were Poppa and Marilyn? How could I ever hope to find them in this crowd? Poppa would be worried about me.

As I searched, I started to cry. My automatic pilot button had gone off and everything was beginning to sink in. "Jake!" I heard a scream in the distance and turned to see Poppa and Marilyn standing on the railroad overpass, waving to me. I broke into a run. I got up to Poppa and threw my arms around him.

"Poppa, they've killed the President," I screamed, as I started crying. I tried to be brave, but I couldn't help it. I started sobbing uncontrollably. Poppa had been crying also. He nodded. He knew they had killed the President. He took the edge of his open raincoat, wrapped it around me and pulled me to his breast, as if to protect me from the storms of the world. He patted my head and kept whispering, "It'll be all right Jake, it'll be all right." I was shaking, trembling, crying.

"Oh, I'm so sorry, Poppa, I'm so sorry," I kept on repeating to him.

"It's all right Jake, let it go." He clutched me tighter. "Marilyn, we need to get the boy home." Marilyn had been crying too.

Poppa took one of my hands and Marilyn took the other as they led me across Dealey Plaza. I don't think I could have walked myself. Poppa helped me into the car. I laid down in the back seat and closed my eyes. The Captain was aiming his rifle at me.

Agent Clint Hill had let down his guard. After the tall buildings and overflow crowds of Main Street, they were almost there. He didn't like the slow, steep angled turns of Dealey Plaza, but they were almost there. Soon he could rest, get some lunch. He was famished.

Riding on the left bumper of the presidential follow-up car, he thought he heard a firecracker, or a backfire from a motorcycle. He looked at the President who seemed to be okay.

Some more firecrackers, or was this a gun? Clint became alarmed. He saw the President reaching for his throat and Hill started to bolt. "Halt!," somebody had screamed from the inside of the follow-up car. He thought it was the Chief, Emory Roberts. The President was slumping forward. *This is crazy! What's going on here? It looks like somebody is shooting the President. What is this halt?* Agent Hill's mind raced. He was about to dash to the President's car when a blast from a gun sent a stream of blood and brains right at him, spraying his suit and the windshield of the motorcycle cop next to him. He saw Jackie Kennedy climbing out of the back of the car, and racing up to the fender of the President's limo, he leaped on. Jackie was reaching for a piece of what looked like the President's head.

"Get back in the vehicle, Mrs. Kennedy, and get down!," Clint screamed, as he shoved her into the back seat on top of the supine President. Clint splayed himself spread eagle above them to shield any further bullets. One look at the President and he could see he was too late.

"Get this car the hell out of here and now, Mr. Greer!," Clint barked at the driver, who seemed to be in a funk. Greer put it in gear and the limo sped off, under the overpass. "Four miles to Parkland Hospital, step on it," Agent Roy Kellerman in the passenger seat shouted at the driver. Greer was accelerating to eighty miles an hour. Clint looked down again. Jackie, in shock, was trying to put the President's head back together with the piece she had found. She was also trying to close a large flap of skin that was protruding from the side of his head. "They've murdered my husband, they've murdered my husband." Over and over again she kept repeating it. Clint looked down at the lifeless body and knew they had.

The dash to Parkland seemed like it was taking an eternity as Clint hung on for dear life. He started pounding his fist on the trunk. His one task, his only duty, and he couldn't even do it right. He had lost the President. *Who had shouted halt? And why?*

With the blare of sirens roaring, the motorcade converged *en masse* on Parkland Hospital. The President's limo came to a screeching halt and Clint jumped off. Agent Kellerman came up to him and asked how the President was. "He's dead, Roy," was Clint's only reply.

Agents Kellerman, Sorrel and Lawton tried to keep the panicked masses away from the car. They started yelling for two stretchers. There was a crush of medics, nurses, reporters, bystanders. Jackie Kennedy sat helplessly in the back seat, all eyes upon her. She was rocking back and forth and cradling her husband's broken head to her breast. There was a vacant look in her eyes.

Clint walked back to the car. "Mrs. Kennedy, please, we've got to get the President to the doctors."

"Mr. Hill, you know he's dead. Let me be."

All the years of discipline and training had hardened Clint to an icy stoicism, but Jackie's brief words pierced his heart. He choked back a sob. He peeled off his suit jacket and offered it to the First Lady. She took it and gently wrapped the President's head. Clint looked back at the waiting stretcher and nodded for it to come forward. After first removing Governor Connally, four agents lifted the President's lifeless body onto the gurney and wheeled it into the hospital. The vigil had begun.

The heavy set man with the brown fedora and dark sunglasses had watched the motorcade screech in. He had been expecting them. He watched as the agents worked feverishly, trying to get stretchers and also control the swelling crowd. There was no chance to get near Kennedy; he'd have to drop the bullet on the ground and hope somebody would discover it. The man pressed in closer. *Connally was wounded also!* An idea.

A Secret Service agent barked at the man to get back. A Dallas cop looked over and assured the agent that the man was okay. He was with them. The agent backed off.

To remove Kennedy, they would have to remove Connally first. The Texan seemed to be conscious. They wheeled the stretcher to the car and placing the semi-ambulatory Governor on it, started wheeling it away. The man with the fedora, approaching from the opposite direction, brushed past, and in a flash, deposited the bullet by Connally's side. He continued moving and, from a distance, peeked into the limo. The man in the back was dead. Hopefully, there would be one more at his club. Jack Ruby had finished his business at Parkland, and was headed back to town. He looked at his watch. 12:39.

With the stretchers bearing the President and the Governor wheeled inside, the growing crowd had nothing to do but wait, hope and pray. They needn't have bothered. John F. Kennedy had died in Dealey Plaza.

Lee sat in the second floor cafeteria waiting for a phone call that would not come. He looked at his watch. 12:30. Noise and commotion below, it must be the President passing. *What the fuck was Ferrie up to this time?* Lee would have liked to have seen the President. Oh well, one o'clock and he'd drop the tape off and be done with the hyperactive nut. The Carousel Club, up on Commerce Street, was a couple of blocks away. Sounded familiar. *That's right*, now he remembered. Ferrie had taken him over there one night, not too long ago. Met the owner, another hyper guy, Jewish, he thought. *What was his name? Rosen*? *Ruby? That's it, Ruby, Jack Ruby.* Now he remembered. He sauntered over to the Coke machine and popped a quarter in.

A pounding up the stairs. Lee turned. A beet red policeman, waving a gun in his face and gasping for air screamed "Halt!" Mr. Truly, the building supervisor, trailed in his wake.

"Do you know this man?," the officer shouted to Truly, who informed him he did, that he worked there. The officer took off down the hall. Truly turned to Oswald standing there, Coke in hand, and whispered, "The President's been shot," then took off down the hall after the policeman.

Lee stared after them in shock. It was Ferrie. What the hell was happening? Some primordial instinct told him something rotten was going on and that Ferrie and Bannister were behind it. He rued the day he had ever met them. Lee's mind raced. Panic started setting in. The hell with the package, no way was he going to the Carousel Club. He needed time to think. Find Mr. Truly and tell him he needed a couple of hours. He was going to do that anyway.

Except Mr. Truly was nowhere to be found. He was busy chasing the policeman around the Depository. *Got to get out of here, got to go somewhere to think.* Lee motored down the stairs and out the front door into the panic and confusion that was Dealey Plaza. *The President's been shot, imagine that*, he thought. *Right here, in Dealey Plaza.* This was not good. *God damn fucking Ferrie. Better get my pistol right now. God damn*

Ferrie. Better go somewhere to think. Gotta get out of here, now.

Lee walked over to the bus stop and got on a waiting bus. It started up but was frozen in the Dealey traffic. *Damn*, thought Lee. Though he hated to pay for it, he had to have a taxi; he had to get out of here. He got off the bus and headed for the taxi stand. Chaos swirled around Dealey Plaza. Lee saw an available cab and headed towards it. An elderly lady stepped three paces behind. Lee, ever the gentleman, stopped in his tracks and graciously offered the woman his cab. She thanked him profusely and got in. He could wait.

By the time the second cab arrived, Lee was in a state of panic. Could it be that Ferrie was setting him up as a patsy in the shooting of the President? Was that what all those public demonstrations as a leftist were about? The mail order rifle? The bogus revolutionary who actually had lived in the Soviet Union and had a Russian wife, to boot? How could he have been so stupid? *Tell me it just can't be so.*

The cab screeched to a halt in front of his rooming house. Lee got out and ran inside. 1.00 P.M. No time to waste. *Gotta think, gotta go somewhere to think. How bad had the President been shot? Would he die? Oh, this just can't be.*

Lee changed his shirt and grabbed his pistol. The weapon had been part of his ceremonial revolutionary garb, but if he saw Ferrie now, God knows, he'd use it. He hoped it worked. And who knew who or what Ferrie might unleash on him. Better safe than sorry. *Where to go. Can't stay here. The park? A movie theatre? Yes, a movie theatre, the Texas Theatre*. It wasn't too far and he could sit in the dark and think. Lee dashed out of the house and headed for the *Texas*. The continuing panic was rapidly depleting his adrenaline.

By one o'clock, Oswald had not appeared at the Carousel Club. White and Benton were getting nervous. The President had been shot, but where was their man? Could this backfire on them somehow? By prior arrangement, White remained behind, in case the unfortunate Oswald decided to appear. Benton took off in his patrol car and headed to Ruby's apartment for further instructions. The officer was starting to have grave misgivings about the whole thing.

When Benton arrived, the sweating Ruby had just gotten back from his mission at Parkland Hospital. The officer informed him that Oswald had failed to show. "Shit," cursed Ruby. *Where was the little weasel?* They phoned White back at the Carousel. No Oswald. Plan B. They'd stop in front of Oswald's rooming house, to see if he was there. It was right down the road. They rushed to the patrol car and headed out for the short drive to Oswald's. They pulled up in front and honked. Nothing. "Let's go inside and see if he's there," Ruby barked. "If he is, you take him out." Ruby started to step out the door.

Officer Benton panicked. "Hold on, Jack, I'm not liking this one little bit. I'm not going inside."

Ruby freaked. "What the hell are we paying you fifty-thousand dollars for? This man has got to be murdered! If he's not, we're all dead, history. Including you. Don't you understand, Benton?" Ruby couldn't believe this was happening.

Benton depressed the accelerator, nearly bouncing Ruby from the car. "It's just not right, Jack, murdering an innocent man. It's just not right." Benton kept repeating this over and over again, while driving in no particular direction. Ruby was in full panic. What if Oswald got away and the police caught him? Unimaginable consequences. This man must be killed. Now. Somehow.

Benton took random lefts and rights. He was in full retreat now. "Jack, I'm going to report the whole damn thing to my superiors. It was wrong from the beginning and I was wrong to accept it. I'll give you your five thousand back. For Christ sakes, Jack, the President's been shot! What do you say, Jack?" Benton stopped the car. He could reason with Ruby.

Ruby was sweating profusely. Not only was there a very real danger of Oswald getting away, but now this self appointed messiah was about to incriminate Ruby in the assassination of the President. Unimaginable consequences. No time to think. "Get out of the car, Officer Benton," Jack ordered.

Benton stared at Ruby. "Whatever you say, boss." Benton slowly got out and stood by his door. His mind was a blaze of confusion. It was wrong. The whole thing was wrong.

Ruby crossed over the front of the car. His eyes were wild. "You fucking Judas Iscariot, I'll be damned if I'm going to fry because of you!" Ruby reached into his coat pocket and pulling out his revolver, quickly pumped four bullets into the bewildered Benton. The officer collapsed in a heap. Ruby looked down at the dying policeman. Jack had to get out of here, he had to flee. "Benton, you dumb motherfucker, why did you make me do this? Oh, Christ."

Ruby fled across a yard, ran down the next street till he got his bearings. He could hear sirens starting to wail in the background. *An alibi, got to think of an alibi.* If only he could get his mind to think straight. *Got to walk slow, nothing suspicious. Slow, back to my apartment. I'll be able to think there. Why didn't I shoot him in the car? Did anybody see me?* Christ, Ruby thought, you just don't react the way you need to react, when you need to. Benton was dead and Oswald was alive. Wasn't it supposed to be the other way around? More Miltown tranquilizers at the apartment. *Got to sort out my thoughts.* He saw an approaching cruiser flashing its lights, speeding toward him. *Oh God, it's the end.* The cruiser sped by, apparently on the way to Benton. Ruby quickened his pace. He walked the remaining eight blocks without incident. He entered his apartment, grabbed a handful of pills and collapsed in a heap on the floor. He started to shake uncontrollably.

In the meantime, a very much alive and panicked Lee Oswald had fled to the safety of the Texas Theatre, trying to gather his thoughts. In his anxiety, he had looked into a shoe store window and then hurried next door into the theatre, forgetting to pay. There would be peace inside, a chance to think. A clerk in the shoe store saw the suspicious looking character, who fit a description broadcast on the radio, slip into the theatre without paying. He called the police.

Oswald sat in the theatre, trying furiously to collect his thoughts. Had Ferrie set him up as a patsy in the shooting of the President? And if so, should he turn himself in? Should he flee?

The house lights brightened. The decision had been made for him. Somebody yelled, "There he is," as policemen converged on him from every direction. Oswald panicked, and as the first officer approached him, got up and slugged the cop. Lee was wrestled down and pinned to the ground. Surrounded by thirty cops, Oswald was read his rights and heard something about shooting a policeman.

A policeman? What policeman?

The morning had been long and ponderous as Carlos stared at the phalanx of windbag lawyers flooding the courtroom floor. What time was it? 1:00 P.M. He should have heard something by now. *Don't tell me they aborted the fucking thing again.* Carlos grimaced at the thought.

Out of the corner of his eye, Carlos caught the onrushing form of a court officer making a beeline to the judge. *Could this be it?* The judge leaned forward as the officer approached and with great annoyance queried, "what is it, Mr. Brown?" Mr. Brown stepped up to the judge and whispered something. The judge went white and silently mouthed, "Oh, my God." He straightened up and cleared his throat. *Was this it? It must be it.*

"Ladies and gentlemen, I have some very disturbing news to report. President Kennedy has just been shot in Dallas. His condition remains uncertain." Pandemonium broke loose in the courtroom. The judge pounded his gavel. "Order in the court! Order in the court!"

People really say that, mused a suddenly relieved Carlos. Maybe the day won't be so bad, after all. *Shot, they said, not killed. No time to relax yet.*

The judge regained his composure and announced an hour recess. Regardless of the President's condition, court would continue. There was a trial in process and the judge was getting damned tired of it. He made this abundantly clear to the retreating masses.

Carlos stepped back into a little anteroom by the side of the courtroom. He joined a group of people hanging on every word pouring from a scratchy transistor radio. The President's condition was apparently serious. Very serious. There was a haunting silence in the room. And then the word. The President had died. People stood there in stunned disbelief. It was incomprehensible. This vision of youth, health, hope—suddenly dead, like that, at the snap of a finger. Muffled weeping broke out, followed by uncontrollable sobbing, as the undeniable reality of it started to sink in. This one was going to hurt real bad.

Carlos stared straight ahead, no expression. He took in the scene around him. *They better get Oswald*, he thought to himself. He'd hate to have to pay the price if they didn't.

The judge was ready. The lawyers finished their concluding statements half heartedly. Nobody wanted to be there. The jury adjourned and returned in less than five minutes. Carlos was a free man, cleared of all charges. The murder of the President had provided an unexpected benefit. Carlos and his petty venality were penny-ante stuff compared to the monstrous events of the hour. The courtroom cleared out as if there had been a bomb scare. People went their scattered ways to grieve, pray and immerse themselves in the minimal unfolding information of the event. The country had come to a standstill.

Carlos sped back to his bayou estate. He snapped on the TV. Weeping crowds. Pictures of Dealey Plaza and the Depository building. No suspects apprehended. No word about Corsicans. A rifle found on the sixth floor. What were the police telling or not telling?

Shouldn't they have found Oswald's body by now? Carlos started to worry again. Some word came about a police officer being shot and killed, a patrolman named Benton. Carlos leaned forward. *Wasn't that one of the men Ruby was supposed to use?* Carlos couldn't be sure.

The phone rang. Carlos jumped up and dashed over to it.

"Mr. Marcello, this is Ferrie."

"Yes, David." Carlos couldn't wait. "Did the police get Oswald?"

"Yes, Mr. Marcello, the police got Oswald."

Carlos heaved a sigh of relief. Maybe he was going to come out of this unscathed, after all.

"Thank God," whispered Carlos. "Thank you for everything, David."

Ferrie hesitated, uncomprehending. "Thank you, Mr. Marcello?"

Now Carlos was confused. "Yeah, thank you. You just told me the police got Oswald."

Ferrie understood. “They did. He’s alive.”

"Get that body out of there. I don't care if you have to run over the bastards with the casket!" J. Edgar Hoover was screaming into the phone. Carlos had done his part. Hoover would be damned if things were going to fall apart on his watch.

"Mr. Director, they're offering a lot of resistance. It could get ugly."

"Let me tell you about ugly, Mr. Youngblood. If you and your agents don't get that casket out of there, you can forget about your pensions, or coming to work on Monday, for that matter. Do I make myself clear?"

"Right, Mr. Director. It will be done." The line buzzed in Youngblood's ear as the Director slammed the phone down. The agent shook his head in disgust. This was going to get ugly.

He walked back to the casket, which was presently involved in a tug of war between the Texas authorities and the men from Washington. Literally. Youngblood looked at the scene in disbelief. Orders were orders. The President was going back to Washington.

County medical examiner Earl Rose was standing in front of the casket and would not move. *We're going to have to shoot that bastard,* thought Youngblood. Hoover had impressed upon him the haste that was necessary in removing the slain President's body from Dallas. *What was the Director so afraid of?*

Rose was screaming. "This man was murdered in Texas and by Texas law we must have an autopsy. We can not release the remains without it!" His face flushed with anger, sweat pouring down, Rose became the unmovable object. He was about to meet the irresistible force.

The agents gathered. The President's private physician, Dr. George Burkley, who had been traveling with the motorcade, tried to reason with the intransigent Texan. "Dr. Rose, this is the President of the United States. We must get him back to Washington. Certainly you can make an exception in this case." Rose was adamant. This man was murdered in Texas, he would have a Texas autopsy. No exceptions. Facing a steely eyed phalanx of Secret Service agents and Kennedy aides, this was not the yellow Rose of Texas.

Youngblood had had enough. The Secret Service drew their guns. Six beefy agents lined the back and sides of the President's casket. They had been in Dallas too long already. They would leave over Rose's dead body, if necessary. As the casket sped forward, Rose flew to the side. Even though the law was the law, Rose was not prepared to die for it, not just yet anyway.

And so the getaway, er, cover-up, began. It would be the first of many bizarre events designed to deny and overlook the hordes of eyewitnesses, testimony, medical evidence, and logical reconstructions of the events of November 22nd, 1963. It was the beginning of mysterious heart attacks, bizarre accidents and typed suicide notes of long departed individuals, whose only illness was that they knew too much, saw too much, or talked too much.

Who would have thought you could sit on an atom bomb? But after thirty years, the roasted *derrieres* of the shadow government show that it can be done. It hasn't been easy, but it can be done. Carlos may have set in motion the tragic events of November 22nd, 1963, but without the considerable and continuing assistance of his strange bedfellows, peppered throughout the subterranean caverns of the governmental ganglia, he never could have pulled it off. Nope. Not the Crime of the Century, he couldn't.

IV.

The Aftermath

After dropping Marilyn off, Poppa and I got home around two thirty. My mother greeted us at the door. She had been watching TV and crying. "Did you see the President?," she asked. Poppa and I nodded. We had seen the President. Did we know he had been shot? Yes, we knew he had been shot. Did we know that he had just died? This we had not heard. We thought he had died a couple of hours earlier, anyway. Poppa told my mother that I wasn't feeling well and led me to the bedroom to lie down. I lay there, shaking uncontrollably. I was afraid to close my eyes. I was afraid of the Captain.

Poppa went back to the kitchen and sat down with Mom. He told her what had happened. She couldn't believe it. Poppa shrugged his shoulders. He didn't want to be there. He just happened to be. With me. We just wanted to see the President. My Father would be home soon; he would talk to me. Poppa seemed to be okay. Mom and Poppa went over to the TV. Some policeman had just been shot.

My father came home about three o'clock. This must have been an unusual day. We never saw Dad before six or seven. He knew that Poppa and I had gone to see the President. He wanted to know if we were all right. One look at my mother told him we weren't.

They all sat down at the table. Poppa explained to Dad that we had been in Dealey Plaza. Had we seen anything? Yes, said Poppa, we had seen everything. Had it on film too, he thought. My father whistled and sighed, "Oh, boy. Jake's going to need some counseling, I think."

I heard Dad's steps approaching. It was the Captain coming from behind the picket fence. I pulled my blanket over my eyes.

"Jake?" He sat down on the side of my bed. "Jake, it's all right, it's me." I pulled the cover down over one eye. It wasn't the Captain; it was Dad. I gave him a weak smile.

"Jake, Poppa told me what happened. I'm very sorry, but there's nothing any of us can do about it, we just have to accept it. Did you see the President get shot?" I nodded my head yes. I couldn't speak. My father shook his head in dismay.

"Jake, now what you saw was very painful and causes something we call trauma. It will hurt for a while, but you'll get better in time. Do you understand?" I nodded yes and Dad continued. "I saw it in World War II in Germany. A soldier would see somebody get shot or a friend get killed, and it would be very painful for them. But with time and a little counseling, they would get better. Do you know Dr. Baumgarten?" I shook my head no. "Well, she's a psychologist and she's very good. She can help you deal with what you saw. And Mommy and Poppa and I will be here to look after you. You'll be okay, Jake." Dad leaned over and kissed me on the forehead. I wanted to tell him about the Captain, but I couldn't speak.

He returned to the kitchen. "He's in shock. I've seen it before. I'll call Dr. Baumgarten and see how soon she can see him." Dad went to the phone and dialed. Dr. Baumgarten wasn't in, so Dad left a message. He retired to the TV with my mother, Poppa, and my older sister, who had just come home. About five o'clock I discovered that my legs worked again and I went and stood at the edge of the kitchen. Everybody looked over and smiled at me to come in. The dead had arisen.

The biographies of Kennedy were showing, interspersed with dribs and drabs of news. We watched in disbelief, scenes of people watching in disbelief, crying, wailing, stunned. The country was numb. It seemed that this man, for whatever reason, had been the embodiment of so many hopes for the future. Hopes that had been snatched away in one stunning, incomprehensible blow.

A suspect had been nabbed in the Texas Theatre. A short, slight, balding guy who worked in the Book Depository, somebody they were calling Harvey Lee Oswald. He looked most unimpressive with his rumpled hair, white T-shirt and blackened eye. They had found his rifle on the sixth floor of that building, with three spent cartridges lying next to the southeast corner window. Incriminating photographs had also been discovered at his rooming house. My father shook his head.

"Who could imagine that one scrawny little guy like that, acting by himself, could kill the President of the United States?"

I turned to my father, able to speak for the first time in hours.

"That man didn't kill the President, Dad."

"How can you be so sure of that, Jake?"

"Because I saw the man who did."

The getaway caravan sped out of Dealey Plaza and raced to the safe house in North Dallas, dispensing its charges one by one. This nondescript ranch house was to be their domicile for the next ten days while the enormous events of that afternoon died down. Robert arrived first, quickly followed by Lucien, and finally a disconsolate Giancarlo. Not only had he not hit the President, he had hit the other man twice, and he knew it. Hopefully, Lucien and Robert did not.

Lucien's hands were still shaking. He needed whiskey, now. Anything. Wine, if necessary. His gracious host, Novello, offered up a brimming glass of Johnny Walker Red which Lucien quickly dispatched of. There was no euphoria. There were just frazzled nerves coupled with the attendant adrenaline produced by the momentous and spine-tingling execution of the plot. Whiskey was needed. Copious amounts. Now.

After draining his third glass, Lucien snapped on the TV. Although he was fluent in French and Spanish, as well as his native Italian, his English was halting, at best. But the scannings of Dealey Plaza and the repeated pans of the Depository building, Lucien understood. They had found the rifle on the sixth floor. There were no pictures of the picket fence, although one or two witnesses had pointed in that direction. Mostly there was the Depository.

Lucien waited. *Why hadn't they found the body of the patsy? And what was this about a police officer getting killed? Was that connected somehow? Would there be flashing lights around Novello's safe house after all?* A hidden sub-basement had been prepared for such an eventuality, though Lucien prayed they wouldn't have to use it. All they could do was wait. They had done their part.

The whiskey was beginning to take effect. Robert was getting boisterous. He knew he had hit the President, twice he thought, once in the back and once in the head. He couldn't be sure about the head shot because the President's head had exploded from another direction, which he knew had to be Lucien's shot. They all knew Lucien had delivered the *coup de grace*, but as the point man, from fifty feet, he was supposed to. Lucien began to relax a little. Yes, in fact, he had fired the shot that would be remembered throughout history. Too bad the consequences for taking public credit for it would be disastrous. Lucien's greatest achievement would have to remain clandestine. When Lucien found himself resenting the credit that this fool Oswald would get for his alleged handiwork, he quickly reminded himself of the price Oswald would have to pay.

The three hitmen remained glued to the TV. Amid the relaxation, their concerns began to grow. *Shouldn't the patsy's body have been found by now?* After all, the rifle and the shells had been discovered. The body was supposed to be coordinated with that; it was part of the plan. The Carousel Club was only a few blocks away from the Depository.

And what about this policeman getting shot? Was he one of the officers connected with the patsy? Lucien hadn't been told any names. He was just assured the deed would be done.

What was this flashing on the screen? Somebody being arrested at the Texas Theatre. The patsy! He was alive! How did he escape? The patsy in police custody! Unimaginable. They would all be dead men now.

Novello raced to the phone. He dialed up Marcello. Nofio picked up. Did they know that Oswald was alive and in police custody?

"Yes," sighed Nofio, they knew. They were working on it right now. Nofio paused. "Have the Corsicans returned?"

"Yes," nodded Novello. "All three of them."

Marcello grabbed the phone.

"Get them in the sub-basement. Now!"

The capture of Lee Oswald had set off a nine alarm panic in the far reaching, disparate corners of the country. The pre-conspirators, co-conspirators, and post-conspirators had been thrown a major league curve ball. Two men were supposed to be dead, and two men were. Only they were the wrong two men. Well, one of them, anyway.

J. Edgar Hoover quickly swung into action. There would be no tape recordings of any interrogations of Oswald, no public information issued. What about the Dallas police? "Fuck the Dallas police." Jackson Casey, Chief of Police, might prove troublesome, but Earl Cabell, the Mayor of Dallas, was the brother of the post-assassination coordinator. Casey would quickly fall into line. Hoover knew of Oswald and his activities first hand. The ex-marine was a time bomb waiting to go off. He must be tried, sentenced, and executed, post-haste. Executed? He must be executed before the execution. Somehow. Some way.

Mysterious leaks about Oswald's past appeared moments after his arrest. In an hour the American public knew his life history. Mighty fine detective work. Mighty fine. Except the details were supposed to be released after his death. His continued survival was sort of ruining everything.

The plants had been planted and found. The rifle and three shells on the sixth floor of the Depository. The slightly disfigured bullet on Connally's stretcher. A picture of the smiling face of a gun toting Oswald, hoisted atop a borrowed body. The limp hanging blanket in the garage where Marina told police Lee's gun was. Everything had worked so beautifully. Open and shut case. Except that the star attraction was noticeably devoid of the *rigor mortis* that was scheduled to be setting in, just about now.

Hoover ruminated. He would conceal Oswald's interrogation under the guise of national security. That had always worked well in the past. They would need lots of national security on this one. Lots.

The phone rang in Jack Ruby's apartment just about when he expected it to. His TV had just flashed out the picture of the manacled and bruised Oswald being led away from the Texas Theatre.

The quivering mass of nerves went over to the phone to pick it up. Where could he run?

It was Ferrie. What happened? Oswald didn't show, plain and simple, shrugged Ruby. He didn't know why. Ferrie cursed himself. Oswald had always cooperated before. Why now, of all times? What happened to Benton? No sense in fudging with these piranhas. They'd fillet him soon enough, anyway.

"Benton went berserk. He was going to blow the whole thing, turn us all in. I had to silence him."

"Hmm," Ferrie murmured to himself. "Leverage." Carlos had been listening on the wired phone. He motioned to Ferrie to hand him the receiver.

"Jack, this is Marcello." Jack didn't need an introduction. He knew who it was. "Jack, I'm aware of your cooperation and good intentions. And as far as I'm concerned, the deal is still on. I will have Ferrie personally come up and deliver the cash to you." *Great,* thought Jack. *Have him deliver it to Memorial Cemetery,* he mused.

Carlos paused and then continued. Somehow Jack figured he would. "As you know Jack, we've now got a problem on our hands. A serious problem." *Understatement of the century, Mafia breath.* Yes, Jack agreed they had a serious problem.

"Jack, Oswald has to be eliminated, and as soon as possible. You're the only one we know who can get into Dallas Police headquarters. We don't think your buddy Roscoe is gonna shoot him in front of his comrades." Marcello laughed at his warped joke.

"You want me to shoot Oswald inside police headquarters,?" Ruby gasped. This was crazy. Absolutely crazy. "How do you expect me to get away?"

Carlos hesitated. "We don't."

Ruby paused, trying to absorb the enormity of Marcello's words. His head was spinning. This was all just crazy. Absolutely insane.

"And what if I don't do it?" Self preservation had started to kick in.

Marcello flew into a rage, but tried to control himself. "Jack, there is no 'what if.' You just do it. This is an order."

"Okay," replied Ruby, weakly. Marcello knew he wasn't convinced.

"Jack, you have two choices. Let me make them abundantly clear to you. We know there are two people in your life that mean anything to you. Your sister and your boyfriend, George." *Christ, these guys have good information,* thought Ruby. They were right on.

Marcello continued. "Now we are prepared to take care of both of them in fine style for the remainder of their natural lives. We will also pay for all your legal defenses. I have spoken to my attorneys, and they think it shouldn't be that difficult to prove insanity, in view of the extraordinary circumstances. A couple of years in the nuthouse, good conduct, rational behavior, and, bingo, you're a free man. At which time we support you like a king for the rest of your life." Marcello continued, without pausing. "Now Jack, if you decide unwisely to not follow this choice, let me outline the other possibility. We will take care of your sister and your boyfriend for the rest of their natural lives. Which should be about a month."

"Now Jack, do you remember Action Jackson?" Jack shuddered. Action Jackson had been a Mafioso up in Chicago who had turned informant. Unfortunately, he had fallen back into Mob hands, where he was subsequently tortured, deballed, burned alive, dismembered, and finally left hanging on a meat hook. He had set a new standard for Mob excellence. Very unpleasant stuff.

"Do you remember Action Jackson?," Carlos wanted to know. Yes, Jack remembered Action Jackson. "Well once we've attended to your sister and your boyfriend, we will treat you to a delightful performance on your person that will make Action Jackson look like child's play. Do you understand, Jack?" Carlos was impressed with his facility to convey menace. Jack understood.

"Now Jack, we know you are a reasonable man. Please do not decide unwisely. There is also the messy business of Officer Benton to be aware of. We will give you time to consider. It's now five thirty. Call David here by six o'clock. We trust you will decide wisely." Click.

Carlos turned to Ferrie. "David, as soon as Ruby calls, which he will, I want you to head up to Dallas to make sure he honors his commitment. Take the money we've promised him and deposit it in this account I've set up." Marcello handed him a slip of paper. "I don't want him to think I'm not a man of my word." Ferrie nodded. He had every incentive to insure Ruby's compliance. If the stocky Jewish gangster failed to deliver, he was next.

Ruby looked up at the spinning room turning swiftly around him. Sweat poured down his pale white forehead. He looked down at his calendar. Easy schedule for today, November 22nd. Plant a bullet. It seemed so simple. He picked up the receiver to phone Ferrie.

When the first shots rang out, one man, following three cars behind, knew they weren't firecrackers. Lyndon Johnson quickly ducked, as instructed. He needn't have bothered. Agent Rufus Youngblood sprang up and was hanging spread eagle over him like flattened road kill. Something instinctive told the veteran agent that this was more than firecrackers. It had better be, or he would be damned embarrassed. Damned embarrassed.

Lyndon had been anxious all morning, awaiting the fateful moment. Today was the day and he knew it. He had quarreled with Kennedy the night before about seating arrangements for the motorcade. Johnson was lobbying hard to switch his friend and protégé, Texas Governor John Connally, slated to ride with Kennedy, to the Veep's car. In the Governor's place he would put arch-enemy, Senator Ralph Yarborough. A two-fer. Kennedy would not have it. Johnson stormed from the room. "You'll get yours soon enough, you Harvard son-of-a-bitch," Johnson murmured to himself. "Sorry Governor, I tried. Them's the breaks."

Kennedy had made a note to himself. The barely tolerable Johnson had become unbearable. He had scarcely helped win Texas in 1960 and would not be necessary in '64. He was setting so many records for vice presidential scandals, that even subsequent bagman Spiro Agnew, would be green with envy. The latest adventure involved Johnson's neighbor and friend, Bobby Baker, a $20,000 a year legislative assistant, who had somehow managed to take control of three and a half million dollars worth of vending machine business at various defense contractors' plants across America. This feat of legerdemain was so impressive that it had made the cover of *Life Magazine* several weeks before. You never knew where Ole Lyndon was going to stick his grubby little fingers next. Kennedy wasn't about to find out. He issued an order to his secretary, Evelyn Lincoln, noting that Johnson was off the ticket. Period. It was the last order he was ever to issue.

Lyndon had been in a funk all morning and throughout the motorcade. There would be much work to do that afternoon and damn little time to do it. Not to mention having to keep a somber comportment throughout. As the cars approached Dealey Plaza, Lyndon was twisting and turning, fiddling with a walkie talkie. *What the hell is he doing*, wondered the barely civil Yarborough, from across the seat.

Shots rang out. Lyndon spent the frantic trip to Parkland cushioned below Agent Youngblood's splayed torso. It wouldn't be the last time he would use a Secret Service agent as a human shield, but at least this time he wasn't urinating.

Johnson was quickly led into a side closet off the operating room. Nervous agents, worrying about a mass conspiracy, anxiously urged him to leave the hospital, to get out of harm's way. Lyndon wasn't going anywhere until he received the confirmation he was looking for. Somehow the threat of worldwide conspiracy and gunmen roaming the halls of Parkland Hospital didn't worry him. The confirmation came at 1:13. Johnson hightailed it back to Air Force One, Dallas Police Chief Jackson Casey in tow. *Had they found the patsy's body?* No word yet, offered Casey. Nothing to do but sit and wait.

They didn't have to wait long. They found Oswald. Alive and in police custody. This could unravel the whole thing. One minor blip and the whole house of cards would fall down. Johnson wouldn't have it. Get Edgar on the phone. Now.

Did Edgar know that Oswald was alive and in police custody? Edgar knew. He was working on it, right now. And where the hell was Kennedy's body, anyway? Lyndon wasn't going anywhere without it. They were working on that, too. "Well, get it done," fumed Johnson. He slammed the phone down.

Hoover phoned back in fifteen minutes. Kennedy's body was on the way, and if Oswald could be exposed at police headquarters for two to three minutes, he could be taken care of, as well. Johnson looked over to Police Chief Casey. Could he do it? Casey nodded back. It would be messy, but he could do it if it needed to be done. Johnson smiled back at him. It needed to be done.

Johnson glanced out the cabin window and saw the body of the slain President being loaded aboard, accompanied by the beautiful and bloodstained Jackie. *Thank you, Edgar, I'll talk to you in Washington.* Lyndon was ready to go.

He bid farewell to Chief Casey and reminded him of the solemnity of his task, and the consequences that failure would engender. He beckoned the grieving widow to come forward to be by his side for the swearing in. And with that, Lyndon Johnson raised his right hand and became the 36th President of the United States.

Lee didn't know exactly what had hit him. But judging by the number of law enforcement officials swarming around him, it wasn't good. Whatever thinking he had to do would be done inside the Dallas city jail.

Cruising into the back of that institution, hordes of newsmen pressed against the car, flash bulbs popping. Shouted questions bounced in muted tones off the sealed windows. Lee was led inside and quickly whisked up to the third floor. He was beginning to suspect the worst.

Outside, the Dallas police were starting to build their open and shut case against the defendant. A rifle and some shells had been found. A bullet at Parkland. Pictures of the subject with the weapon. They had their man, all right.

Lee was hustled into a backroom. No reporters. No cameras. No tape recorders. What, he wanted to know, was he being detained for? The murder of a policeman. And suspicion of involvement in the shooting of the President. Lee shook his head. *Fucking Ferrie. The God damned FBI.* He couldn't believe this was happening.

FBI Dallas field agent, James Hosty, entered the room and introduced himself. Lee went ballistic. This was the same weasel who had attempted to question Marina in his absence. Lee let loose a torrent of expletives directed at that revered agency and its beloved director that could have peeled the paint off the walls. His fury was uncontrollable. Agent Hosty beat a hasty retreat.

So this is it, thought Oswald. This is what all the leftist crap, all the leafleting and public demonstrations were all about. The secret trip to Mexico. The mail order rifle. He should have known. *Well, fuck 'em.* Two could play this game. Lee could name names. Names of people who knew and did a whole lot more than his petty shenanigans in the pay of the U.S. Government. *Don't say anything. Get a lawyer.* The media wanted him? They would get him. Boy, would they get him. The Ferries and the Bannisters and the Hostys and the Hoovers would rue the day they messed with Lee Oswald. *Bring 'em on.*

Lee scoped the room. Throughout the course of the interrogation, no note pads appeared, no tape recorders whirred; just a couple of Dallas' Finest sitting there, flapping their gums at him. *Very strange,* thought Lee. *Got to get a lawyer.* There was this fellow in New York who Lee was familiar with, who had made a name for himself in the '50s defending cases that the Government had brought, in which they charged conspiracy. *What was his name? Abt, that was it, John Abt. Got to get in touch with him.* Lee clammed up. He asked for a lawyer. A burly cop in the corner handed him a phone. Lee quickly dialed up Ruth Williams' number, at the house where Marina was staying. Marina had just unwittingly directed authorities to Lee's rifle in the garage. When the wrapped-up weapon was lifted, it proved to be a limp hanging blanket. Marina was worried.

Ruth Williams answered the phone and Lee, speaking matter of factly, asked her to try to find Attorney John Abt in New York. Williams was flabbergasted at Lee's nonchalance, in the face of the momentous events swirling around him, but she agreed to try to get the lawyer. Then she put a hysterical Marina on the phone.

"Lee, what is going on, what has happened? They are saying all these awful things. Please tell me."

Lee did his best to be reassuring. "Please don't worry, Marina. It's all a terrible mistake. Things will be fine once they get sorted out. Please take care of the children and don't worry about me." Lee spoke with the perfect conviction of one not troubled by guilt. He was an innocent man. He just needed the time and the opportunity to prove it.

"But what about the rifle, Lee?"

"Don't worry about the rifle or any other thing. This whole thing is a set-up. Time will prove me right, Marina. I love you. Take care of the children."

It was time to move to the cell. As Lee headed down the hall, he was inundated by a crush of media, flash bulbs, and shouted questions. *Did he kill the President?* Lee laughed to himself. Absurd. The whole scene was absurd. If the police wouldn't give him a lawyer, maybe the media would. "I didn't shoot anybody. I'm just a patsy. These people have given me a hearing without legal representation. I would like someone to come forward to offer legal assistance." Lee could trust the media. They would respond to a reasonable request. If the Ferries and Hoovers of the world were going to lay their weird machinations at his feet, he would fight them off, through the media, in public. He could wait. He had time. His innocence would prevail, of that Lee had no doubt.

The shaking had stopped. In its place, a peaceful serenity had descended. Jack Ruby was a dead man and he knew it. Oh sure, his body might live on for a few years, but this would merely be coincidental. For all intents and purposes, Jack was dead. Time to say farewells. He called his estranged brother in Chicago, who he hadn't seen in years. *No, nothing in particular, just called to say hello, just called to chat. Okay. Too bad about the President. Got me nostalgic. Anybody else?* A few old acquaintances. Jack dialed.

It was Friday night. Jack hadn't been to Temple in years. The Rabbi was surprised to see him, but grateful for the congregant, despite his checkered past. They were all sad about the President. They prayed. A group gathered around Abraham Zuckerman to get a first hand account. Jack listened in, without comment. Jack was ready to face his God, although he could not stay for cake and coffee. He had an appointment at the Dallas Police Station.

Late that evening Lee was led down stairs for a "press conference." Except there were no questions allowed, which was unusual for a press conference. Several of the law enforcement personnel were concerned that Oswald, who by this point had achieved the notoriety of Hitler and Stalin combined, would be left unprotected, a gross security violation. Not necessary, they were told. *Okay, whatever you say.*

Oswald peered at the crowd. The crowd peered back. The bespectacled Jewish gangster, fresh from Temple, clutched his gun in the back of the room. Failure of nerve. He just couldn't do it. He eased off the trigger. Action Jackson flashed through his mind, along with visions of his dead sister and lover. He clutched the gun again. *Just couldn't do it.* Maybe if he got closer. Or maybe he just couldn't do it. Jack agonized.

After two or three minutes the inevitable happened. A reporter asked a question. Exactly the wrong question, did Oswald shoot the President? Lee started to answer. "No, I didn't shoot anybody. In fact, that's the first time that anybody has mentioned that to me." He was quickly cut off. *Hey, don't you know there's no questions. This is a press conference, damnit*! What the hell was wrong with Ruby? Ample time, ample opportunity. *We've got us a real problem here, a real problem*. End of press conference.

The calls started coming in that night. The Mafia. The Government. The FBI, via the Mafia. Ferrie, and then Ferrie again. Jack had twenty four hours or he and his clan were dead meat. Did he understand? Yes, he understood.

Texas state law required the transfer of a prisoner charged with a felony to a county facility within twelve hours. Oswald was charged with Kennedy's murder at 11 P. M. Friday night. But things being what they were, this technicality was quickly bypassed. Sunday morning would be an opportune time to transfer and expose the prisoner at the same time. It would be the last crack at him, and it needed to be successful. Lots of powerful people were depending on it.

Lee spent an active Saturday being interrogated, shuffled around, and passed through lineups, as the star in residence amidst the pandemonium of Dallas Police Headquarters. Still no tape recorders, no notes taken, no record of any of his statements. And no response from lawyer John Abt, on vacation from New York. Overnight, Lee had gone from a complete nonentity to a deranged killer. His life history, or differing versions of it, flashed from media outlets around the country. High school dropout. Dishonorable discharge. Defector. Russian wife. What was this madman doing on the loose with the President coming to town, anyway?

The madman was starting to enjoy the limelight. He had never asked to be put in this position, but now that he was in it, he would take advantage. A book. A movie, maybe. Once his innocence was proven, oh what a story he would have to tell! And names he could name. Maybe he could help in the investigation. Who knew where the trail from Ferrie and Bannister led? The potential for revenue, fame and intrigue, was unlimited. Maybe Lee could provide for his family, after all. Could this be the lucky break he had been waiting for, in the wake of this tragedy? Lee waited for his lawyer and dreamed of the possibilities. Still no record of his interrogations. He'd have to get his story out to the media by himself.

Jack's testicles were in a vise. The Sunday morning transfer would be it. It was then or never. Ruby would drop a telegram at the Western Union office, which was visible from police headquarters. As he left that office, the signal for the transfer would be sent. He would be let in a side door, proceed through headquarters to a back stairway and down the staircase to the garage. He would have access to an unshielded Oswald walking to the transfer vehicle in the basement. It would be broadcast on national TV. Jack was going to murder the accused assassin of the President of the United States on national TV, and there was no way out, except suicide, perhaps. Jack considered. Maybe he could get the transfer changed or called off. In the dead of night, he phoned Dallas Police Headquarters and anonymously warned that Oswald would be murdered during the transfer. The

Sergeant on duty made a quick note of it and promptly fell back to sleep. The transfer was on.

Lee arose Sunday morning after a much needed good night's rest. Vindication was his once he got out of this hell-hole, and today was the day. A book and a movie. Fancy clothes for Marina. A new car, if he ever learned how to drive. Maybe a house. And time to spend with his little girls. Lee snapped to attention. He shaved and showered and put on a fresh set of clothes. He felt great. Today was the first day of his new life.

Jack Ruby walked out of the Western Union office at 11:18 in the morning. A signal passed from the third floor of police headquarters. Get the prisoner moving. Lee's morning questioning was abruptly interrupted. It was time to go. Though Lee had been surrounded by a human shield when he was brought in as a suspect in an officer's slaying, he was given a two man escort on the way out, as the accused assassin of the President of the United States. Was the media lobbying for a good shot? They couldn't have had a better one if they had been. Ruby slipped in the side door and headed for the basement. Zero hour. The lamb was on the way to the slaughter.

Oswald stepped out of the elevator manacled to two deputies, one on each side. He was an innocent man, at peace with himself. He walked calmly as he reached the garage.

The cameras rolled. *Here he comes, Oswald, the accused assassin.* The nation looked at the slight, balding, serene young man, stepping forward. It just didn't compute. Something was wrong.

Ruby had finished his last *Shema Israel.* His time had come. Unlike Oswald, at least he knew it. He pounced forward, the stocky avenger. Lee turned his head. *Aaargh!* The bullet ripped through his abdomen as Lee crashed to the floor. Ruby was firing madly as his friends and compatriots wrestled him to the ground. *Jack, you stupid son of a bitch, what in the hell are you doing? Isn't there enough shame on Dallas already?* He was quickly subdued, handcuffed, and led off to Oswald's vacant cell, by a score of pissed off and double crossed associates. *We thought we could trust you, you were one of us.* Dallas' infamy was deepening.

Lee lay dying on the basement floor. A conveniently placed ambulance was parked close by. Lee was on his way to Parkland. He was delirious. As the ambulance siren roared, Lee's fading consciousness raced. *Marina and the children. It was all so unfair.* He just wanted to be a good husband and father, that's all he ever wanted to be. Why wouldn't they let him? He had to live, he had to tell his story. Almost forty eight hours in captivity and not a note, not a recording, not a word of his protestations had been brought to light, illuminated, captured for posterity.

The pulse was weak. Vindication was so close. *I can't die a vilified patsy. The world must know. It's all so unfair.* Lee Oswald was rolled into operating room #2, twenty yards from where the President of the United States had died two days earlier. The new President of the United States was on the line. He wanted a death bed confession from the accused assassin. *Mr. President, in all due respect, there will be no death bed confession from Lee Harvey Oswald today. He died at 1:07 P.M., Central Standard Time.*

And so Lee Harvey Oswald's fifteen minutes of fame had ended. Somehow, in almost two days of capture, not a statement was recorded, not a word was preserved. A grieving nation watched in stunned silence. It was all so incomprehensible, all so bizarre.

The system moved without delay. The FBI impounded and sealed up the evidence. It was taking over the investigation. The Justice Department, with the prime suspect murdered, considered the case closed. Carlos relaxed. Edgar relaxed. Lyndon relaxed. Lucien came up from the sub-basement. The President of the United States had been murdered by a man calmly sipping a Coke from a second floor lunchroom. The rest was merely technicalities.

Like millions of other Americans, we sat around the TV that bright Sunday morning in November for a glimpse of the assassin. We had been glued to the set since Friday afternoon. I had recovered a bit from my initial shock, but I couldn't get the Captain's face out of my mind. People from Time-Life were coming this afternoon to look at Poppa's film. It turned out that Poppa had captured the key moments of the assassination on film, and that the nation's tragedy might turn out to be a financial boon to him. The FBI had requested that he turn over the tape, which he did, after keeping a copy for himself. They were not pleased with this arrangement, but were not at the point of breaking knuckles yet, much to their later regret.

Poppa, Dad and I leaned forward in our chairs as the TV screen flashed a picture of the cops bringing the composed, unimposing, wisp of a man from the elevator to the basement. Dad shook his head. "That man doesn't look like he would hurt a fly," he started to say. Then "BLAM!," and a mass of confusion. Oswald had been shot on national TV! Dad, Poppa, and I, leaped up in amazement. *This was crazy*. On top of the outrageous events of Friday, now this. Unbelievable. We watched while pandemonium reigned in the police station basement, as the ambulance came to whisk Oswald off to Parkland. They quickly led Oswald's assailant away, someone apparently many of the officials knew, named Jack Ruby.

'"Ruby!," Poppa cursed. "That low life." Poppa had met him a few times at Temple; he seemed like a shady character. In fact, Poppa thought he might have seen him Friday night, but couldn't be certain. But that wasn't what upset Poppa. He was ashamed that a Jew had gotten mixed up in this sordid affair.

Amid the delirium from Parkland Hospital and the somber scenes from Washington, flashing from the TV screen, the Time-Life people arrived. Poppa had set up the projector in the living room and my mother was serving coffee. I went outside to shoot hoops. I wasn't ready to see this yet. I had seen all I needed to.

Poppa let the film roll. I heard a groan coming from the living room. Nobody, including Poppa, had seen it before.

Apparently it was very graphic. Mom left the room, sick. Dad walked away, shaking his head. He suddenly knew that all this crap he had been hearing about Oswald being the lone assassin shooting from the back, was just that, a lot of crap. Why were the police so adamant? Anybody who looked at this film could clearly see that the shot that took the President's head off came from the front and the side.

Poppa rewound the film for the Time-Life people, who wanted him to run it again and again in slow motion. Dad didn't want to see it again. Once was enough. The three men watched the slow moving ghastly scene time and time again. *Old man Zuckerman really had something here, something a lot of people would pay money to see, or not see.* They retired to caucus in the den. They were prepared to pay Poppa a substantial amount of money for the "rights" to the film. Could Poppa keep a copy? Certainly, as long as the "rights" remained with them. They were prepared to pay $25,000. Poppa calculated that was about $1,000 per second. He whistled and told them he needed to conference with Dad.

Poppa didn't feel right making money off the tragedy. He could always use it, God knows, but it didn't seem right to him. Dad felt otherwise. First of all, these people had more money than God and would probably make a hundred times what they were offering Poppa. Secondly, if they made the film available to the American public, people could actually see the events of that day and judge for themselves. Dad strongly suspected that, based on the film and what I had told him, the public wasn't getting it straight. If Poppa's film could help achieve some modicum of the truth, so much the better. They returned to the living room. They would take the $25,000, Time-Life could have the rights. They shook hands and the men departed.

Since Friday, Poppa had been besieged for interviews. What had he seen? He had gone to a Dallas TV station Friday afternoon and described the events he had viewed through his camera lens. I knew he had been totally preoccupied with his movie camera and hadn't seen the Captain at all. A few of the reporters had questioned Marilyn, who reported essentially the same thing as Poppa. Nobody thought to ask me what I saw, which was just as well, because I could barely bring myself to think about it, much less talk about it. Except that I couldn't get the Captain out of my mind.

Poppa went off to take his afternoon nap. Dad stepped outside to join me for some hoops. He was clearly upset by Poppa's film, and concerned about me. He motioned for me to come over to the picnic table in the corner of the yard. He wanted to talk. I tucked the ball under my arm and followed him over.

"How you feeling Jake, you seem to be doing better than Friday." I had to acknowledge that I was. But it still hurt and I couldn't stop thinking about the Captain, or the President's exploding head. I suspected I wouldn't for a long time.

"Now Jake, I don't know exactly what you saw, but I don't doubt that you saw something extraordinary." An understatement, if ever I heard one.

"There's something not right about this whole thing, what we're seeing and hearing on TV. You know it and now that I've seen Poppa's film, I know it. Hopefully, when the American people see the film, they'll know it, too. Now you saw something that very few people saw, that maybe nobody else saw. Do you know that's true, Jake?" I nodded. I knew it was true.

"Now what you saw, you obviously weren't supposed to see or at least know about. Do you follow me, Jake?" *Sort of.* Dad went on.

"Do you know what the word discrepancy means?" I shook my head no.

"Well discrepancy describes a situation where what you hear differs significantly from what you've seen. At least that's one form of it. Now everything we've heard since Friday is that the President was shot from behind by this man Oswald and that he was the only one doing the shooting. They seem to be adamant about it." Dad looked down at me. He had seen that "adamant" had glazed my eyeballs. He laughed.

"What I mean Jake, is the police seem to be determined to convey, er, to show, that this is what happened and that it's important for the public to believe it. They seem to be trying awfully hard to make sure the public believes it. Now you and I know that this 'Oswald shooting from behind by himself' is not necessarily true, but that is what the police are saying. They must have some important reason for saying it." I nodded. Dad was good with words. He wasn't a lawyer, but he could have been. He made things make sense.

"Now Jake, assuming the police and other people want the American public to believe that this man Oswald killed the President all by himself, there must be some very powerful reasons for them to do so. So powerful that it was important enough for them to let Mr. Oswald be shot so he couldn't tell his side of the story. Do you follow me?" Unfortunately, I did.

"Now whoever has the power to allow the accused assassin of the President of the United States to be murdered on national television is somebody or bodies you don't want to fool around with. That man could have been protected. Given the events that have just occurred, he would have to be protected. Unless somebody didn't want him to be, unless someone wanted to make sure he stayed silent. Set him up as the killer and then silenced him before he could talk." Dad looked down at me. "Are you still with me?" I nodded that I was.

"Well that's exactly what I think happened here. I don't know why it happened or who wanted the President killed, but that's what I think happened. And whoever has the power to kill a president and then control the police and whoever else gets in their way, is very dangerous and will stop at nothing to make sure people don't find out. Bear with me Jake, because this is the important part. Although Poppa's film may help shed some light on the situation, you saw things that the police and some very powerful people don't want the public to know. If somebody gets in their way with contradictory evidence,"... Dad stopped and looked at me. "I mean with proof that what they're saying is not so, they will not necessarily believe that person. They may want to make sure that that person remains silent, and they will go out of their way to make sure he does. Do you follow me Jake?" I nodded again.

"Now obviously Mr. Oswald knew things the police did not want people to know. Or at least he knew what they were saying about him wasn't true, and given the chance, could probably prove it easily. But it was important to somebody that he not be given the chance. Now Jake, what you saw was frightening and certainly very real, but like Mr. Oswald, there are some very powerful people who don't want you to tell anybody what you saw. It's important to them that you not tell anyone. Now I'm not saying that they're going to shoot you like they did Mr. Oswald, but I don't think they would hesitate to make sure you kept your mouth shut. It is hard to walk away and be silent about what we know to be true, but sometimes our survival depends on it. And I think this is one of those times. So what I'm telling you Jake, in a very roundabout way, is that it is very important that you not talk about what you saw with anybody. Let's keep it between us. If you need to talk about it, you can talk to me. You know I'll believe you. I hope you understand why I am saying this to you and why it is important for you to do as I'm saying. You must not talk about what you saw with anybody."

"Not even Poppa?" Tears were starting to stream down my face. I always talked to Poppa.

"Especially Poppa. Look, Jake, you've seen how the reporters have been all over Poppa. If he tells them you saw this, it may be dragged out in the open. You don't want to get involved in this, believe me. Do you know if Poppa saw the man?" I knew he hadn't or he would have mentioned it. It wasn't like Poppa to keep quiet about what he saw. Besides, he was so busy messing with his camera, I'm sure the only thing he saw was what was recorded on his film.

"Did Marilyn see the man?" No, I laughed, she was too busy holding up Poppa.

"Will Poppa be safe?"

"Your grandfather will be fine. Nobody is going to mess with a man who has publicly sold a movie to Time-Life. All Poppa is saying is what he saw, and what he saw is exactly what's on the film. He'll be fine."

"Now Jake, you've heard me out and I hope you understand what I'm saying and why I'm saying it to you. I want you to promise me that you won't tell anybody but me what you saw. Do you promise?"

I looked up at Dad, my lips quivering, my eyes washed in tears. I knew that for whatever reason he was saying what he was saying, it was for my protection and safety. I promised.

"Good." Dad stood up as if he had just laid down his closing statement.

"Now Jake, as a special treat to help overcome what you've just been through, I'm going to make a promise to you. The first time the Dodgers come to St. Louis next season, we'll go up there and take in the entire series. Doesn't matter if it's three or four games or if you have school. Just me and you. How's that sound?" Dad knew how to bribe me. It sounded great. He put his arm around me and we walked slowly back to the house as the recently liberated basketball rolled steadily down the driveway and into the street.

On November 24th, 1963, Dad couldn't have known how right he had been. He couldn't have known that the President's brain would be secretly removed at Walter Reed Hospital before his body was silently flown to Bethesda for an alleged autopsy barely suitable for a pauper, much less a president. He couldn't have known that not one word of Lee Oswald's almost forty eight hours of incarceration and interrogation had been recorded or preserved. He couldn't have known that the film they had seen in our living room that afternoon would not be seen by the general public for more than a decade, and even then, in a doctored form only. He couldn't have known that in the next twenty years almost one hundred people tangentially connected with witnessing, or having knowledge of the assassination, would perish in a series of bizarre illnesses, accidents and questionable suicides. Probably, thanks to the promise I made, I wasn't one of them.

No, Dad couldn't have known how close he had been to the pulse of the whole affair that was later to become known as The Crime of the Century. And he couldn't have known, through his concern for my safety and protection, that he had sentenced me to the Secret of it.

At the safehouse in North Dallas, only three blocks from the Zuckermans, Lucien popped the top off a bottle of champagne. It was two o'clock Sunday afternoon and Marcello had kept his word. Lee Oswald was dead. Lucien was a free man.

The three Corsicans had spent the last two days holed up in the sub-basement watching TV. It was getting damned uncomfortable, although the TV had been fascinating. Lucien's bullet had brought the world to a standstill.

The swarthy trio had no idea of the magnitude of the cataclysm that the success of their venture would bring. They knew it would be big, but they were amazed at just how big it was turning out to be. And though they appreciated the grandeur of it, they knew that this grandeur would be matched by a proportionally sized man hunt. Or so it seemed. But somehow the police and the FBI wanted to aid them. The law enforcement authorities seemed to be determined to bottle the investigation, to focus on the lone nut who had fired three shots from the rear, despite the hundreds of eyewitnesses who said otherwise. And now that the lone nut was gone, would the authorities continue their vigilant protection of the truth surfacing? Lucien seemed to think so. It called for a drink.

Lucien had seen the poor schmuck Oswald on TV. The Corsican shook his head. Was the American public really going to buy that this wretched excuse of a man actually pulled off, by himself, what it had taken Lucien, Giancarlo, Robert, scores of associates, unlimited caches of money and material, and hours of careful and diligent planning, to accomplish? Lucien was torn. He was insulted that such a major accomplishment could be railroaded into such a minimal and trivialized corner. He, goddamnit, was the man who brought the world to a standstill, not this squirrel Oswald, who was simply set up to take the fall. And yet, Lucien was grateful for the security that Oswald provided. Without him or his equivalent, Lucien's *magnum opus* would not have been possible. He just wished he could have gotten a little credit for it.

In fact, Lucien had received credit for it, at least in the clandestine circles that safe credit allowed. For unlike a firing squad, where anonymity was essential to the overall objective, nobody had any doubt who had delivered the blow that had dispatched the President to the great beyond. Lucien was becoming a cult hero in his insular little world. Would it be enough?

Eight more days in the safe house. They were scheduled to depart by private plane the following Monday. Enough time would have passed by then for things to cool down. In the meantime they would watch TV and pass the time as palatably as possible. So far the TV had been riveting.

They watched the grief of the American public. They watched the somber shots from Washington, the biographies of Kennedy's life, the quickly patched together life of Lee Oswald. At times, seeing the long lines of grieving mourners filing past Kennedy's coffin, Lucien almost felt remorse. Almost. But then he thought about the police, the Mafia and the hidden government. It seemed he was doing a lot of people a favor and they were willing to pay him well for it. Lucien didn't quite understand it. He thought the President was popular. How could the man have possibly pissed off this many people?

Lucien marveled at the cast of luminaries he had sent scurrying to America. Haile Selassi. Prince Phillip. Chancellor Erhard. Charles DeGaulle. The icy titan himself. *It could have been you,* reminisced a reflective Lucien. Somehow the presence of the great French stoneface had validated the act in Lucien's mind. This was homage. Intended for Kennedy, Lucien co-opted it for himself. The French President's presence was redemption beyond his wildest dreams for the Corsican's previous failed attempt.

Like millions of Americans, Lucien watched the crusty old form of Cardinal Cushing barking out his solemn prayers in that strange accent of his, as the bevy of world leaders surrounded the grave site of the fallen Chief. The somber, shrouded Jackie and the crushed Robert, peeking out from hooded eyes. The tolling of bells. The firing of rifles. The planes flying overhead. Lucien watched America's and the world's grief in amazement. They all did. There was no celebrating, no euphoria, just amazement. Amazement at the amount of grief, amazement at the depth of pain, amazement at the universality of it all, amazement at the enormity of the thing. They had no idea. No idea at all.

They had caught America and the world by surprise and snuffed out its brightest hope. They were just doing a job. Granted, a big job, but a job just the same. They weren't supposed to get emotionally involved with it and didn't, before the fact. But the overwhelming reaction afterward made it impossible not to be. Even for trained hitmen.

There was fear. What was this going to set off? Massive police hunts? It didn't seem to. The American press and the authorities seemed to be most cooperative in this area so far. Would it continue?

There was also a weird sense of pride. They had caused this momentous event, they had created it; without them nothing would be happening. And, yet, it was paramount that nobody know. Lucien looked at the grieving mourners lining the streets, the visiting dignitaries, all thinking that some lone malcontent, this poor misguided Oswald, had precipitated the tragedy. Nobody had a clue otherwise. Oswald had been arrested, tried, and executed in two days. Neatly tucked away, robbing Lucien of the credit, but also of the responsibility. Lucien weighed the equation with mixed emotions.

Was there guilt, remorse, shame in these cold blooded killers, as they watched a nation's sadness? At moments, twinges of it. So many people so sad. So many people acting like a member of their immediate family, a favorite brother, a father, a son, had just been taken from them, without warning, without regard, without a cushioning of the blow. So many people with so much pain. Lucien had no idea what his act would engender. It was just a job, he reminded himself, just a job. Could he kill again? Probably, if necessary. But he, Robert and Giancarlo were set for life. Lucien was glad that this lack of economic necessity might remove him from that decision. After the sobering events of the last few days, he wasn't looking forward to testing his will.

As the President's body was lowered into the grave, Lucien came to attention. He snapped off a salute to the slain Commander. Robert and Giancarlo stared in amazement. A tear trickled down Lucien's cheek. He was saluting the great Man, who, like himself, was master of his game, although very different games they were.

As the final bell tolled and the first shovel of dirt was tossed into the grave, Lucien stared blankly at the TV and saw the smiling face of John Kennedy moving slowly down Elm Street, right at him. He looked through his scope at the beautiful glow, the tousled chestnut hair, the wide ivory smile, the reddish bronze skin. Lucien squeezed and exploded the most beautiful head he had ever seen in his life. And nobody knew. Nobody knew. Nobody saw him. Except for maybe the boy. *Ah, the goddamned little boy.* Lucien snapped off the set, turned on his heels and retreated to a cot in the basement. He lay down and sobbed for an hour.

V.

On The Razor's Edge

Despite the gloom that descended upon the nation on November 22nd, the real grieving didn't start till the Tuesday following the President's funeral. With all the pomp and ceremony attending those somber events, the public's attention was absorbed and its grief deflected. But with last Friday's vigorous President planted in the ground by Monday afternoon, Tuesday dawned dark and brooding. There was nowhere to go to hide our grief.

And nowhere was that grief greater than Dallas. The nation turned its hate to Dallas. Reactionary, nest of vipers, unbelievably incompetent Dallas. Not only could it not protect the President, it couldn't even protect his alleged assassin. Dallas would take a long time to live this one down and its shame was manifest on the gloomy countenances of many of its citizens. Especially the students at Sam Houston Junior High. They, more than others, had shared in the final moments of the fallen President, now quickly on his way to immortality. He had touched them, literally, and now those golden moments had compounded the heartbreak. Wealthy, largely Jewish, Sam Houston had been an oasis of Kennedy country in the middle of right wing heaven.

Randy Epstein had developed his pictures of JFK's historic plunge into his assembled classmates. Arms reaching, touching, crying out for the smiling President. Randy was going to use them to torture his friend and Kennedy-phile, Jake Zuckerman, who had forsaken his classmates for a better view. But all this changed when the class returned to school and heard the tragic news. Jake did not come back.

Randy rushed home from school to call his friend. *Was Jake all right?* Not really, replied his mother; he had been in Dealey Plaza.

"Oh my God," screeched Randy. "Did he see it?"

"Yes, unfortunately, it sounds like he did. Jake's not feeling too well right now. Maybe you could give him a call tomorrow to see how he's doing. I think he would appreciate that."

Ever the dutiful soul, Randy quickly agreed, adding "if there's anything I can do, Mrs. Zuckerman, please let me know."

"That's very thoughtful, Randy. We'll keep that in mind. I'm glad that Jake has a good friend like you. Thanks for calling."

Randy called Saturday and then again Sunday. Jake couldn't come to the phone. Was he mad at him? Randy figured he would wait till Tuesday; he would see Jake at school. The President's funeral on Monday had cancelled classes. Knowing how much Jake loved the President, and what he probably saw, Randy vowed he would help Jake however he could. It was the least he could do for his best friend.

After the funeral, I lay on my bed and stared up at the ceiling. Even my twerp little brother, running in and out of the room, couldn't get me riled. I had thought about riding my bike out to the Oswald funeral, but I knew my father would never allow it. Not to mention a zillion Secret Service agents. But as I lay on my bed that Monday afternoon, I started to form the obsession that would dominate my life for the next thirty years. Little did I realize that I would be joined by thousands of others, mostly young men, my age and older. All of us were somehow mysteriously invested in the Kennedy phenomena, and his death had diminished us in a very real and tangible way. It was palpable. It was the end of innocence. It was the opening of the floodgates of disillusionment that would manifest itself in the Vietnam War, the urban riots, the Robert Kennedy and Martin Luther King assassinations, Kent State, and would finally culminate in Watergate. But as I lay there on my bed after my idol had been laid to rest, this was all an intellectual abstraction. All I knew was that I felt sad, very sad. It hurt to move, it hurt to talk, it hurt to be. So I did the only thing that my psyche would allow: I got on my bike and rode. I didn't ride, I flew. Miles and miles. My parents had bought me a three speed Rudge, English racers they called them back then, and the two of us had become inseparable. When I wanted to think, I rode. When I wanted to be alone, I rode. When I wanted to hang out with my friends we rode, mostly past the houses of the girls we had crushes on.

I thought for a minute of going down to Dealey Plaza, but my curiosity was overmatched by my fear. I wasn't ready to face it yet. So I hopped on my cycle and headed out to the open fields north of Dallas. I rode for hours. Tomorrow would be school. Would I go? My parents had offered to let me stay home for a week, if I wasn't up to it. But what would I do if I stayed home? Lie around the house? The word had spread that I had been in Dealey Plaza and had a front row seat to the assassination. Good old Randy. Kids would want to know everything. But with the agreement I made with my father, I could tell them almost nothing, which was probably just as well since I was having trouble talking, period. Dr. Baumgarten had finally called back, but based on what we saw on TV on Sunday, Dad felt it best to keep our little secret between us. I seemed to be coping okay; I just couldn't get the Captain out of my mind.

As these myriads of thoughts were flashing through my mind, I pedaled out to the rolling farmland surrounding Dallas and twilight descended. Oh, my God, I realized; I must be twenty five miles from my house! My parents would be worried. I wheeled frantically on my back tire and sprinted back into town. I zoomed past hills and farms, legs furiously pumping. By the time I reached the city limits, total blackness had encompassed the neighborhood. I kept on pedaling.

I was three blocks from my house when I saw it out of the corner of my eye. I screeched to a halt. *Could it be?* I backed up, moved past it and turned back around to get a closer look. *Oh my God, it was!* Illinois license plate WE6-YEY, a white Rambler station wagon. The Captain's car. The Captain's car was parked three blocks from my house! I hopped on my bike and sped away.

If there was one thing I didn't need, it was the Captain seeing me eyeballing his license plate. Probably had the gun pointed right at me. I raced furiously the rest of the way home. I was gasping for breath when I rode up the driveway. My father met me with a combination of worry and anger. Dinner had been consumed long ago.

"Where the hell have you been? Your mother and I have been worried half to death about you," my father screamed.

"I know, I know, I'm sorry. I just started riding and I forgot the time." It had never occurred to me to call them from a pay phone, which was just as well since I didn't have any money anyway.

My father, regaining his composure, said "that's all right, as long as you're okay." He looked at me. "You are okay, aren't you?"

"Yeah, I'm okay. I just forgot the time. I need something to eat." I was starved.

"Did you decide whether you're going to school tomorrow?"

"Yeah, I'm gonna go. I have to go sometime."

"Good then. Let's get you something to eat." He put his arm around me and we walked inside.

It was like a Sunday night, only it was Monday. My sister had barricaded herself in her room to study, a process that repeated itself regularly for six hours at a stretch. My daily output totaled about half an hour, but I managed to be a pretty good student anyway, especially in social studies and math. I sucked the stuff up. My mother and brother were watching TV and Poppa was reading. Or attempting to, anyway. He had been exhausted after all the interviews and the book had found its way to the bottom of his sweater where it was slowly and rhythmically moving up and down. Dad was doing paper work. I scarfed down my food and stood up to go.

"Where are you going?"

"I thought I would take a walk."

"You've been out all day. Are you set for school tomorrow?"

"I think so." As if it mattered.

"Well, it's getting late. Why don't you try going to bed early and get some rest?"

Before my brother? Unthinkable. But my father's relentless logic was wearing me down. Okay, I would go to bed. And in a half hour sneak out the bedroom window. I lay down on the bed and started to figure my plan. A wave of sleepiness engulfed me. When I awoke it was time for school.

The staff of Sam Houston Junior High was braced for a bunch of mental cripples Tuesday morning. They got them. The elation of last Friday's motorcade, where half the eighth grade had gotten to socialize with the late President, was long past. The school arranged to have several psychologists available on short notice, in case they were needed. Mostly there was just gloom, hushed tones, and a going through the motions. Except for The Star. Everybody wanted to talk to The Star. The kid who had been in Dealey Plaza. The kid who had seen it, or so they heard. He was besieged.

But The Star wasn't in a wanting to be besieged kind of mood. The Star wasn't used to being besieged. The Star was used to playing baseball, riding his bike, and longing for the young *shiksas* who weren't available to him. But The Star could not quell the surging mob of its curiosity. The Star considered holding a press conference so he could explain things once and get them over with. Maybe this would win some points with the soft breasted cheerleader he had squeezed close at the last youth center dance. Before the Captain had appeared, he couldn't get her out of his mind and she didn't even have a rifle. *Funny how things change,* The Star mused to himself. No, he would not capitalize on the tragedy. He would tell his story and be done with it. The modified version, at least.

Did he see the whole thing? Yes, he saw the whole thing. *Did he see who did it?* No, he didn't see who did it, he lied.

Where was the President hit? In the head. The crowd groaned. *Was it ghastly?* Yes, it was ghastly. It was incredibly ghastly.

Did he see where the shots came from? It was hard to tell. There was so much confusion. A partial truth. He hadn't seen where all the shots came from.

Was the President in pain? "I don't think so. He looked confused. I don't think he ever knew what hit him."

The crowd hung on every word. He looked for his blue eyed beauty, but she was nowhere to be seen. But Bruce Cohen was there and he was in a doubting kind of mood. "I don't think you really saw it. I don't think you were even there."

"That's what you think, pizza face. I was there." Figures. The only boy in eighth grade who was shorter than me. I had been his understudy in *Rumpelstiltskin* several years earlier and Bruce was having trouble with the attention I was getting, desired or not.

"Besides, my grandfather sold his film of the whole thing to Time-Life. You'll see it soon enough." The crowd was impressed. Bruce backed off. The press conference was over.

I started striding down the hall when Randy Epstein flagged me down from behind. "Jake, I've been calling you. Didn't your mother tell you? Are you mad at me?" I looked up at the gawky string bean that was Randy. I smiled.

"No Randy, I'm not mad at you. I just wasn't ready to see anybody yet."

"Must have been something, huh Jake?"

"Yeah, it was something, Randy. It was something all right."

"Did you hear that he got out of the car and shook hands with a lot of us up by Lemon Street?" Yeah, I had heard that. Randy had told my mother.

"I took some pictures for you. I figured you'd really be sorry that you missed him until we heard what happened. I've still got them if you want some. I developed them that night." Maybe I would take a few. I would have to think about it. "Well whatever you want Jake, whatever you want." Randy was handling me with kid gloves.

"Now that you mention it Randy, can you show me how to develop a picture?"

"Sure Jake, we can do it after school if you want. Pictures of Lois Hymanson?" Randy gave me that "you dirty dog" look. Lois had stripped for us in my backyard pool two summers before. Eighty pounds of flat chested Jewish sensuality. Randy's usually agile mind had failed to make the connection. Lois would be a good dodge as long as Randy didn't demand to see the pictures. I gave him a sly look back. "Can't do it today, Randy, maybe soon."

"Whatever you want Jake. See you later." Randy ambled off to class.

My father quizzed me at dinner that night, but that wasn't unusual; it was part of the routine. *Was school okay? Were the kids curious?* Yes, to both. He corralled me afterwards. *Did I keep my promise?* Yes, Dad, I kept my promise. I gave them a partial version, the part I could tell without getting in trouble.

"Good. That's for the best I think, Jake. You got homework?"

"A little. I'm going out for a walk."

"Don't be back late. You know there's school tomorrow." Dad looked at me with a concerned eye and figured I'd be all right. Maybe the boy needed some time alone, some time to walk and think. Maybe he's even got a date. Dad understood.

I strolled out into the night. The boy had a date all right. With the Captain.

"I tell you Edgar, I just don't like it. I don't like it one little bit." The anxiety ridden new Chief Executive was pacing the freshly laundered carpet of his recently acquired office. In front of him was the one man whose unwavering cooperation he would need. He would not be disappointed.

"There's just too many loose ends, too much left to chance. Plus, these bastards in Congress are all over my ass to start some kind of investigation. I tell you Edgar, I just don't know what I'm going to do." Johnson was inconsolable. The *coup* of benign neglect had not gone as well as planned and though the bulk of the American public seemed satisfied, even desirous of the quick and convenient explanation offered, many constituents were not. Once the initial shock started wearing off, there were many questions to be answered. Questions that would not go away. Purported events that just didn't add up. Explanations that would not stand the light of day. If they were given the chance to see the light of day. It was the job of the two exalted personages present to make sure they did not.

"Mr. President, in all due respect, the 'fallout' from the 'situation' has been limited and contained as well as possible considering the magnitude of the event."

"Well I guess that's true Edgar, but we've got to do more. We've got to be sure that the American public is sold, hook, line and sinker, that Oswald was the assassin and that he was acting alone. These committees and investigations scare the shit out of me." As well they should. Without the passive cooperation of this dynamic duo, the "situation" would never have occurred to begin with, and without their combined active participation, it would never remain covered up.

"Mr. President, I have sealed off the investigation by the Dallas Police and impounded all the evidence. The Justice Department considers the case closed and is content to let us run the investigation, which means it remains in my control. The lone purported assassin is dead. It is inevitable that there be some minor exigencies evolving from such a situation, but those exigencies are being contained, even as we speak."

"How?"

"With the impounding of evidence, for example, the sworn secrecy of the Dallas physicians and the Bethesda autopsy team. Shall I name more?"

"No, I understand what you're saying Edgar, and I appreciate it. But what are you going to do about the eyewitnesses and the media? I understand that several people have come forward to say they heard shots from the top of the grassy knoll. What do we do about them? We can't shoot them all, can we?" Hoover looked at Johnson, who he thought might be seriously considering this alternative for a moment. "No, we can't shoot 'em, I guess," Johnson chuckled. Hoover heaved a sigh of relief.

"Mr. President, I respectfully submit, that if the Congress and a portion of the American public want an investigation, you give them one. But on your terms, before you are forced or railroaded into one."

"What do you mean, Edgar?"

"Well, Mr. President, it seems inevitable that there will be a demand for some kind of investigation. After all, it is the assassination of an American president we are talking about. You could initiate such an investigation on terms favorable to yourself, using widely respected persons who have, let us say, an incentive to reach a desired outcome. Your call for the investigation would be a show of good faith to the Congress and the public that you are actively pursuing it. And with the right parties chasing the facts, that investigation could have both the credibility and the outcome necessary to reassure the American people that what was supposed to have happened actually did."

Johnson glanced over at Hoover admiringly. A man whose cynicism could match his own.

"Well, Edgar, that sounds all well and good. But what do you do about the facts and the witnesses that don't match your predetermined conclusion? How do you deal with that?"

"With all due respect, Mr. President, we ignore them. We are trying to reconstruct a certain situation leading to a desired conclusion. Those facts that support your theory, you include. Those that don't, you throw out."

"You can do that?"

Hoover was shocked by the President's *naiveté*. *I guess politics isn't like investigating, after all*, the Director thought to himself.

"Mr. President, it is done all the time. Whenever an answer is needed to quell a particular situation, it is better to come up with a proximate one, that will soothe the public's curiosity, rather than to leave an open festering sore which will only incite the populace and eventually threaten national security."

Lyndon knew that Hoover would hit on national security sooner or later. *He really believes that crap*, thought Johnson to himself.

"National security. Sounds good to me, Edgar. Do you think it will fly?"

"I think it is appropriate given the situation, Sir."

"National security, national security," Johnson kept repeating to himself. "I like that. Who do you suppose we could get for such a committee?" Hoover leaned forward, anticipating the question, obviously having already considered the idea.

"There are several names that come to mind, Mr. President, names that would provide a commission with credibility and would interact favorably with us."

"Like who?"

"Well, one is our old friend Allen Dulles. He has a fifty year background in the investigative area and directed the CIA for eight years before your predecessor disposed of him and threatened to dismember his agency. I think Congress would okay him in a heartbeat."

Johnson nodded. "Good choice. Who else?"

"Well, the Bureau works closely with Representative Ford. He has always been very cooperative with any of our requests and I don't see any reason why this situation should be any different."

Hmm, thought Johnson. *Gerald R. Ford. Not too bright, but he seems to be popular in the House. And Hoover says he's malleable. Put a stamp on him, too.*

Lyndon hesitated for a second. "What about the Supreme Court? Now we're talking some real credibility. Got any ideas over there?" Hoover looked back at him.

"Ideas, Mr. President?"

"You got any goods on anybody over there, Mr. Director? I know how complete your files are. Anything on the Chief Justice?"

"Well, as a matter of fact, I..."

"Good," interrupted Johnson, "I'll have him over here and we'll make him an offer he can't refuse." Ole Lyndon was getting into it. Edgar was really onto something here.

As they sat looking out at the gloaming, just as the two brothers had done a week and a half earlier from the hallowed reverie of the White House, the two lofty conspirators parried and jabbed, thrusted and feinted and honed the details of the forthcoming connivance. Cassius and Brutus couldn't have done it any better. And so, on a gray November afternoon, deep within the sanctified bowels of the Oval Office, the Warren Commission was born.

Magazine Street. A few more steps and I'd be there. An anxiety ridden boy, I was too timid to ride a roller coaster or a Ferris wheel. But somehow I was possessed by the incredible event I had seen last Friday. It made me transcend all bounds of fear and personal safety. It had literally taken me over and I was marching to its tune. Men who would assassinate the president of the United States in broad daylight probably shouldn't be trifled with, but my reason had been shut down on this one. I was obsessed.

I turned the corner. There it was, three houses in. The white Rambler station wagon with the Illinois plates, parked in front. I strolled casually past. An older man with a mustache, reading the paper and glancing out the picture window through slightly parted curtains. Nothing unusual, nothing to arouse or create suspicion. *Sentry duty,* I guessed. I continued walking to the end of the block. There had been a row of bushes separating the house from its neighbors and a line of houses with opposing backyards on the next street over. I formulated my plan. I would circle around the block, cut through the backdoor neighbor's property and hide in the bushes on the side of the house. There were two sides, two sets of bushes; maybe I could see something from one of them.

I reached the house with the opposing backyard. My heart was pounding. No lights, a good sign. I started stepping quietly across the lawn. A cold November night with a crescent moon and wind. Cold, but good cover. Halfway into the backyard, a dog from the house diagonal to the Captain's started barking. I froze. The dog stopped. After five minutes, I started crawling again and slid into the Captain's backyard. No dog. I saw a big side window, with light pouring out. If I moved fifteen feet forward and crouched in the bushes, I could see into the window. I edged slowly forward, hanging by the bushes. Five more feet and I'd be there. My heart was thumping out of my body. I crawled on my hands and knees, slowly, quietly. *The fucking dog again!*

I flattened myself to the ground. No sign of movement from the house. I waited. The dog stopped. I prayed that if there was anything to see, it would be on this side of the house, because I sure as hell didn't want to have to repeat this process again.

I inched forward and stopped. *Voila!* There were people inside! Not the Captain, but people. Two men sitting at a table, a bottle between them. A large heavy set man with dark skin and dark hair and a slighter man with a similar complexion. I could barely hear their muffled conversation, but the little I could, clearly was not be transacted in English. It was Italian or French or something similar, but not English. I watched and I listened, frozen in my tracks.

A third man approached. This man looked vaguely familiar. Younger and blonder. Was he the man I had seen a half block ahead of the Captain, who flashed the Captain some kind of sign and then sped off in his getaway car? I couldn't be sure; I had only seen him for a few seconds. It might be him. But no Captain. The Captain I would know. I watched as the three men laughed and drank. They seemed to be having a whale of a good time, sipping and gesticulating amid their animated gibberish. I waited. A fourth man brushed into view and then disappeared. I only caught the back of his head. He reappeared and turned. And there, with the unadulterated smile of evil incarnate, he was, the Captain! I thought my heart would burst from my chest. The Captain wheeled and spun and staggered to the table. The Captain was feeling no pain. He joined in the impassioned waving of arms and hands of his inebriated compatriots, and I watched as the four men poured from the bottle and played out their besotted ritual. I was too far away to hear anything but muted tones and laughter, and even if I could, I wouldn't have understood it. I had found the goddamned Captain and he wasn't even speaking English! My mind raced furiously. There was a shallow metal well directly underneath the window where the Captain and his friends were splitting their joyous memories with the help of a bottle. If I could only get into the well with a tape recorder!

Yes, that was it. I didn't need to see them. I already knew who they were. If I could just record them, I would find out everything. My father had a little portable tape recorder. If I could just get into the well and turn the tape up all the way, maybe, just maybe, I could capture their conversation. And since it wasn't in English, maybe I could get somebody to interpret it for me. It was worth a try. I glanced at my watch. 10:30. My parents would be starting to worry. I would have to come back tomorrow night and hope that the Captain would still be there. Nothing left to do tonight. I started my slow spider-like crawl backwards into the neighbor's yard. *Please, no dog!* I stayed low, moved silently forward, ever forward, until the liberation of the street. Like MacArthur, I vowed, I shall return. *Please, Captain, oh my Captain, please be there.*

I saw his eyeballs floating around in the pan first. I could not forget those eyeballs, those searing eyeballs. As they continued floating in the wretched waters fuming out of the container, the eyeballs were joined by a smooth chiseled jaw, slightly hawked nose, scrunched up apricot ears, close cropped brown hair and arched, even eyebrows. All in all, the Captain wasn't a bad looking man. Looked almost more Jewish than French or Italian. *But, oh those eyeballs! Laser jets of death. Piercing irises.* It was almost hard to look the picture in the eye.

Randy had proved to be most accommodating to my secret project. He showed me how to use each pan, how to process the negatives and make copies, all with no questions asked. No doubt he was hoping for a complete set of the unexpurgated follies of that sultry eleven year old sex goddess, Lois Hymanson. I had let the carrot dangle, with no commitments.

What I had laying in the pan in front of me was remarkable. Four pictures, each as clear as a bell, dramatizing what were surely some of the greatest secret moments in history. The Captain aiming and firing the fatal shot; the Captain tossing the gun to the railroad man with the large open toolbox; a full frontal close up of the Captain stepping toward me, moments after murdering the President. And a back view of a white Rambler station wagon, Illinois license plate WE6-YEY, with a side view of the Captain's head inside. I developed four sets and thanked Randy. He smiled at me quizzically and I was on my way.

I stashed the first set of prints with the negatives in a small child's safe I kept in my room. Brother proof. The second set I hid in a folder under my bed and the third set I stuck on a ledge out of reach in the unfinished part of the basement. The fourth set I put inside my wallet. Safety in division, I thought, showing a healthy paranoia well beyond my years.

I gobbled down dinner. My parents looked at me with concern but I seemed to be functioning okay. I was a man with a mission. I excused myself from the table and went rummaging through my father's desk for the small portable tape recorder. I captured the little beauty and took it out to the garage to test. Perfect. I pocketed a spare tape and was on my way.

As I approached Magazine Street, I looked up. Less moon than last night. Good. But less wind, too. I would have to be really careful not to make any noise, especially as I was going for the metal well right beneath the house. I repeated last night's ritual. Same paper reading guard peering from a crack in the picture window. White Rambler out front. Same house with no lights directly behind the Captain's. I wasn't going to find out if there was the same dog. I moved as slowly and quietly as an Indian in the forest. In a while I reached the viewing bush. The boys were at it again, louder and more boisterous than the night before. I pressed my body hard to the ground and crawled, crablike, across the open gap of ten feet and hopped into the well. I clicked on the recorder.

By Wednesday Lucien and the Corsicans were getting antsy to get out of Dallas. The drama and intensity of the assassination and its subsequent events had played out. They were emotionally drained and ready to move on. Boredom set in and with it, restlessness. They slept by day. With nothing to do at night they drank and watched TV. They consumed copious amounts of both.

The TV coverage had become less and less, but what they saw still amazed them. Just six days after the assassination, the media seemed to be determined to close the case, much to the Corsicans' delight. But, oh, what they were selling the American public! Lucien had to shake his head. Three bullets, all from behind. They laughed. Robert and Giancarlo had fired three shots each, and Lucien two. Wasn't there a police recording anywhere to indicate this? Oswald had gone from helpless patsy to super leftist psycho. Scheming mastermind. Marksman *extraordinaire*. Oswald had become in death everything he wasn't in life. And all thanks to a few plants and some doctored photographs. Lucien joked that if Marcello had known he would get this much aid from the authorities and the media, the Mafia boss could have done it himself and saved a few million dollars. They all laughed.

Giancarlo was getting a bad rap. They knew he had hit Connally by accident. He thought he might have hit him twice and missed Kennedy altogether. Lucien had cut a picture of Governor Connally from the paper and written "President Kennedy" across the chest and hung it on the refrigerator. He and Robert were having a good laugh over it. Giancarlo looked at them. For his four hundred thousand dollar share, they could laugh at him all they wanted. Fuck 'em. He had his villa picked out.

Lucien looked forward to the flight to Montreal and then to moving on to Marseille. Four more days. He could make it. They didn't seem to be under any threat at all. But Gavinet had been adamant. Ten days in the safehouse, regardless. Lucien would have to wait. He worried about the boy. Would he come back to haunt him? What had the boy seen to boldly photograph him like that? There must have been something. The goddamned boy. If it weren't for the boy, it would have been perfection. Did the boy pose a threat in anyway? Lucien couldn't know. He just wanted to get the hell out of here.

SCREEEEECH! There was a loud, high pitched noise from the side of the house like a railroad car grinding to a halt. The men froze in their places. The sound quickly disappeared. It was replaced by a barking dog. Lucien tiptoed to the window like a cat and peered out. Nothing but darkness. They dimmed the lights. Still darkness. Lucien indicated to Novello to go around to the side of the house to check it out. It had all been too easy. As the three Corsicans huddled around the table, frozen in silence and darkness, a pall of anxiety engulfed them. Was the gig up?

I had settled in the well and put my recorder in motion. It wasn't comfortable, but it was bearable. And if I couldn't understand them, at least I could hear them, through a small crack in the window. I figured my recorder could too, and comprehension would come later, at my convenience.

It was weird, in the middle of all this mumbo jumbo, certain recognizable words and names kept repeating. Kennedy. Connally. Mar-say. New Orleans. Lucien. Giancarlo. Ro-bear. Marcello. Gavin-yay. Dallas. Lyndon Johnson. I made a note to myself to listen to the tape and breakdown how many times each one of these was mentioned. I figured I could gauge the relative importance of each according to the frequency of its appearance. I filled the first hour, as the tape ground to a halt in its casing. I hit the reverse switch and it started recording the second hour flawlessly. More of the same, except a little louder, a little more inebriated. The second hour quickly filled up. I looked at my watch. 10:30 again. I had enough. But I had an extra tape. Who knew what they might say and what I might miss? It was late, but I was wide awake. I flipped the old tape out and popped the new one in. What the hell, I would go for it. I pressed the record button.

SCREEECH! Shit, something had jammed! I fumbled furiously. It seemed like an eternity, but I popped the right button and the screeching stopped. Fuck, I cursed myself, I couldn't leave well enough alone. Wasn't two hours enough? The light darkened in the Captain's house. The dog started barking. This was the end of my life, all thirteen and a half glorious years. Oh, how I wished I had gotten a chance to say goodbye to Mom, Dad, and Poppa. "Boy found dead in North Dallas backyard," I saw the morning headlines. I froze. If anybody came, I would be completely silent. If they saw me, I would bolt. What else could I do?

The front door clicked and I heard soft shuffling footsteps descending the stairs. The Captain. I was a dead man. I crouched lower. The footsteps were coming closer.

My heart was bursting from my chest. The footsteps came to within five feet of the well and stopped. I made ready to spring. The footsteps popped on a flashlight and swept a pan across the bushes. Nothing. The light panned back across the bushes. Still nothing. The footsteps paused. I was sure they could hear the sweat popping out on my brow. Should I just surrender, without a fight?

The footsteps turned and swung the light around and stopped. Nothing. The footsteps slowly shuffled past. "*Our Father, who art in heaven...*" The footsteps were moving further away. They reached the end of the house and turned. I waited. The door reopened. The footsteps were gone. I raised myself out of the well and sidled along the bushes. I made a mad dash across the neighbor's backyard and didn't stop running till I reached my driveway. I slipped into the house, tiptoed to my bedroom, flung myself down on my bed and started shaking and sobbing, till I cried myself to sleep. My days of bravery were over.

The last Jewish Republican in North America was coming to dinner. At least that's what Dad called him. Mr. Solomon Berkowitz, handyman *extraordinaire*, prankster nonpareil, and all around mischievous grandfather from Houston, Texas, would be gracing our house with his presence this Thanksgiving. And what a Thanksgiving it was! Just six days after the nation's phenomenal loss, it was the most somber holiday I could remember. And, yet, the joy inherent in the gathering of the family, helped soothe our pain, and we took comfort in each other's company. It was fun having everyone around.

Solomon had not been a fan of the late President, but he was shocked like everyone else. Even more so when he found out that Poppa and I had been there. Solomon followed politics and had scoured the papers thoroughly. Like most Americans who received all their information through the media, Solomon had reached the conclusion that Oswald had acted alone. After all, it wasn't unprecedented. Solomon pointed out that when he was exactly my age, a single assassin had shot and killed President McKinley in Buffalo, New York. Solomon remembered following the story of the ebbing President in *The New York Times*. And just barely twenty years earlier, another lone nut had shot the newly elected James A. Garfield, in a Washington train station. The former Civil War hero lingered for eighty days before finally succumbing to his wounds. And even though the Lincoln assassination was clearly a conspiracy, it was obvious that one man acting alone, had shot and killed *The Ancient*. Solomon knew his history and like many people his age, the lone nut theory was not so hard to believe.

Except that Poppa and I had been there. History meant little. There were motorcades and TVs and airplanes and interactive radios in 1963. The technology of assassinations and their potential settings had changed substantially since 1901. There were even movie cameras with zoom lenses to capture such events. In fact, we had one such example on film, which I still hadn't seen. Would Solomon like to see it? Solomon agreed, but the demure Mrs. Berkowitz and everyone else chose to pass.

As Poppa set up the projector, I looked over at my maternal grandfather. Solomon, I had been told, had been a brooding despot when my mother was growing up and had raised quite the dysfunctional family. But apparently he had mellowed in his old age into the puckish sage he was today. With his huge beaked nose and gargantuan ears, he could have passed for a Jewish version of Lyndon Johnson. There was an aura of mischief surrounding his whole persona. I liked every little thing about this man. Like me, he loved history and politics. He had promised to take me to Washington and the Smithsonian this Christmas, barely a month away. It was his version of Dad's baseball trip, and boy, was I excited. I had never been to Washington. It seemed like the Promised Land to me. More than anything, I wanted to see the President's grave.

Poppa had finished threading the projector. He warned me and Solomon that it was very graphic. What could be more graphic than what I saw?, I thought. Solomon was ready. Poppa sprang the projector and the film rolled. Kennedy approaching, waving, disappearing from view, reappearing, clutching his throat, bending forward and falling to his left; and suddenly, BLAM! Solomon winced. I recoiled in horror. It brought it all back. Mrs. Kennedy climbed on the back of the car, another man mounted it and pushed her back inside, and they sped off. End of film. Did Solomon want to see it again? No, that was all right.

Solomon asked Poppa what he thought. Poppa told him he was too busy filming to really absorb what happened, but it seemed to him that the film showed Kennedy being hit from the side and being thrown back. Poppa also thought that he had heard a couple of shots over his right shoulder coming from the picket fence area, but he couldn't be sure. It was all so instantaneous and confusing. Once you realized what was happening, it was over. Solomon turned to me and asked me what I thought. I echoed Poppa that it had been very confusing. I couldn't really be sure what happened. Dad would have been proud. Solomon stayed convinced of the lone assassin. It was more comfortable that way.

I spent one of the happiest weekends of my life, arguing politics and reliving history with my two grandfathers, the Socialist and the Republican. I loved my home and I loved my family and I especially loved my dueling Poppas. For the first time in a week, I felt a little faith restored in my world. Maybe everything would be okay, after all. I kissed Solomon goodbye on Sunday afternoon and told him I was counting on him. *Washington or bust.* He assured me not to worry.

The following Wednesday I was sitting in Earth Science, listening to Mr. Remotich babble on about igneous rocks or some such nonsense. My mind was far away, thinking about Washington, Dallas, President McKinley, and the like. A messenger came into the class and whispered something in Mr. Remotich's ear. He looked up. Could Jake Zuckerman please proceed to the Principal's office with the messenger? *Oh Christ, what now? Did somebody find my pictures and tapes?*

Mom was sitting in the Principal's office, crying. I would not be going to Washington after all. The last Jewish Republican in North America, age 75, had succumbed to a massive heart attack. In less than two weeks, I had lost my second hero.

Thanksgiving 1963 was not a sad time for all people. Lyndon Johnson glanced around his new office and his living quarters and decided he had a lot to be thankful for. J. Edgar toasted Clyde at his private residence. The new President was going to waive the Director's mandatory retirement. He had a new lease. Lyndon would name him Director for Life. There was much to be thankful for.

But the biggest holiday bash would involve the weirdest amalgam of people imaginable, taking place near Tampa, Florida. Santos Traficante, wintering on the Gulf Coast, had invited the recently liberated troops of the Syndicate to a gala event at the Don Cesar Hotel on St. Petersburg Beach. No expense would be spared. There was a celebration to be had. They all came. All the doubters, all the naysayers, all the skeptics. Most said it couldn't be done, but they had done it! Carlos arrived, the conquering hero. Handshakes and cigars all around. They had pulled it off, The Crime of the Century. The anxious moments had passed. The remainder was merely details. Carlos had done his part. The rest was up to Hoover and Johnson. The Corsicans were still in Dallas, but they'd be out soon. Oswald was dead, Ruby was silent. The case was closed. Robert Kennedy lived, but in body only. Nineteen-sixty-four was going to be a very good year. The boys soaked up the salubrious breezes the Gulf of Mexico offered. A very good year, indeed.

Since my brush with mortality Wednesday night, I had agonized. I knew *what* I had promised Dad, and *that* I had promised Dad. But that was before I had stumbled on the Captain's house. I had seen the man who had killed the President and I knew where he was. I had audio and video evidence. Didn't that mean anything? Didn't I have an obligation? But I had promised Dad. A promise was a promise.

All Thanksgiving day I agonized. When I saw Poppa's film, I decided. I couldn't live with myself if I didn't. There was no school that Friday so I spent the morning copying the tape. When I had finished, I hopped on my bicycle and headed downtown. I was going to Dallas Police Headquarters. I parked my bike out front and headed for the door. I stopped and retreated. Three times I did this, and finally I crossed the street and went into Woolworths to agonize over a soda. *Goddamnit*, I was going to do it. Why should I be the only one to suffer with the knowledge of the assassination? The only pre-uninformed one, that was. Didn't I have an obligation to share it, especially when the criminals were at hand?

I stormed out of Woolworths determined not to break stride till I had reached my destination. Fingering the photographs and touching the pocket recorder, I marched up the steps of Dallas Police Headquarters and went in. A beefy sergeant sat in front of me. "What can I do for you, son?"

"I want to see the man in charge."

"What's it concerning?"

"It's very important. I can't tell you."

The sergeant shot me a sideways glance and with a "suit yourself" look, picked up the phone and asked for the Chief. He put the phone down.

"Have a seat son, the Chief will be right with you."

I retired to the bench and waited. Ten minutes later in strode Jackson Casey himself. I had seen him on TV all week. He pulled a chair up across from me.

The sergeant made the introductions. "This young gentleman says he has something he wants to see you about. Says its important."

Casey looked me up and down. He looked just like he had on TV. "What is it I can help you with, son?"

I looked up at the Police Chief, all solemnity.

"Well Sir, I, I, I..." I saw my father's face slowly coalesce in the back of Chief Casey's head and steadily move forward till it covered his face like a Halloween mask.

"Well what is it, son?" Casey was not a man of patience.

"I, I..." I couldn't speak. I stood up.

"I'm terribly sorry Sir, to have wasted your time. I apologize." With that I turned to go. Casey looked over at the sergeant, and heaving a sigh of relief, watched me head toward the door. I closed it behind me and ran down the steps. Within seconds I was on my bike, sobbing and racing toward home.

The sergeant looked over at Casey. "Wasn't that the kid who was with Zuckerman at the assassination? He sure as hell looks like the one from the pictures we've seen."

Casey stared at the sergeant. "So what if it is?"

"Well maybe he was trying to tell us something about the assassination. If it's him, he certainly had a bird's eye view. Maybe we should call him back. Relax him. See what he knows."

"I don't think that will be necessary, Sergeant."

"Why not? What have we got to lose?"

Casey glanced at the clock on the wall. 12:30 P.M., Friday, November 29th. One week, to the minute.

"Because Sergeant, that...is ancient history."

VI.

The Hunt

As the traumatic events of November 22nd, 1963, started fading from memory, I began the uneventful task of growing up. My life consisted of a mundane sampling of school, sports, friends, and unfulfilled teenage sexual longings. But never, not for a day, an hour, a minute, were the President and the Captain far from my thoughts. With the death of my Grandpa Berkowitz and the promise to my father, I had put the momentous events of that day on the back burner, hoping they would slowly disappear. It almost worked.

There was a flurry of activity surrounding the assassination for the following year, which seemed to die down after the '64 election and then fall from the face of the earth completely. The Warren Commission had traveled to Dallas, interviewed over five hundred sources and introduced its voluminous findings six weeks before the election. I sat there and read them beginning to end with an intensity and absorption that most of my peers reserved for *Playboy* and *Esquire.* Either I didn't see what I knew I saw, or somebody was lying big time. At times it made me doubt my sanity. Could I have possibly been so mistaken in what I saw transpire that I imagined the whole thing? I thought about it and concluded that it was not possible. I had the pictures, I had the tape recording. I didn't make them up. Poppa had his film, which, except for a couple of still frames published in *Life* magazine, had not been released to the public.

Could I have been the only witness who saw something different than what the scores of people in the Warren Report said they saw? I was to find out years later that I was not, that those people whose testimony differed in any way from the "Oswald acting *alone from behind* scenario," were completely ignored. It's a good thing I didn't testify, because I would have been one of them. Funny thing, once again, nobody asked me to.

The Commission's report itself was ludicrous. Even the still pictures from Poppa's film, which were made available to the public, showed the President clutching his throat in response to a shot from the front. And the one bullet supposedly causing seven wounds in both Kennedy and Connally and then emerging unscathed on a Parkland Hospital stretcher, was preposterous. *Were people really supposed to believe this?* Either the Warren Commission people were incredibly stupid, or they were liars. There was no other possibility. For sure, they expected us to be just as stupid to believe this crap. And yet, there seemed to be no uprising, no outcry. I guess the country wanted to finish grieving for the late President and get on with things.

There were some good books and articles that sustained what little faith I still had left. One book in particular, called *Rush to Judgment*, by Mark Lane, had captured my attention. Lane seemed to have found all the people the Warren Commission had missed. And though there was no direct mention of the Captain, a lot of people had seemed to sense something coming from the grassy knoll. I considered contacting Lane with my pictures and recording, but as a fifteen year old kid without resources or confidence, I quickly nixed the idea. Besides, there was the promise to my father, and after reading the Warren Report, my feeling was, "What good would it do, anyway?" I had come around to my father's viewpoint. There were some very important people with some very good reasons for not wanting the public to know the truth. My contradictory viewpoint would have about as much impact as a pebble in a stream. Maybe someday, but not now.

Either I was becoming more disillusioned the older I got, or the country had gone into a downward spiral. Everything that was so positive when the President was alive seemed to start falling apart after his death. That whole sense of optimism, of hope, that had surrounded his presidency, quickly dissipated. The new President attacked his agenda with unparalleled fury and there were some dramatic advances in areas such as health care and civil rights. But it just wasn't the same. Despite the Beatles being sent to us to compensate for the optimism of Camelot, things quickly started going downhill.

The country had become embroiled in the Vietnam quagmire, a war that many people questioned. College campuses went up in revolt, followed by the blighted ghettos of the urban areas. The country seemed to be falling apart at the seams. Whether as a cause or result of this chaos, American youth turned on to a whole new realm of drugs and hallucinogens. The age of Peace and Love was born.

Things reached their tumultuous zenith in the climactic year of 1968. Poppa, Dad and I reacted in horror to the assassination of Martin Luther King, quickly followed by that of the fallen President's own brother, Robert. Lyndon Johnson was forced to abdicate. The outrageous Democratic convention from Chicago, which was riddled with violence, was followed by the coronation of pure evil itself: Richard Nixon, back from the dead, nominated at the Republican convention in Miami. My father shook his head. He saw nothing but ominous signs from all directions. Events started taking their toll on Poppa's health.

The President's assassination seemed to have disappeared for a couple of years but started making a comeback in 1967. Despite William Manchester's best selling *The Death of a President*, a bigger piece of fiction than the Warren Report, if possible, little holes and chinks in the armor of the cover-up began to appear. Perhaps the American people were ready to face it. In New Orleans, District Attorney Jim Garrison forced a trial for conspiracy in the assassination, implicating the CIA. I followed this with a passion. Despite having several key witnesses mysteriously die during the course of the trial, the charges were quickly dismissed. Cynics said it was just a show by Garrison to keep the "authorities" from the real culprits, the New Orleans Mafia. The Syndicate's backing was allegedly instrumental to Garrison's political ambitions. I didn't know. All I knew was the Captain. And that on my tape, New Orleans had come up quite a bit, although in what context, I had no idea. But nonetheless, a ground swell of doubt about the assassination had begun and I watched with great interest. Maybe my time would come yet, although if it did, it damn well seemed I better proceed with extreme caution.

As I entered high school, I started to think about my future. Maybe, just maybe, somehow I could carry out the dreams of my fallen idol. Or maybe I just needed to get out of Dallas. In either case, I found myself in the fall of '68 on the hallowed grounds of Harvard University, with the intention of studying history and politics, followed by law. Who knew, maybe I could be the first Jewish president, the same way Kennedy had been the first Catholic one. A boy could dream. No open motorcades, though.

I took to Boston like it was the lost city I was meant to be in. Although it was cold and rainy much of the time, there was something, some texture about it, that was totally lacking in Dallas. I loved Harvard Square, the outdoor cafes, the bookstores, the walk along the Charles, the view of the Boston skyline. It felt like home. If only I could move my family there, life would be perfect.

When people heard I was from Dallas and that my name was Zuckerman, the first question they asked was about the assassination. Was I there? I deferentially answered that I was close by. If only they knew how close. I took a part time job at Bramble's Burger Cottage, across from Harvard Yard. Various Kennedy offspring came in, mostly Bobby's kids, and they all had that same healthy glow I had seen on the President that day. I felt a strange kinship to them and at times wanted to show them my pictures, not that they asked.

And talk about *shiksas*! Harvard Square was *shiksa* heaven. I had grown surprisingly tall given my family's standards and had inherited the killer green eyes that ran on my father's side. My education was not confined to history. Solomon Berkowitz would not have approved.

The unbridled celebration of my newly emerging manhood was rudely interrupted one night by an urgent phone call. Poppa's health was slipping fast. I was on the next plane to Dallas. When I reached his bedside, Poppa was breathing peacefully, remembering a life well lived. Tears filled my eyes. "Boychick," was all Poppa said. I held his hand in mine.

"Poppa, I love you."

Poppa looked up. He talked in halting breaths. We laughed. We cried. He was calling for Rickel Dora, his long departed wife.

I had never told a soul. But I must tell Poppa, before he died. Poppa sat up. I recreated the scene at Dealey Plaza. Poppa's eyes twinkled. I told Poppa about the Captain. I told him about the promise I had made to Dad. Poppa rolled his eyeballs as he thought of his only son. *"Oy, Mendel."* Mendel was always so practical. Mendel was a slave to practicality. Poppa was a seeker of truth and therein lie the difference.

Poppa sat up on his pillow. "Jake-a-la, I have left you the money that the Time-Life people gave me. You must promise me something. We cannot walk away from the truth. For some reason, God wanted us to see what we saw. That's why I must have known to leave the money for you. Because that's what God wanted. Jake-a-la, use the money to find out what happened. Let that be your mission. Will you promise me?" Poppa leaned back. The breathing was more uneven now. I was confronted with the promise I had made to my father and with Poppa's dictum. Practicality versus truth. I had been practical long enough.

"Poppa, I promise."

With that, the gentle spirit and great soul of Abraham Zuckerman departed this world. I cried for three days straight.

Every family has one. Ours was Aunt Katya. Dad's older sister was an animated little woman with no shortage of brains or eccentricity. Or scandal.

Katya was six years older than my father and the pride of Abe and Rickel Dora's life, as she whizzed through school chalking up honors like paper clips. Grade school valedictorian. Class Treasurer. Writing awards. Math awards. And languages. Katya soaked up languages like a sponge and by the time she was fourteen, she had absorbed and mastered over ten of them in the polyglot that was New York. This lingual agility was to prove an invaluable skill throughout her event filled life.

To provide supplemental income for the family, the thirteen year old Katya had taken a job teaching night school to the scores of first generation Americans hoping to improve their lot in the New York of the late '20s. Jews, Poles, Russians, Italians; Katya peddled English to them the same way Uncle Chaimkeever had peddled fish down at the Fulton Fish Market a generation earlier. Katya was good and her students loved her. One of them, a dapper young Italian gent, loved her too much. He impregnated the fourteen year old Katya.

Filled with the horror of the disgrace of their fallen genius, Abe and Rickel Dora followed the traditional practice of the day and shipped her off to Europe to have the baby, who was subsequently put up for adoption. Katya returned to New York, *sans* child, and continued her studies, but not her night classes. She became her high school valedictorian and went on to Brooklyn College, where she duplicated that feat there in 1937, majoring in languages. Katya had just completed her Doctorate on a full scholarship to Columbia and was about to start a brilliant career as a professor of Linguistics, when she and the rest of the country were rudely interrupted by Pearl Harbor.

Actually, with the countries of the world raging at war, the demand for Katya's skills was never greater. She was quickly snapped up by the War Department and sent to Europe where her life of intrigue began. Katya was used as a liaison with the Russians and the French, and also worked decoding German and

Italian communiqués. The need for her services kept her hopping around Europe during the war and immediately afterwards. She was one of the first women into Germany, trying to sort out the chaos and tragedy that the Fuhrer had left for his country. Katya saw first hand the horror of the German concentration camps and could only imagine what terror lay in Russian-occupied Poland, where the major extermination camps had been located. Poppa had had some younger brothers and sisters who hadn't made it out of the Ukraine by the time the mass exodus of Jews to America had stopped, with the onset of World War I. He, himself, had only made it out of the Pale of Settlement by a year. Katya wondered if any of the relatives or their families were still left alive. Seeing what she saw, she doubted it, and this brought out a strong Zionist instinct in her. She adopted the original family name of Zuckosky and thought about going to Israel. Instead, she went to Washington.

With the Marshall Plan going full steam and the Red menace running wild, the State Department recruited Katya for a hodge podge of assignments: dealing with the steady stream of displaced and sometimes questionable immigrants coming into America; deciphering the fractured and limited communications with the Russians; and coordinating French and American communication in Berlin. She flew from Europe to Washington and back so often that she considered the trip a shuttle run.

Katya blossomed in Washington. Although tiny, she had the bright green Zuckerman eyes and was comely and alive. Her company was sought after and many a Capitol cocktail party was enlivened by her presence. But despite her attractiveness and no lack of suitors, Katya had no intention of settling down. She was a free spirit who liked to come and go as she pleased, much to Abe and Rickel Dora's chagrin.

Sometime in the early '50s, Katya received a transfer to Paris, which ended up being more or less permanent. She seemed not to want for money and Europe was particularly suited to her eclectic and migratory soul. There was no shortage of government missions there as tensions with the Russians continued to rise all during this period.

I had only met Katya once, when she came to Dallas for Rickel Dora's funeral in 1956. I felt in her a kindred spirit. With my interest in politics and history awakened, we became pen pals. Katya was a walking textbook of everything I was interested in and we talked of me going to Europe to visit her. At least I talked of it.

As a high level functionary at the American Embassy in Paris, Katya got to rub elbows with the rich and powerful of Europe and America. She sent me pictures of her with DeGaulle, Churchill, Adenauer, and the like. But the greatest prize she sent was a picture of her with President Kennedy in Berlin, taken right after the "Ich Bin Ein Berliner" speech, one of the Chief Executive's greatest moments. The President had his arm around Katya's shoulder and they were toasting the triumph of the trip, along with a number of State Department officials. I begged Katya for an autographed copy, but she refused. Too tacky, she said. I'd have to settle for the toast. I placed the picture next to the photos of Ken Boyer and John David Crowe, the other holy relics of my collection.

Katya seemed to be very saddened by the Kennedy assassination. It almost seemed that he had been a personal friend of hers. She was amazed that Poppa and I, of all people, had witnessed it and that Poppa had filmed it. She was hungry for details, but Poppa seemed confused by the whole matter and I was sworn to secrecy. Poppa sent her a copy of the film with strict instructions that it was for her viewing only. He didn't want to violate the "rights" agreement he had made with Time-Life. With the death of Kennedy, Katya and I drifted apart for several years but when I reached high school, with my awakened interest in the events of World War II, we started corresponding again, and Katya promised she would take me on a grand historical tour of the battle torn continent of Europe someday soon.

The only good thing about Poppa dying in the fall of '69, was that it brought Katya to America. Now that my grandfather's wish had liberated me from the promise to my father, I could share my secret with a sympathetic and understanding soul who had actually known the President. And there was even a more practical aspect to her visit. She could translate my long held tapes of the Captain and his associates. Maybe even, with her friends and connections in the State Department, we could work on solving the case together. I anxiously awaited her arrival.

After the funeral, Katya and I retired to the local McDonalds. I had told her I had something I wanted her to hear which required some privacy. Neither of us could think of a place where our anonymity could be more assured.

We sat down over steaming coffee and cheeseburgers. An old lady and young girl lingered two booths away but didn't seem to pose any major security threat. I hunched closer to Katya.

"Remember the Kennedy assassination and Poppa's film?," I began.

"How could I not?" Katya looked sad, pained by the memory.

"Well I know a lot more than I could tell you then. I've been dying to tell somebody, and I think you can help me."

Katya was all ears. She seemed to have a keen interest. I told her about the Captain and my subsequent promises to my father and grandfather. I told her that I could barely stand it anymore and that Poppa's okay and her presence were almost like signs to me. Katya listened so intently I could almost feel it. I took out the pictures of the Captain in action. Katya could scarcely believe what she saw. Imagine sitting on something like this for six years. She sympathized.

There was more. I took out the tape and my small tape recorder and explained to her about the Captain's house and my tape in French, which needed translation. I pushed a pad toward her.

Katya took the recorder, clipped on earphones and started listening. She burst out laughing. The old woman and little girl turned around.

"What's so funny?"

"I'm sorry, Jake, I just wasn't expecting it. The tape's in Italian."

"Oh, I'm sorry, I thought it was French."

"That's okay, let me readjust and we'll find out what it means."

Katya plugged back in. She started scribbling furiously, repeating murmured *hmms* and *uh-huhs* to herself. She kept shaking her head in amazement. After fifteen minutes she clicked the tape to a stop and looked up.

"Well?"

"Well, they're definitely talking about the Kennedy assassination, all right. Sounds like they were being paid for it by somebody. I'll have to listen to more to get the gist."

"Please Aunt Katya, listen to the whole thing. I need to know what it says."

Katya went back to work, writing frantically and clicking the tape on and off. After three hours the tape came to a grinding halt. Katya looked up, seeming almost overwhelmed. "Intense," was all she could manage to say. I waited patiently, concealing my anxiety.

"Well?"

Katya drew a deep breath and collecting herself, looked over at me.

"Well Jake, I'd say you've been sitting on some dynamite here. Basically, these three men are apparently Corsicans who live or lived in Marseille on the French Riviera. They were hired by a man named Carlos Marcello, who heads the Mafia in New Orleans, to assassinate the President for two million dollars. There is a fourth man named Novello, who seems to be a host, maybe it was his house they were staying in, but our three Corsicans are named Robert, Giancarlo and Lucien. Lucien seems to be the leader and the one who delivered the fatal shot. He and

Robert are making fun of the other one for hitting Governor Connally. The three of them seem pretty drunk and are looking forward to getting out of the country and back to Marseille. They seem to be anxious about getting caught as long as they remain in Dallas. There is some talk about the media and the authorities helping with the cover-up, and even, depending on your interpretation, Lyndon Johnson and J. Edgar Hoover having knowledge of the plot."

Katya couldn't believe it all. She was overwhelmed.

Katya continued. "They are incredulous that the public has bought all this business about Oswald and were apparently very concerned about his capture prior to his killing. That's what convinced them that the authorities and the media were on their side. They knew that Oswald didn't and couldn't do it and were surprised at how easy it was to fool the public. They almost seem to be jealous of Oswald."

Katya put her head phones down and continued to shake her head. "Amazing," was all she could say, over and over again. She was clearly shaken.

"Aunt Katya, I think we owe it to the country to come forward with this. This is much better evidence than Garrison ever had. It could blow the whole case wide open."

Katya looked at me. "I'm not sure the country wants to know. Especially after listening to this tape, I'm sure the Government doesn't."

"Well, you work for the Government. What do you think?"

"Those are two different things Jake, working for the Government and what I think. But I will tell you. I don't think these fellows could have pulled off the post assassination activity without governmental help. I think they know that, as well.

As far as the Government goes, the "Government" is not a monolith. It is comprised of many different areas, agencies and individuals. But the elements of government that are alluded to here, seem that while they're not actively plotting with the conspirators, are passively cooperating with their mission. And if that is indeed the case, then it doesn't seem like they would go out of their way to try to discover whatever mystery lies behind it. Do you see what I'm saying, Jake?"

Unfortunately, I did. Who is going to investigate themselves? But I could not leave well enough alone. Here were the Garrisons of the world, scratching around with all kinds of peripheral evidence while I was sitting on documented audio and video representations of the central core of the whole thing. How could I not pursue it?

I asked Katya to assist me. I wanted to go to Marseille to track down the Corsicans myself. Maybe next summer. Would she help me?

What if I found them, Katya wanted to know. What good would it do?

I hadn't thought that far ahead. I just reacted viscerally, and this is what came out. Why not go to the FBI now?, Katya suggested. I didn't feel right about doing that. It didn't seem to help anybody in the past, why would they believe me now, especially if they had a vested interest not to do so? Katya couldn't disagree with me, based on what she had seen and heard. *But who were we? A bunch of vigilantes?* These were dangerous men. I pondered this thought. I liked it. I turned to Katya.

"Yes, in fact, we are vigilantes. And if the Government doesn't like it, tough shit. We'll rub their noses in it till they can't hide. If they don't want to solve The Crime of the Century, then goddamnit, we'll solve it for them."

Katya smiled at me and we shook hands. She looked over at me.

"I know you got Bar Mitzvahed at thirteen Jake, but today you have become a man."

Three summers had passed since my fateful meeting with Katya, summers that had seen interest in the Kennedy assassination wane as the failed Garrison trial ended and the ascendancy of Richard Nixon transpired. As the Vietnam War continued unabated, the Great Satan derived the draft lottery and I was unfortunate enough to be blessed with number thirty two. To this day, I still don't know how I got out. The lottery did successfully deflect a lot of anti-war activity, as two thirds of the former eligibles now had their asses removed from the fire. A master stroke by the *bejowled* one. The war raged. Cambodia and North Vietnam came under unparalleled bombardment.

Katya had returned to Europe, and I continued my studies at Harvard, graduating in 1972. It had been my plan to take a year off and travel before continuing on to law school. Katya had promised to shepherd me throughout Europe to the many historical points I wanted to see. She also agreed, reluctantly, to meet me in Marseille if I tracked down the Corsicans, and to act as interpreter in any public eavesdropping I might be able to arrange. Katya, as a government employee, seemed reluctant to get involved in what her senses told her was something the Government would not want her involved in. It was not a question of morality. In fact, Katya believed there was a moral imperative to pursue it. It was a question of practicality. After many years as a representative of her country, she knew what could and couldn't be done and what was desired or not desired, despite any prevailing public statements. Everything about this situation told her it couldn't be done, and wasn't desired, despite our best intentions. Still, I pushed on.

I had arranged to travel to Paris, in the summer of '72, when Katya was unexpectedly called away. It seemed that her long lost child, the one she had given birth to at fifteen, some forty years earlier, had died suddenly in Mexico City. Failing any record of a father, the Government of Italy, where her son was a legal resident with no known descendants, had no intention of reclaiming their recently deceased citizen. The task fell to Katya, whom they had chased down through some ancient birth certificate, to deal with the remains. Through a sense of duty, and wanting to avoid further scandal, Katya quickly headed out to Mexico City to dispose of the matter. Having done so, she looped up to Dallas. She was a much older, sadder Katya, aged more than the three years our separation had warranted. And though I was happy to see her, I was saddened by her appearance. Would she still indulge me? Maybe the traveling would cheer her up. Well, she would show me Europe. She just didn't know about Marseille.

I arrived in Paris for my World War II—Mozart—Holocaust tour on July 7, 1972. Katya and I proceeded to make a circle in my rented Ford of Paris, Verdun, Munich, Salzburg, Vienna, Cracow, Berlin and Amsterdam. Along the way we stopped at such fabled places as the Ossiary, the haunting illuminated bone pavilion where the 350,000 dead at Verdun, history's most fatal battle, were honored; at Berchtesgaden, where Hitler had consorted with the gods; at Auschwitz, where Hitler had dictated to the gods; and Berlin, where the gods had finally extracted their vengeance. I was overwhelmed by the expanse of European history. America was a mere babe in the woods, by comparison.

We landed back in Paris, exhausted and satiated. It was the trip of a lifetime. I mentioned Marseille but Katya begged off, looking for a vacation from my ceaseless nomadic demands. But I was wound up. My real mission lay ahead of me.

Most tourists go the Riviera for the sun, the beach, and the night life. In the summer of '72, these trappings were wasted on me. I had waited for nine years and I was ready. If I needed to track these Corsican motherfuckers half way around the world, so be it. They had given me enough grief already.

I rented a small room overlooking the Mediterranean and waited. I looked day and night. I didn't wait long. I saw a familiar looking figure amble along the harbor front and then slip into the Mediterenee Bar. I followed and watched him from a table as he quaffed the first of many brews at the bar. It was him, I was pretty sure, the older, heavyset one. He had aged and put on some more weight, and I couldn't be certain.

Certainty arrived two hours later. The blond man I had seen nine years earlier, walked through the doors and joined the stout fellow. He looked exactly the same as I remembered. He sat down with the heavyset man, and as the two of them laughed, I sat there staring. Imagine, I thought to myself, two men who had fired the bullets that had killed the President of the United States, casually meeting for an after work drink, like millions across the world, and nobody knew. Nobody knew. They could have been two construction workers, two firefighters, two policemen, happily reminiscing about past events over a beer or two. And what past events to reminisce about. They must be enjoying a good laugh on the world.

But as I waited and watched, still no Captain. One hour, two hours, nothing. I moved closer and grabbed a bar stool at the quickly filling pub. The Corsicans had never seen me. Who was I to them? I switched on the recorder hidden in my coat pocket.

I got back to the hotel room at 11:30 and turned on the tape for playback. Nothing but muffled tones and loud noises from throughout the bar emerged. Totally useless. Despite her reluctance, I would need Katya. I just needed to find out if this was a regular meeting, before I sent for her.

The next night I returned to the Mediterenee, and sure enough, encountered the two compatriots. Still no Captain. Curious, I thought. One more night, just to be certain. Same thing. Time to send for Katya.

After much hemming and hawing, Katya agreed to meet me after the weekend, in Marseille. She wasn't sure what I hoped to prove, but she reluctantly agreed to my demands as a family duty and because of her understanding of what I had gone through. I had a suite of three small rooms, so there would be no problem with accommodations.

When I met Katya that Monday afternoon, she looked pale and ashen. She had seemed to be on a gradual decline since I had seen her at Poppa's funeral, but she appeared to be dropping precipitously since the beginning of the summer. I tried my best to cheer her and she responded with some half-hearted smiles.

Who knew what went on in that brainy interior of hers? I couldn't understand her total reluctance about my mission, which she had embraced, if only mildly, three years earlier. But I was determined. I was tired of being burdened with it.

We waited till dusk fell and strolled to the Mediterenee. It was a beautiful August night. As we entered, there sat the blond man and the fat one, getting properly toasted, right on schedule. We took a table no more than three feet from them, and conversed, read the paper, and sipped espresso. I could get into the European mode of existence. Still no Captain. Katya's eyes flitted around like a bird's as she attempted to follow the conversation through the noisy din. Three hours we hovered and sipped till Katya indicated she had had enough. The boys were slurring their words by now. As we strolled back to the hotel, I awaited anxiously. *Well?*

"Well, if you want to know about hookers, horses and hangovers, then these are your men," she responded. "But if you want to know about anything of substance, or the Kennedy assassination, forget it. I mean why would they be discussing it in public anyway?" Maybe Katya was right. It was ancient history. These were just a couple of good friends, of limited capacity, enjoying a night out. What of it? Let it rest in peace. Katya was dour.

Well, maybe we could tape their voices and have it applied to my original recording and have the FBI do some audiographic or whatever analysis and see if it matched. I mean, why not? And where the hell was the Captain, anyway? Katya just shrugged. He hadn't come up in the conversation.

Katya was pessimistic and downcast. Basically, she said, "What's the point? Who would care? The whole thing was almost nine years ago."

I thought about it. *Who would care?* Kennedy, and even his brother, were long gone. J. Edgar Hoover had just died and Lyndon Johnson would soon be dead also. What relevance did it have anymore? I despaired. *God damnit, no.* I knew what I saw. I wouldn't let it go that easy.

Katya and I returned to the hotel and retired to our respective rooms. I clicked on the TV and sat back in the rocker that the hotel provided, swaying back and forth. I slipped in and out of waking consciousness. The TV buzzed back at me in test patterns and bee fights.

AAAAAH! I awoke with a start. Standing in front of me in his sharply pressed police uniform, was the evil countenance of the Captain, grinning ear to ear. The laser eyes looked down from the barrel of a thinly penciled rifle aimed straight at my cranium. I had better be ready to die, because I was going to.

The Captain chortled. "So we meet again, my little pus sucker." The Captain smiled widely. I was chilled to the bone.

"Any last requests before you die?"

I stammered for my breath. "But, but, but..."

"But nothing, you little weasel. You think you can fool me, you think you can trick me? You think I don't know what you know. And you think I'm going to let you get away with it? I, Lucien Sartee myself, killed the President of the United States. You are just small potatoes. Do you think I don't know? Do you think I'm going to let you get away with it? HAH! The nerve of you following me here. You will die like the dog you are!"

The Captain cocked the trigger. He focused his aim.

"But I, I, I..." Too late. The Captain smiled. *Click.*

AAAAARGH!

The bullet crashed into my right temple and threw me back against the chair. My brain exploded upward and backward. The Captain had hit me with the same shot as he had hit the President. I started to fade off into the great white light that pulled me forward, when a figure emerged. It was Jackie Kennedy crawling back on the bed in her pink matching outfit, collecting the splattered bits of my brain to piece together my head. She shook me violently. *Wake up! Wake up! Don't die!*

I awoke in a sweat, my heart thumping mercilessly. Aunt Katya stood before me, shaking and pounding me with all the frightened might her pink nightgowned body could muster. I was gasping and wailing, slipping in and out of eternity's grasp. "He killed me, he killed me!," I screamed. I was hysterical. Katya cradled and comforted me. After fifteen minutes, my sobs returned to a manageable level.

"Now, now," over and over again, Katya repeated to my declining blubbering. I embraced her and sat still in total silence.

"Thank you, Aunt Katya, I'm so sorry. The Captain had killed me and you have brought me back to life," I whimpered.

Katya cuddled me. "It's just a bad nightmare, a really bad nightmare, you'll be okay. Now now." Over and over again. I started to regain my composure. I held Katya close.

"It's just that it was so real, Aunt Katya, he was right there, he was sneering at me and pulled the trigger and killed me just like the President. I swear. It was so real. I could feel it. I thought I was dead. Oh, I'm scared."

"It's okay, it's okay," Katya soothed. "You'll be okay. Just get some rest. It was all a bad dream."

"But it was all so real, Aunt Katya, all so real. I saw him standing there, right in front of me. I know it was him."

"I'm sure you did, dear. It will be okay."

I got scared. What if the Captain had been stalking me all along, just waiting to pounce? Was this a premonition? I was the only thing that stood in his way of the perfect crime.

"What if the Captain is stalking me, Aunt Katya? What if he's stalking me, just waiting to strike?"

Katya shook her head back and forth. "The Captain isn't stalking you Jake, I can assure you of that."

"How can you be so sure, Aunt Katya?"

Katya looked at me straight on, green eyes blazing. "Because he died in Mexico City this June."

Nineteen seventy-three should have been a banner year for Aunt Katya. As one of the highest ranking dignitaries at the State Department in the city that was hosting the Paris peace talks, her work was more vital than ever. But somehow, she had been shunted aside by the Nixon administration's hand picked team. It was as if they intuitively recognized the enemy.

Katya had become unhinged with the discovery of her son and who he was, even though his identity would remain hidden to the world. Katya knew, and that was enough. I tried talking to her, consoling her, telling her it wasn't her fault, all to no avail. Katya was inconsolable and didn't want to talk about it. It was the great unmentionable. The fact that I knew only deepened her pain.

As for myself, the hair raising thought that this creature, this cold eyed killer, had been somehow related to me, was unfathomable. What quirk of fate had brought us together at so strange a meeting? And yet as time passed, I grew philosophical about it. I had no more chosen to have this psychopath for a cousin than I had chosen my chance encounter with him in Dealey Plaza. It had just happened. I had not engineered either event. If only I could transfer a little of this acceptance and resignation to Aunt Katya, I thought.

Thanksgiving was coming up and we invited Katya to stay with us. Maybe a visit with her family would cheer her up. Who knew? We were willing to try anything.

I was home from my first semester of law school when I picked up Katya at the airport. Considering how she had been, she looked remarkably good. It seemed that the spirit, or at least a hint of it, had been reborn in her. I regaled her with tales of *1L*, of sadistic little men in bow ties, of vicious Socratic questioning, of seating charts and all-nighters, and we both roared with laughter. Funny that torture should be the preferred method of passage for those pursuing the legal arena, she mused. There must be an easier way. There must be, but probably not one as enjoyable for the pompous purveyors of credentials, and sometimes, knowledge. We both chuckled.

Thanksgiving that year fell ten years to the day of those tragic events that had so invaded our lives. I had not ventured back into Dealey Plaza, but Katya was curious. We enjoyed a big Thanksgiving meal with what remaining family we had left: Mrs. Solomon Berkowitz, my only surviving grandparent; my mother's two sisters, their respective spouses and two of their children; my sister, my brother, myself, Katya and, of course, my parents. There was much to be thankful for. We all had our health and all of us, despite the occasional downs, were thriving reasonably well. And we had the pleasure of each other's company. Although day to day living together had brought the inevitable tensions that a family experiences, our going off to college had dispersed these unpleasantries and made the occasional get together all the more meaningful. And this year we had a distinguished guest from Paris to revel with us in the bosom of the family. It was the happiest Thanksgiving any of us could remember.

As dusk fell, Katya began to stir. She wanted to see Dealey Plaza. My father looked concerned, despite being unaware of the Captain's significance. "Not to worry," parried Katya. "It's something I want to do. You can go on without me." Reluctantly, I offered to drive her in. I still had an aversion to the place which was why I had not been back in ten years. "No, that's all right," Katya said. She wanted to be alone. She could take a taxi and would be back soon. I kissed her at the door.

Katya disembarked from the cab at the door of the School Book Depository, now a Texas state building. Everything looked just like the pictures. Being the tenth anniversary, there was a considerable crowd milling around the area. Katya strolled the breadth and width of the Plaza. She stood on the overpass, moved behind the picket fence, walked across Elm Street to the small patch of green between the roads. She envisioned Poppa's film, pictured Lucien standing there, taking aim. She had named him Louis before the agency took him from her. Katya knew so much more than the others present, knowledge that was painful and intensely personal. She was trying to exorcise her demons.

She approached the Depository building. She wanted to see the *sniper's nest.* "Sorry, ma'am, the building's not open to the public," sneered the security officer on duty. She flashed her State Department credentials at the beefy guard, who eyed them suspiciously. He would be a moment; he had to make a phone call. He slowly ambled back and gave Katya the okay. "For fifteen minutes only," he grumbled.

"Fine," Katya said.

The guard pointed toward the elevator. "Sixth floor, ma'am."

"Yes, I know," replied Katya. She walked over to the elevator, pushed the button and quickly arrived at the now notorious floor.

Exiting the elevator, she wandered through the vast empty space of the warehouse till she reached the other side and moved to the southeast corner, otherwise known as the sniper's nest. The boxes were still assembled the way they had been on that fateful day. The window was still half open, as it also had been.

Katya stared down at the milling crowds below. They were pointing, gesticulating, recreating the possible scenarios and directions. America's great tragedy and America's great mystery, rolled into one. Katya watched them swarming like bees over the grassy flanks of the Plaza. Katya smiled. She was the Queen Bee, directing from above, possessing much of the painful answer so eagerly scurried for below. She was at peace.

The last of light was flickering across Dealey Plaza. Katya raised the heavy sill and felt the cool breeze splash across her skin. She looked out to her right and down to the picket fence where Lucien stood, rifle at the ready. He looked up and winked. Her eyes scanned to the little abutment where Poppa, Marilyn and I were standing precariously balanced, excitedly awaiting the approaching limousine. She waved down at us and we waved back. She looked straight down as the big Lincoln carrying the Golden Man turned the corner. She smiled down beatifically on her unsuspecting friend, who was now relaxing to the cheers of the crowd. The limo started its slow descent down Elm Street. The elevator across the floor clicked open. The guard started strolling the expanse of floor, calling out, "Ma'am, your time is up." Katya watched as he slowly approached and miraculously turned into Lee Oswald, calmly stepping and smiling toward her, and just as quickly reconfigured back into the guard.

"Yes, it most certainly is," she replied. Katya stepped out on the ledge and plunged six stories to her death.

After a childhood spent rooting for far away franchises, Dallas had finally made the Majors, just when I was leaving town. The Cowboys had been there since the early sixties and they had been recently joined by the second incarnation of the Senators, the Texas Rangers. If Washington was doing nothing else, it was spawning baseball teams for the hinterlands. I was sitting back watching the highlights of the Cowboys' Thanksgiving Day game when I saw the flashing blue light appear in the driveway. My heart sank to my feet. There was a knock on the door, some garbled words and the next thing I knew I heard my mother scream. I went running out. My father appeared numb.

"WHAT?"

My father turned to me, glassy eyed.

"Katya's dead. She jumped from the School Book Depository."

No. No. No. No. It just can't be. That damn fucking Dealey Plaza, the place was cursed. Oh God, no, tell me it just isn't so. Tell me that it didn't really happen. Katya, my soulmate.

It had really happened. The two policemen were standing there, expressionless, the blue light flashing behind them. A crowd of curious neighbors began to congregate on the perimeter of the lawn. It had really happened.

"Who's Jake?," one of the two blue automatons inquired. My father pointed at me.

"She left a note and some pictures for you. We can let you look at them, but we're going to need to impound them as evidence until the autopsy's over. We also need somebody to claim the remains." My father volunteered for that unpleasant duty as the officer handed the packet to me. I retired to my bedroom to hide my tears and try to understand Aunt Katya's last moments. I unwrapped her letter.

"Dear Jake,

Please don't grieve for me. I have led a long and full life and love you all very much. I know you love me too, and it is the knowledge of that love that I bring to eternity with me. Life, as they say, works in strange and unusual ways, ways that can show us the greatest joys as well as boundless sorrows. Strange events may occur that involve you, but which you have no control over. I think you know what I mean.

I am leaving our little secret with you, from whence it came. It is yours to do as you choose with. I know I leave it in wise and loving hands.

I want you to scatter my ashes over Dealey Plaza. You may think me morbid, but this is what I wish. Do this last favor for me, nephew. Please don't think me selfish. We all seek our freedom and this is my way of finding mine.

Give my love to everyone. Tell them I am at peace.

Katya"

I looked at the note in disbelief. As soon as I came to, this was going to hurt. A lot.

Folded inside the note were some pictures. The picture of the Captain stepping toward me, that I had given her; a picture of me looking out over the harbor in Marseille, taken in front of the *Mediterenee*. And finally, a small portrait of the unlikeliest of all people, President Kennedy. What a strange trio Katya had gathered in her final possession. All I could do was shake my head and stare at the floor.

My father came into the room and wanted to know if I was okay. He always wanted to know if I was okay. Well, at least he cared. Yeah, I was okay. *Could he see the note?* I hesitated for a second. *Why not?* It was his sister, after all.

He scanned the note, pursing his brow. Several "Hmms," escaped his lips. He paused. "What does she mean by our little secret? Is that about what you saw?"

"No Dad, not really," I mumbled.

"You haven't told anybody, have you?"

"No, I haven't told anybody." *At least not yet,* I thought to myself.

"Well, I still think that it's best that we keep that under wraps, don't you agree?"

"Do you really think this is the time to talk about it, Dad?"

"Well, maybe not. I'm just concerned for your welfare, Jake, that's all."

"Okay Dad, I understand that. Look, just don't worry about it. Okay?"

"I'll try not to."

"Fine." My silence indicated that the topic was closed for discussion.

"Who's the policeman in this picture?" Dad pointed toward the Captain. I had originally told him about my pictures but based on his reaction, I had never shown him them.

"I don't know. Probably just a friend."

"It's not like Katya to have a policeman as a friend. Besides, that looks like the Depository in the background."

I remained mute. Dad let the topic drop. He knew more than he was letting on.

"Get some rest, Jake. We'll start preparing for the funeral tomorrow. I'm going down to the police station with the captain. Are you all set with these?," he said, pointing to the pictures and the note. I nodded my head yes. Going to the police station with the captain. How appropriate.

The small family funeral was held at the North Side Jewish Center on Monday, November 25th, ten years to the day of the President's funeral. Through these hallowed walls had passed the bodies of Abraham Zuckerman and Jack Ruby. Katya was joining some mixed company. The rabbi waxed eloquent about what a good and full life Katya had led, only to be undone by a few demons. "Let us remember the good things," he stated. I stared at the tiny coffin which would house Katya's remains until cremation. It had been a good and full life. The shock and violence of the end of it had brought the tragedy and the sadness.

Separate out that and one could feel good about and for Katya. I would try to concentrate on that.

Two days later my father handed me a small wooden box. It was Katya. I hopped into the car and headed down to Dealey Plaza, Katya on the front seat beside me. I got to within two blocks of the Depository and stopped. I couldn't do it. I parked and sat for a half hour. I still couldn't do it. I turned my car around and sped toward home.

I carried Katya to my room and placed her on my bed. I picked her up and smelled the lush cedar fragrance. I clutched her to my chest and cradled her in my arms. The big warm tears rolled down unimpeded, staining the dark, beautiful wood. I was watering Katya.

I awoke three hours later, still clutching the moistened box to my chest. I reached down below my bed and lifted out the safe. Swiftly dialing the combination, I opened the door. I placed a loving kiss on top of the box and put Katya in the safe next to the Captain and the tape recording. I kept her there for the next eighteen years.

The death of Katya had taken the wind out of my sails. I needed a rest, a break from responsibility, emotional intensity, and more than anything, from the Kennedy assassination. I figured I would need to gird myself for whatever November 22nd, 1983, might bring. I asked for and received a leave of absence from law school.

The mood of the country granted me a reprieve. Watergate was coming to full fruition and Nixon *agonistes* had pushed most everything, including the assassination, to the back burner. The spirit of disillusionment triggered by that fateful day in Dallas, came to its glorious climax with the bagman Agnew receiving monthly installments in Blair House and Richard-the-Liar-Hearted scrambling fast to upgrade his crumbling image to the lofty status of *unidentified co-conspirator*. Hey, everything is relative.

A few failed love affairs had produced in me the necessary depression to create some fairly good songs, which I recorded in a state of the art four track studio. Wanting to be free from thought, I headed out to vacuity central, Los Angeles, where I circulated my tapes and played in local coffeehouses. Although my tapes received considerable airplay at local college stations, nothing serious developed with them. This vagabond life was too much a means to an end to sustain my continued attention, however, and after two years of Southern California beaches, volleyball, and folk clubs, I was once again ready to resume serious life.

While making good on the political compromise of the decade by pardoning his fallen predecessor, Gerald Ford announced that our long national nightmare was over. It seemed like this new era of innocuousness would be a good time to finish law school and I enrolled at Northeastern University in Boston, which had an interesting experimental co-op program that intrigued me. Besides, I was tired of being tortured by little men in bow ties. Despite the cold and the rain, it was good to be back in the center of the universe, and the unchallenged heart of *shiksa* heaven. Much to my parents' ambivalence, I got seriously involved with a round featured, blond haired, blue eyed maiden, whose lineage dated back to the Mayflower. Nancy's easy manner and grace tempered my Jewish intensity and compulsiveness as we bicycled the rolling hills of Vermont, climbed the gentle peaks of New Hampshire and frolicked on the soft sand beaches of Cape Cod. New England could be fun when it wasn't busy being brutal. I even went outside one winter day to try skiing, but two runs on a chilling lift convinced me that my time between November and April was best spent inside. I took up racquetball.

Thoughts of the Kennedy assassination resurfaced in my mind every now and then, but with the Warren Commission conspirator, Gerald Ford, in the White House, the time didn't seem right to act. Recovering from Watergate and Vietnam, the country didn't seem ready for it yet. Maybe the assassination would just go away, both in my mind and in the national consciousness. Maybe.

As we entered 1977, both the country and I took major steps forward. I graduated from Northeastern Law and got married. The real world at last, I guess. The election of 1976 consigned Gerald the Mediocre to a footnote in history and propelled a crinkly Robert Kennedyesque look alike, Jimmy Carter, to the White House.

There were changes in the air. And one of those changes was interesting, very interesting. Now that Ford was gone and our long national nightmare was truly over, interest in the Kennedy assassination began to surface again. After thirteen years of unmitigated disillusionment, our great national tragedy, precipitating the deluge, was ripe for investigation. So ripe that Congress was actually forming a committee to investigate it. "Speak now or forever hold your peace," I told myself. "Speak now or forever hold your peace."

Over a carefully planned Sunday brunch at the Cambridge Galleria, I told the newly pregnant Nancy the whole sordid tale, from A to Z. She sat there for two hours, her mouth wide open. This hadn't been in the plans. I told her what I needed to do, what I had wanted to do for so long, but the time just never seemed right. She smiled at me beatifically. "Do what you need to do," she told me. God, I love the *goyim*. They're so understanding.

So, with the blessings of my new wife, I called a friend in D. C. I had information on the assassination, new information that would blow the lid off the case. Would the FBI be interested, the Congress?

I called my D. C. cohort, a friend from Harvard days, *Deep Throat*. What the hell, it had worked once before. *Tell them that Zuckerman had the real Zuckerman film. The story behind the story, as it were. Were they interested?* Throat would let me know.

Deep Throat phoned back. The FBI was skeptical. They had seen the film. Did I really have anything to add? Throat, my man, you disappoint me. Arrange a meeting. Tell them I have everything to add. Tell them to hike up their garter belts. I was going to knock their socks off. Trust me.

I entered the hallowed halls of the J. Edgar Hoover FBI building on a chilly late fall day. I re-checked my appointment book and laughed to myself. Tuesday, November 22nd, 1977. I couldn't seem to get away from it. I hoped I would symbolically unburden myself and the country. What was the statute of limitations on tragedy, anyway, I wondered.

I walked down the long marble hallway, pictures in hand, recording in pocket, Throat by my side. The A-team. The steely eyes and bull terrier jaw of J. Edgar Hoover glowered down upon us from a giant portrait at the end of a long corridor. An elevator ride up to the sixth floor and a quick usher into the plush anteroom of the political assassinations unit. As Throat and I sank into the soft backed couches, I mused. Imagine, a whole unit designed to *not* find out what happened. I was not without skepticism. But as a newly licensed practitioner of the legal profession, I vowed I would go to the proper authorities, despite my apprehensions. It was the law.

Mrs. Beverly Kimmel busied herself at the typewriter. She informed us that Mr. Sullivan and Mr. Quisling would be with us shortly.

Quisling. Why would anybody named Quisling not change his name? I mean how many Hitlers were there left after the war? Okay, granted, there weren't too many before it. All the Adolfs, however, suddenly became Dolfs. The man put the name out of commission, for God's sake.

But I never understood how people could not unburden themselves of such ridiculous surnames. I had known a Lipschitz and a Finklestein growing up, both of whom had been teased unmercifully. Didn't these people know what they were condemning their children to? Its not like a name change was financially prohibitive. Or would the Royal House of Lipschitz be deeply offended?

And now Quisling at spymaster central. I shook my head. Would wonders never cease? In any case, Throat had assured me that they were top level agents. Mid level functionaries, I translated. We would see.

The intercom buzzed. The two *monsieurs* were ready for us. I had told Throat the story and shown him the pictures only a week before. He had been shaken. As another freshly minted lawyer, vintage Georgetown, with minor political connections, he remained certain that the Bureau would be interested. My extensive reading on the assassination and the Bureau's relationship to it made me more cynical than my usual cynical self. I would try to give them the benefit of the doubt.

Sullivan was an older fellow, about fifty, tall, thin, silver haired, elegant and nattily dressed. A benign presence. Career bureaucrat, I figured. The aforementioned Quisling was younger, heavier, shorter. Only a few years our senior, I surmised. He conveyed an intensity lacking in Sullivan, but it was not an unfriendly one. Maybe this would be worthwhile after all.

The usual pleasantries were exchanged as Mr. Sullivan, the senior agent, motioned us to a corner table. I plunked my leather binder down and took a seat. The meeting had come to order. Sullivan, as the senior, spoke first.

"Your friend Mr. Lefkowitz tells us you have important new information on the Kennedy assassination, Mr. Zuckerman. We are always looking for leads, but I must caution you. The Bureau has seen and analyzed your grandfather's film many times." *Great,* I thought, the disclaimer. *Get ready to hang on to the floor, bureaucracy breath.*

"With all due respect, Mr. Sullivan, what I have with me has nothing to do with my grandfather's film. The only connection is that I was with him and standing two feet away when he filmed it. I have pictures of my own, taken at the moment of the assassination, and subsequent recordings of the perpetrators' conversations. Pictures and recordings never seen or heard by any investigative body before. Would the Bureau be interested?"

Sullivan's and Quisling's attention had been captured. "Please proceed, Mr. Zuckerman."

I took out a manila envelope from my binder and opened it. I commenced telling them the story of the Captain, the hard hat, the railroad man, and the getaway car. I circulated the photos. Sullivan appeared to start to tremble. Quisling's mouth hung open. "Unbelievable," he kept on repeating to himself. "Absolutely unbelievable."

Sullivan, who had prepared for a quick dispatch of the rehashed Zuckerman film, was clearly unnerved.

"And the tape?," he uttered, voice quivering.

"Well, it's in Italian, but I've got a complete transcript here," I offered, pushing forward Katya's thick binder.

Sullivan browsed through it and then handed it to Quisling who did the same. I placed the cued up tape recorder on the table in case either man wanted to try his hand at the romance languages.

Sullivan cleared his throat. "Would you mind if Mr. Quisling and I could have a few minutes alone to review the evidence. Can you leave it with us for fifteen minutes?"

I looked over at Throat and back to Sullivan. "Fine, Sir. Where should we wait?" No problem. I had several copies of each item.

Sullivan pushed a button on his oversized desk. "Mrs. Kimmel, could you walk Mr. Zuckerman and Mr. Lefkowitz to the reception area?" Sullivan cupped his hand over the speaker. "This won't be more than fifteen minutes, gentlemen. We appreciate your indulgence."

Mrs. Kimmel ushered us to the reception area. "Would you gentlemen like some coffee?" Why not, I thought. It was nice having the FBI by the balls. I was going to savor it.

Throat was excited. "Did you see the look on that honky's face? I thought he was going to shit in his pants." Throat pumped his fist.

"Now you know what it's been like to sit on this stuff for the last fourteen years. I hope one of these bastards takes us seriously and decides to do something. The country's suffered enough already." My outraged sense of patriotism had clicked in. I was tired of getting fucked by the Government.

"I told you I would knock their socks off, Throat."

Throat looked over at me. He wasn't sure he liked this Throat business and told me so. I parried back. "Come on, this is exciting, cloak and dagger stuff. Besides, it beats the hell out of Gerald Lefkowitz."

Throat gave me his best shit-eating grin, as if to say, "Fine, you want me to be Throat, Throat it will be." Jewish male bonding at its most intimate juncture. Me and Throat against the world.

We sat sipping our coffee. Mrs. Kimmel came to fetch us. "They are ready for you, Mr. Zuckerman. Agent Sullivan has requested that Mr. Lefkowitz remain in the reception area." I looked at the impassive stolidity of the middle aged block of granite. She would have played well at the Kremlin.

"He comes with me," I responded. It was time for the Clint Eastwood stuff.

"Suit yourself," Mrs. Beverly Kimmel sneered back. We followed the immovable force who led us back into Sullivan's holy chambers. Only Quisling was gone. In his place was a heavyset steely eyed gent of sixty or so, who conveyed the very essence of menace. I wondered if he had eaten Quisling.

Agent Sullivan stepped forward. "Gentlemen, this is Agent Corbin, Chief of Internal Security. He has requested that Mr. Lefkowitz remain in the reception area."

I countered. "If you don't mind, Mr. Sullivan, I would like my associate to join in the meeting." Super Agent Corbin cleared his throat, smoke emanating from his ears. He was clearly getting annoyed by my intransigence.

"Mr. Zuckerman, this is not a request, it is a demand. There are sensitive matters of national security at stake here." The forces of evil had spoken. I was wondering how long the all pervasive theme of national security would take to kick in. I looked over at Throat and shrugged my shoulders. Round one to the Bureau. Throat sheepishly retreated.

"Wait for me outside," I called after him. I might need somebody to deposit my dismembered corpse somewhere. The door clicked shut.

Corbin was not one for small talk. He glowered down at me. "Mr. Zuckerman, what you have here are some very disturbing items, very disturbing. And *if* they are true, they would pose a great threat to internal security." I sat up, deeply offended.

"What do you mean 'if' they are true? Do you think I am making this stuff up? Do you think this is all forged?" I glowered back at the stonefaced malevolence. I'd be damned if I was going to be intimidated by some arbiter of "security." This was the truth, God damnit.

"Mr. Zuckerman, have you ever considered the possibility that somebody looking at this 'stuff' from the outside, might consider it unauthentic? Might it not be possible that as a citizen of Dallas who had regular access to Dealey Plaza, you could have quite easily staged these photos, as well as the purported conversation?" Corbin let it rest and filter down in heavy silence. He had a point. There were no other people in my pictures but the principles. I must admit that I had never conceived of this possibility.

Somewhat taken aback, I stammered, "Chief Corbin, don't you people have visual and audio tests you can run to verify the validity of these? Don't you want to know? I mean there are existing pictures taken of me standing next to my grandfather at the time of the shooting."

"Our tests, your evidence and our wanting to know are all different issues. Yes, of course we want to know. And certainly there are tests available to help confirm the validity of your evidence. Help that is, not necessarily confirm. And we will put both the photos and the tape to the test, Mr. Zuckerman, I can assure you. But I think you're missing an important point." Corbin stopped and let it hang heavy in the air.

"Which is?"

He glared over at me, as if to say, "Are you ignorant, or just obstinate, you little piece of dung?" I stared back.

"Which is that the Kennedy assassination is a matter of tremendous volatility that continues to threaten the possibility of ripping open the stable underpinnings of the nation. It is our responsibility at the Bureau to see that this does not happen."

"Is it your responsibility to suppress the truth?"

"I didn't say that. We will pursue the truth, as we have, but in a cautious, responsible and non-public manner, everything the so called conspiracy theorists refuse to do."

"And if you find the truth?"

"Assuming that there is a different truth than the one that has already been found, we will bring the guilty parties to justice, as it is our mission to do. But we will do it in a way that does not bring destabilization to the nation. Do you understand that, Mr. Zuckerman?"

Corbin was good, very good. And damned evil.

"So what are you going to do with the evidence I have brought you?"

"We will impound it, of course, review it, and take the appropriate actions. I assume you have copies?" My silence confirmed that I did.

"How do I know that you're not just going to sit on it? I mean for purposes of national security and the like?"

More smoke belched from Corbin's ears. "You don't. But as a practicing attorney in the nation's legal system, you must have some faith in the chief investigative body of your country."

Boy, I'm glad I didn't have to testify to that one in a court of law. And whatever faith I did have was rapidly slipping away.

"So that's it?" I threw up my hands. Agent Corbin glanced over at the silent Sullivan. The Master had finished his part.

Sullivan cleared his throat. It was time for the functionary to take over.

"Mr. Zuckerman," he started in a shaky voice. "The Agency needs your complete cooperation in this matter. We are prepared to pay you fifty thousand dollars for it."

So there it was. The price of my silence. This was all out of a grade B movie. And yet it was really happening.

"Mr. Sullivan, has it ever occurred to you that it's not money I'm after, but the truth?"

Sullivan, sweat popping out on his brow, stared over at Corbin. The ominous one remained impassive. Sullivan licked his lips and began again. "I'm sure it is Mr. Zuckerman, I'm sure it is. But on a matter as sensitive as this one, it is necessary for the Bureau to preserve the highest confidentiality. And we are prepared to offer incentive to insure it. Say $100,000?"

Sullivan had to be one of the world's worst poker players. If I were into this game, I wondered how high I could make him go.

"Mr. Sullivan, I think you miss my point. It's not the amount of money that I'm interested in, it's the truth. If I had wanted to make money on this, I could have sold these pictures to some publisher for a lot more than what you're offering me now. I didn't come here for money. I came here for your help in solving a tragedy that is a continuing scar on the nation. That is what I'm interested in. Do you know what it's been like to live with this for the last fourteen years?"

Sullivan looked back at me. "What makes you think a publisher would assume that these photographs were legitimate?" He was getting sidetracked.

"I really hadn't thought about it, to tell you the truth. But assuming they know who my grandfather was and that there are pictures of me standing next to him, holding a camera, which there are, I think there's a good possibility they would be interested. But that's not the point, not the point at all."

"Then what is the point, Mr. Zuckerman?" Sullivan was prattling. Corbin, eyeballs flashing, had lost it.

"All right gentlemen, that's enough. Let's cut the bullshit. Listen, Zuckerman, the Bureau has made you an attractive offer. You can take it or leave it, I don't give a shit either way. We will investigate the material in the way that we best see fit. If you don't like that, tough boogers. If you are tempted to go to an outside source with your 'evidence,' there will be serious consequences to pay, very serious consequences, trust me."

"Is that a threat, Chief Corbin?"

"Call it what you want. Just mark the solemnity of my words. I don't fuck around on these matters."

I was quite certain he didn't. I decided to test him. "And what kind of consequences would those be, Chief?"

Corbin turned beet red. He couldn't believe my unmitigated gall, or perhaps it was my unparalleled obtuseness. In either case, his limited reserve of patience had long since expired.

"Since you seem to require us to be exceedingly explicit, Mr. Zuckerman, we will oblige you. There are several people in your life, specifically your father and your pregnant wife, whose security we could not guarantee. In fact, their existence might become extremely precarious. Extremely precarious. Is that explicit enough for you?"

I couldn't believe this was happening. The FBI was threatening the lives of the people most important to me if I considered pursuing the truth with people who actually cared and wanted to know about the assassination. *Oh, what a terrible mistake this had been!* I should have known. Everything about the last fourteen years told me this was a bad move. So much for the sanctity of the law, so much for the proper authorities. So much for the benefit of the doubt. I stared out, shaking my head, my mouth hanging open.

Corbin sat there with a malicious little grin on his smug face, seeing that he had gotten to me for the first time. He was about to deliver the *coup de grace*.

"Jake, may I call you Jake?" The evil being was putting on his best paternal tone.

"Uh-huh." I sat there slack-jawed, barely able to speak.

"We think you may have another vested interest in this matter, independent of the truth. Maybe your motives aren't as pure as they seem." Corbin was coming totally out of left field now.

"What do you mean?"

"Does the name Katya Zuckosky mean anything to you, Jake?"

Shit. They know about Lucien and don't care. Wait, they're going to blackmail me with it. No, how could they blackmail me, I was trying to expose him anyway. My mind was a jumble of panicked thoughts. *What in the hell did this mean?*

"Of course I know Katya Zuckosky. She is, er, was, my aunt."

Corbin paused. He smiled. "You know Jake, not all things are as they seem. Like your little pictures here, perhaps." He pulled out a small slip of paper from the folder in front of him and placed another page over it, covering everything but the very top. He turned it upside down, and continuing clutching it, put it under my nose. It was an official document of some kind.

"Does the date on the top mean anything to you?"

April 1, 1950. My birthday. "That's the date of my birth."

"April Fools Day, how appropriate Jake. Now follow with me." Corbin slipped the cover page down one line.

City of Washington, Walter Reed Hospital. It was a birth certificate.

Name of child: Jacob Zuckosky

Holy shit, this can't be happening.

"You still with me, Jake?"

"Uh-huh."

"Good." Corbin slipped the cover down another line.

Mother's name: Katya Zuckosky, State Department

"Oh, I can't believe this, I just can't believe this. You mean...I mean...Is this...What I mean is..."

Corbin was having the time of his life. "You ain't seen the half of it yet, Jakey." He lowered the paper another line, almost to the bottom.

Father's name: John F. Kennedy, U.S. Congress, Massachusetts

I stared from hollow unbelieving eyeballs.

Corbin stood up and grinned. "How you like them apples?"

VII.

The Resolution

I needed to be alone. I needed time to think. Or not think. I just wanted to get in my car and drive.

Logistics could be a problem. In two days I was due back in Boston, or more specifically, Longmeadow, Massachusetts, for Thanksgiving at Nancy's parents. The good Dr. Butterworth and his patient wife Ruth, had extended their annual holiday greetings, and I was expected to be the obliging son-in-law. My relationship with them was tenuous at best. Dr. Butterworth had not been pleased when his only daughter and the apple of his eye, had shown up with a man who didn't even remotely resemble a Todd or a Biff. And though law credentials helped mitigate things a bit, the unrelenting Doctor only begrudgingly gave us his blessings after it was clear he had no choice. It was the price of seeing his daughter.

Nancy's two older siblings had turned out to be vegetables. The oldest was highly medicated and living in a halfway house somewhere in upstate New York. The middle child had followed his father to Brown and Yale, earning an MD, and was now living on a farm in Vermont, not doing much of anything. Nobody was quite sure what his problem was. To ease her pain, Nancy's long suffering mother had recently found God, whatever that was. I promised Nancy I wouldn't be confrontational about it. In consideration of these facts, I didn't understand why Dr. Butterworth wasn't more accepting. After all, a law degree ought to mean something. I wondered if being all Jewish, or half Catholic and half Jewish, or a President's illegitimate son, would cause him the greatest discomfort. The situation was fraught with delicious possibilities.

Lefkowitz was the first to see the hollow shell that emerged from Sullivan's office. "What's wrong?," he shouted as he jumped up, a look of concern crossing his face. I tried to talk. I couldn't. I motioned for him to follow me. We hustled out of Bureau headquarters and into the streets of Foggy Bottom. Government buildings as far as the eye could see. I walked hunched over, my hands shoved into my pockets, my head down.

After two miles or so, Lefkowitz couldn't take it anymore. "What the fuck is going on with you, Jake, will you tell me?" I owed him an explanation. I wondered if I could talk.

"Some strange things happened in there, Gerald. Things that I really can't talk about right now."

"Gerald? What about Throat? I thought it was Throat?"

"No Throat, Gerald, at least not for now, anyway. Gerald, I'm going to need you to help me."

"You name it, my man." Gerald loved being black. As outcast Jews at Harvard undergrad, we knew we weren't white.

"Gerald, I'm going to need to spend some time alone. I'm going to tell Nancy that I'm staying with you and working on this thing and that it needed more, unexpected time. If she calls, you've got to tell her I'm out and will call her back when I get in. I'll check in with you every eight hours. Can you do that for me?"

"Where are you going?"

"I don't know yet. But I've got to go somewhere and think for a while. I've got to be by myself."

"Can you tell me what's going on?"

"I will Gerald, I swear, shortly. But right now I need to do this."

"Are you going to be safe?"

"Yeah, I'm not in any danger. I just need some time to sort a few things out. Can you help me with this, Gerald?"

We had reached my car. I peeled off a freshly planted parking ticket. Gerald looked over at me. "Hey, you're my main man. Whatever you want, Bro." He had raised a high five for me to slap. Gerald, who had been raised in the sprawling barrio of East Meadow, Long Island, was rapidly slipping into his major ethnic oppression mode. I figured I'd better get going before he put on a dashiki and started sprouting an Afro. I dropped him off at the subway and told him that I would call him that night. I drove off in search of a pay phone.

Nancy was not pleased. Things weren't that great with her parents to begin with and this was the worst possible PR move I could make with them, especially with her being pregnant and all. I understood. But this was unavoidable. She knew what I working on. Surely she could understand.

What would she tell her parents? That I was working on the Kennedy assassination with the FBI over Thanksgiving?

"No, obviously, you can't tell them that. Tell them I had to go to an emergency conference. A complication in a case."

"But you don't even have a job!"

Hmm. Good point. Also a source of considerable conflict. "That's it! Tell them it's a job symposium for recent graduates. That's perfect!"

"During Thanksgiving week?"

"Hey, your father thinks lawyers are crazy, anyway. He'll believe it." It would have to do. I couldn't come up with anything better.

"Look Nancy, I'll explain all this when I get back. I'll be back on Sunday. And to make up for it, I'll take you to Club Med on Martinique for a week in January, on me, okay?" More like on my grandfather, but who's counting. That seemed to soften the blow.

"Okay Jake. Be careful. And call me. I love you."

"I love you too, Nance."

11.30 A.M. We had only been with the bastards for an hour, but it had been enough time to totally unhinge my life. I just had to get in the car and drive somewhere. Anywhere. The comfort of motion. But where?

I had an idea. To Solomon Berkowitz, Miami Beach had been the promised land. He never made it there, but my grandmother had a small condominium near the boardwalk. Since she would be in Dallas visiting with my parents over Thanksgiving, the condo would be empty. She had given each of the grandkids a key in case we ever wanted to drop in. I had actually availed myself of this privilege twice. *South Florida.* A nice long beach to walk and think on. Some warm sunshine. A free place to stay with a bed and a refrigerator. It sounded good. I prayed she hadn't changed the lock for any reason.

I nosed my car onto the Arlington Memorial Bridge and headed for I-95 south. Staring me smack dab in the face on an elevated hill in the distance, was the grave of John F. Kennedy. I peered up at it, looking for the eternal flame. I couldn't see it. The thought of this man possibly being my father was incomprehensible to me. Absolutely incomprehensible. I bid him goodbye as I headed into Northern Virginia. He had caused me enough trouble for today.

The mind numbing miles proved to be the perfect antidote for my shock. Somewhere between Richmond and Petersburg, the Northeast ended and the rolling eternity of southern farms began. Hot baked red flat fields with low lying crops and grass cover. Decrepit shacks with tin roofs. The soul of Stephen Foster songs started pounding in my veins. I didn't have to wish I was in Dixie. I was. An endless train of billboards began to pop up on either side of the highway. Pancake houses. Drag racing tracks. Plantation museums. Country music on the radio. A foreign land. A large space connecting Florida with the rest of the world.

And yet it was hauntingly beautiful. Unlike the uptight Northeast, the South was peaceful. Unhurried. A body could relax down here. As I entered the Carolinas, I started thinking maybe this wouldn't be such a bad place to be. Chapel Hill. Or maybe Asheville. I'd have to ask Nancy about it. A quiet peaceful life in a warm beautiful surrounding. Somewhere in the dark recesses of my compulsive Northeastern soul I knew it was a fantasy. And yet there was great comfort in thinking about it. I needed peace. More than anything, I needed peace.

As thoughts of the land of cotton filled my mind, I began peeking in my rearview mirror. *Could Corbin actually be telling the truth?* I looked for traces of the President's face. Not around the eyes. I definitely had Katya's and my father's green eyes. And I didn't have those ear lobes attached to my head that seemed to mark a flaw in Kennedy's otherwise perfect features. But from below the eyes down, I had the former President's wide ivory smile and his square jaw. And somehow I had escaped the slightly hooked nose that ran in my family (no pun intended) and had something much more similar to Kennedy's classic straight line model.

If what Corbin was saying was true, it would explain a lot. For one thing, after a slow start, I had grown four or five inches taller than my father and brother, who both topped out at 5' 7". I was right about at Kennedy's six feet. For another, I had never understood why I was only ten-and-a-half months younger than my sister. Possible, I suppose, but seemingly physically uncomfortable. My brother was five years younger. You would have thought my parents could have spaced it better. It would also explain Katya's bundle of pictures. A family album, so to speak, minus Lucien's father.

If this were true, the implications were incredible. As if it wasn't bad enough having Lucien as a cousin, he had now become my half-brother. Which meant that I had seen my half-brother murder my father in front of my grandfather, who was also my father's *de facto* father-in-law as well as the killer's grandfather. Boy, talk about all in the family. And I always thought it had been a national event.

I had to laugh, if only to keep from crying. Talk about homicidal incest. This was a doozy. And who ever said life wasn't ludicrous? Hah! I began to relax for the first time today. I started enjoying being President Kennedy's long lost son. Maybe this explained my almost mystical attraction to Boston. Could such things be transferred in the genes? I could get into being a Kennedy. The hidden Kennedy, I smirked to myself. But I felt like a Zuckerman, or a Zuckosky, at least. I knew who my parents were, even if they weren't. The other set could be auxiliary.

I called Lefkowitz from a rest stop outside of Savannah. Had Nancy called? *Yes. Where was I?* Georgia. *Was I safe?* Yes. *What's going on?* Can't tell you, Gerald. I'll call you when I get to my motel for the night. How late can I call? *Whenever.* Do you mean that? *Yes, I mean that.* Lefkowitz was insulted that his hospitality had been questioned. Okay, I said, it might be anytime.

I dialed up Nancy. *Where was I?* Washington D.C. This charade was going to be hard to pull off. *Why was I outside? You sound like you're on the road.* "I am. I called Gerald and he told me you had called. I'm calling the first chance I had. I just left the FBI building. I'll be at Gerald's soon." *Are you okay?* "Yes, I'm fine. I'll talk to you tomorrow." Something told me Nancy's female intuition wasn't buying this. But it was the best I could do for the time being.

By the time I got to Jacksonville, it was almost 9 P.M. Miami was a million miles away and I was starting to get tired, not to mention hungry. I wasn't ready to settle in for the night, but I sure as hell wasn't going to make Miami. Where could I go? I remembered Lefkowitz, self proclaimed expert on Florida, telling me about Tampa Bay and the West Coast beaches on the Gulf of Mexico. Said they were nicer than the East Coast. Better sand and color, and less crowded. I calculated that Tampa was about three hours and headed out I-10 toward it. After 220 more mind numbing miles, I reached the outskirts of Tampa. I-275. *Where the hell was I?* I drove till I found the strip. Dale Mabry Highway, or something like that. Everything the road vagrant could want. McDonald's. 7-11. Striptease clubs. And lots and lots of cheap motels. I registered at a Travel Lodge right outside of Tampa Stadium, home of the hapless Buccaneers. They had lost every game of their initial season of 1976 and were well on their way to duplicating that feat in their sophomore year. They were a combined 0-24 or something like that. I was hoping this wasn't an omen.

I looked at my watch. 1 A.M. I called Lefkowitz who sounded like I had awakened him from a deep sleep. Anytime, I reminded him. Right. *Where the hell are you?* Tampa. *Tampa! What the fuck are you doing there?* You told me it was a good place to go. *To do what? Golf?* I told Lefkowitz there were lots of beaches around on which I could do some necessary contemplating.

"You know, Nancy called and she was none to pleased that you weren't here. I think you in some big trouble, white boy." Gerald was starting to go black on me again. I could expect tales of honky oppression at any moment.

"What time did she call?"

"Nine-thirty, quarter-to-ten, thereabouts."

"Did she say why she was calling?"

"What do you think, I'm gonna quiz her? You best be calling, my man, pronto." Click. Time to face the music.

I dialed the phone. A frantic Nancy answered after half a ring. "Where the hell are you?" Good thing it wasn't a wrong number. *Tampa, Florida.*

"Tampa, Florida! Jake, are you having an affair?"

"No, Nancy, please calm down. Nothing could be further from the truth. You okay?" No response.

Ten seconds of silence. "So tell me what you're doing in Tampa?" Is this your way of getting out of Thanksgiving with my parents?"

I laughed, which only pissed her off more. I better talk quick.

"Now listen to me Nancy, and listen good. Some very unsettling things happened at the FBI, some very frightening things. Things that I will tell you about shortly. But I need some time alone to sort them out. Trust me, it's true."

"But why Tampa?"

"I don't know. I just got into the car and started driving south. I ended up here."

"You couldn't have driven north?"

"Nancy please, I'm telling you what happened."

"Did they threaten your life? Are you in danger?"

"Not exactly."

"What do you mean not exactly? They either did or they didn't." Nancy sounded like she was rifling through one of the cross examinations I used to practice on her.

"Nancy, it's nothing like that. You're going to have to trust me on this one. I'm at the Buccaneer Travel Lodge, area code 813-624-4410, room 126. That's where I'll be."

"Jake, are you telling me the truth?"

"Yes, I swear."

"And you're not having an affair?"

"No, I also swear to that. After what happened at the FBI today, I can assure you, my penis is totally non functional."

"What does that mean?" I didn't realize she would take me literally.

"Look Nancy, I love you. I want to spend the rest of my life with you. I will be and want to be the father of your children. All I'm asking is that you give me a breathing space of a few days so I can sort things out. I'll call you tomorrow night. You can call me if you want. Is that too much to ask?"

"When will you be home?"

"Tuesday."

"Why so long? I thought you said Sunday?"

"I need a few days down here, and then I have to stop in Washington Monday for something I can't pick up on the weekend." Nancy started to ask what, but thought better of it.

"Look Nancy, I know this is all bizarre, but everything will be all right. I love you."

"I know." She didn't sound convinced.

"Jake?" *Oh, God, what now* I thought.

"What is it, Nance?"

"What do I tell my father?"

"Tell him his esteemed son-in-law sends his regards."

After the shocking revelations and the twelve hour drive, I slept like a rock that night. As consciousness slowly dawned on me the following morning, I sat up in bed. 11:45. Man, had I slept. *What was I doing in a hotel room?* In fact, *where was I?* Then it all started coming back. It was more of a question of who I was that was a function of where I was.

I peered out of the motel window. Blinding sunlight. Palm trees. At the end of November. Tomorrow would be Thanksgiving. How absurd, but no more so than Corbin's revelations of yesterday.

I was famished. In my haste, I had forgotten to eat the day before. The motel clerk directed me down the street to The Village Pancake House, where I dined like a king. I drove across something called the Courtney Campbell Expressway on my way to Clearwater Beach. Tampa Bay was beautiful, and very wide, much wider than I had imagined. The expressway across was lined with palm trees and the sun danced upon the water. The fantasy started again. Maybe this wouldn't be such a bad place. Never cold, never snowy. But wherever I went, I would still be with myself, whoever that was. Besides, this place seemed like a cultural wasteland and the summers were probably the reverse of Massachusetts winters. Pick your poison.

Clearwater Beach didn't provide the measure of solitude I was looking for. There were hordes of college students drinking beer and playing volleyball. Loud radios. A vicious sea gull swooped down on me and literally ripped a hot dog from my hand. Good scouting report, Lefkowitz. Next time I'll listen to a white man. Somebody told me that St. Petersburg Beach was much quieter. Being late in the day, I vowed I would try that tomorrow. I drove back across the Bay and watched the sun set over the water at a place called Ben Davis Beach. Weird, I thought. Florida's the only state with both an east and west coast. Sunsets were definitely better over the latter. And though Boston was technically on the water, you had no sense of it unless you were dining at Anthony's Pier Four. But in this place, or in San Francisco, you couldn't escape it. It was nice.

I topped off my first full day of being a semi-Kennedy with a trip to a striptease joint which had a sign proclaiming, "Talk about Busch Gardens," a reference to another local attraction. The distraction didn't help much, but the beer did. If I was going to be a Kennedy, then damnit, I would act like one. I called Nancy and turned in for the night.

St. Petersburg Beach proved a much better choice than Clearwater. I walked for miles, feeling the soft sand on my feet and staring into the emerald green waters of the Gulf of Mexico. Thanksgiving day. *How weird,* I thought, glancing around at the palm trees.

The shock was starting to wear off. First of all, the story might not be true. Corbin claimed that my photos might be forged, so why not this birth certificate? But how would he have known to prepare it ahead of time? And what was he doing with it in the first place? The only thing I could think of was that Hoover had it in his files to use against Kennedy during the '64 elections. Allegations of sexual impropriety were one thing, but proof of an illegitimate son was something else altogether. A potent political tool.

Or maybe, I thought, in a flash of heightened grandiosity or paranoia, the Bureau suspected that I might have some evidence that contradicted the Warren Report and had pre-set this document to discredit me. Not just me, but anybody who might have witnessed the killing and needed to be compromised if they threatened exposure. Paranoid, but possible.

There were two reasonable checks to make. I assumed that all birth certificates had to be registered, and on Monday I would go to City Hall in Washington to look for it. The second check would not be so easy. I would ask my parents. Surely, if there were something to be known, they would know it. We were due out there at Christmas.

After watching the sunset over Tampa Bay again, I started spending a depressing Thanksgiving evening at my motel on the strip. I needed to get out. The clerk told me that whatever nightlife might exist was over in the historic cigar making district called Ybor City. There were a lot of sidewalk cafes and one or two might be open tonight. I headed out. The district turned out to be delightful. It was just like Harvard Square in June, with all the people changed from Anglo to Latin. It made me think back to the Bay of Pigs and the Cuban Missile Crisis and the whole Kennedy era. The Cubans had been one of the prime suspect groups after the assassination, because of Kennedy's alleged lack of nerve at the Bay of Pigs. But didn't he stare down the Russians during the Missile Crisis? It just didn't compute. *So why Corsicans, anyway?*

As I reflected, sipping a cup of espresso, the answer sat down at the table next to me. During the last few years, several books had started implicating the Mafia as the instrument behind the assassination. It made sense to me. There were no offsetting events like the Bay of Pigs and the Missile Crisis. The Kennedy Brothers had a flat out, unabated war against the Mob, including deportations and imprisonment. The Mafia certainly had the motive. But they didn't have the means to cover it up. This would have had to have been left to Hoover, Johnson and whomever else in the Government with as much motive as the Syndicate to see Kennedy dead. In my mind, the Mafia had executed the event and the Government covered it up. It was the only thing that made sense.

The two elderly gentlemen could have been any couple of pals taking an evening stroll, working off a large Thanksgiving dinner. Which in fact, they were. Then I remembered where I heard the name Ybor City before. Its unofficial Mayor was one Santos Traficante, the bespectacled gentleman presently sipping *cafe latte* next to me. His friend was the eminent Godfather of the New Orleans Mafia, Carlos Marcello. Apparently, this was an old tradition started at the Don Cesar on St. Petersburg Beach in 1963, when the aging entrepreneurs celebrated their first Thanksgiving of freedom there. It had since become an annual visit, with Marcello gracing Traficante's fiefdom to give thanks for deliverance from the tyranny of Kennedy oppression. The fact that conspiratorial murder was the tool of that deliverance was irrelevant. Deliverance was deliverance and Thanksgiving had its own special meaning to the two geriatric mobsters.

As they sipped their hot beverages and watched the steady flow of Latino beauties strut by, I was seized by a desire to clutch my tape recorder, which I still had in my jacket from my encounter with Corbin, and create Berlitz Italian tape number two. But as I parried with myself, I concluded with a mental shrug of the shoulders. I mean, what was the point? Who was going to listen to it, who was going to care? And what were the chances they were talking about anything relevant, anyway? Like Katya said, would they be talking about the Kennedy assassination in public? And even if they were, what could you do, make a citizen's arrest? Besides, they were speaking in English, albeit hushed and broken.

I relaxed. I was not going to make this my burden. I was going to suck in the cool tranquility that the evening offered. How ironic. After traveling a thousand miles into the middle of nowhere, I still couldn't seem to escape the assassination. But I could resist it. *How bizarre,* I thought. Marcello and Traficante out enjoying the night air, just like Robert and Giancarlo had been doing in Marseille. Life goes on. Mine and President Dad's hadn't, but maybe that was the philosophical lesson Santos and Carlos were teaching me at present. There is no justice, but whatever comes your way, take it and run. Sip down an evening brew with an unindicted co-conspirator. Life goes on. That is, with any luck it does.

As I stared over at the aging Mafiosi, a thought came to my mind. What the hell was I doing here? It was 10 P.M. If I drove twelve hours straight I could be in Washington by mid morning and would have most of Friday to search down my alleged birth certificate. Paradise had been exhausted. Two days of this idyllic void was enough.

I stood up. I crossed over past the reposing luminaries and came to a halt. They looked up. I smiled beatifically. "A good Thanksgiving to you, gentlemen." Marcello and Traficante looked at me like I was from another planet, then broke into sheepish smiles. "And to you, Sir." They heaved a collective sigh of relief. *Play along with the weirdo, maybe he'll go away soon.* He did.

Maybe another salutation would have been more appropriate. "Evening gents, John F. Kennedy illegitimate Jr. speaking. Talked to Lucien and the Corsicans recently? Caught your act in Dealey Plaza. Smashing, really smashing. Must be moving on. Cheerio."

With Marcello and Traficante staring in my wake, I climbed into my car and departed Paradise Lost. By 9:45 A.M., I was crossing the Arlington Memorial Bridge. *Put on the black eyed peas, Brother Lefkowitz.*

My search at D.C. Town Hall was fruitless. Would they have a record of all births occurring in the nation's capitol going back to 1950? Most certainly. Was it possible that one could be missing? Anything's possible, but not likely. *You sure?* Yes, we're sure. There was no birth certificate registering a Jacob Zuckosky that year or any other. Was Corbin toying with my mind? Or did J. Edgar have greater power to make records disappear than City Hall had to make them appear? I didn't know, but I certainly wasn't going to find out in Washington D.C. Dallas seemed to contain more hope.

In twenty four hours I was back in the loving of arms of Nancy and Massachusetts. She had survived the wrath of Dr. Butterworth, who managed to savor his Thanksgiving despite my absence, or perhaps because of it. *Just wait till you hear this one, Nance. Just wait till you hear who you're related to.* Butterworth will shit in his pants.

Nancy received the next installment of my hidden life. In my own defense, at least this part had been hidden from me as well. What next, I wondered. Was Lucien actually Lee Oswald's long lost and presumed dead father, or was Jack Ruby my father's brother or maybe Katya's clandestine husband? Jacob F. Kennedy or John Fitzgerald Zuckerman, or maybe both of them, wanted to know. Christmas would be very interesting.

If you've been dreaming of a brown Christmas, Dallas is your place. The crisp winter wind brushed over the open prairie as we touched down at Dallas' Love Field. I looked out the little oval plane window and imagined the visiting dignitaries lining up on the airport tarmac as we awaited the assembling motorcade. Today would be a good day, a day of triumph, as I rode through the streets of downtown Dallas with my beautiful wife beside me. We turned onto Houston, then moved down Elm, heading toward the underpass, when...when a slightly pissed off stewardess awoke me from my reverie to inform me that the last passengers had departed the plane five minutes ago, including my embarrassed wife. Was there something she could help me with?

The only visiting dignitary who turned out to greet me was Mr. Emanuel Zuckerman, late of the Association of Manufacturer's Representatives. We piled into the waiting limousine, a Buick Regal, and departed toward the ancestral homeland at 585 Mead Lane, North Dallas. Before leaving the area, I had lived there all my life.

As we made small talk on the way back from the airport, I looked over at my father. Why didn't he ever tell me? Maybe there was nothing to tell. Who knew? I was determined to find out soon enough, although I was concerned about being gentle. Despite the usual flaws, my parents had basically brought me up with love and concern. If they weren't telling me something, I'm sure it wasn't for malicious reasons. Besides, they had other things to worry about. My sister, who always tended toward the rigid and authoritarian, had become ensconced in a cult. She had found her freedom in bondage, as L. Ron Hubbard laughed at the world. Well, at least she had all the answers and it made her happy, which was more than I could say for myself. My younger brother had been floundering in and out of college and was not a source of great joy either. I felt somewhat responsible for compensatory happiness. With my law degree, I guess I provided some, although this was somewhat diminished by the fact that I had no job. I planned to look for one after the first of the year. With a new baby three months away, I had postponed the inevitable long enough. Poppa's bounty had turned out to be $150,000, not the $25,000 he had indicated. He had forgotten to mention that there were six installments. But even in my cash rich position, I needed to move on.

Like most Jews on Christmas, we gathered as a clan in self defense. Since the rest of the world was unavailable to us, we took pleasure in each other's company. Besides, Nancy had brought a semblance of Christian spirit to our household. It was a nice touch.

After a sumptuous dinner, I told my parents I wanted to speak to them alone in the den. My father looked worried. I told him not to be. There was just some stuff I was curious about. As he put logs in the fireplace, I looked at the family photo history my mother had assembled on the den wall. Old *babushkas* with shawls, bearded gentlemen with long black coats and *yarmulkes*. Nobody hoeing peat however, or praying to the Blarney Stone. "What gives, Jake?," my father asked, as he settled into the overstuffed chair next to the fireplace.

No sense in beating around the bush. I told him about going to the FBI. Had I ever told anybody about the Captain?, he asked. Just Katya. It was time to fill in my mother, who listened with the same kind of amazement as Nancy had, while I retold the whole story.

Having done that, I told my parents about Corbin and the birth certificate. *Was it true?* The furtive glances exchanged by my parents and the uncomfortable silence told me it was. My father sighed. "Jake, it's not that we didn't want to tell you, it's just that with the Kennedy thing and Katya and all, it didn't make any sense to. You seemed to be doing okay without it. Why add to your burden?" As I suspected, it had been a question of concern and not insensitivity or maliciousness.

"Then tell me what happened, Dad."

Well, it seemed that Katya had the bad habit of getting pregnant every twenty years or so by a man who was not only not her husband, but whom she was not particularly involved with. Did I know that she had had a child when she was fifteen, who had been placed for adoption in Europe? Yeah, I knew. Boy, did I know.

Well in the winter of 1949, Katya did it again. This time she came to my parents in a panic. The father was a prominent Washington politician from very good "bloodlines," as Katya put it, and who was a rising star nationally. His family was afraid that this scandal would ruin his blossoming career and had offered to support Katya in lavish style if she agreed to keep silent, leave the country, and give up the baby. Abortion was out of the question, on both sides.

Katya figured she could work a transfer to Europe, which she preferred to America, anyhow, and keeping silent would not be a problem. It was what to do with the baby that was. Rather than give it up for adoption, she was hoping to place it with people she knew and trusted, where she could watch it grow. She had made the mistake of abandonment, albeit not by choice, before, and she wasn't about to do it again.

To sweeten the incentive, Katya offered that the politician's "family" would support the child well. Having a five month old infant themselves, my parents weren't really in a situation to take another child. But it was family. You did what you needed to do. They agreed to take the baby, but not the money, on one unswerving condition: Katya would have to get her tubes tied. She did, and thus Jacob Zuckosky became Jacob Zuckerman.

Had Katya ever told them who the father was? Apart from her comment about bloodlines, no. And my parents never asked. But as both my face and John Kennedy's became more familiar to them, they had a very strong suspicion. When the assassination occurred and especially with my unintended involvement with it, they had decided it would be best to let the whole thing ride. I seemed to be doing okay both socially and in school. Why ruin a good thing?

My parents saw that I was close to Katya, but this bond didn't seem to jeopardize my relationship with them. Katya had assured them that she hadn't told me anything. Finally, when she died and I was left an orphan, unbeknownst to myself, my parents decided that there no longer existed a dichotomy between the biological and the environmental. They were my parents, plain and simple. None of the externals of the biological genesis had gotten in the way in the past, why should they now? Besides, Katya had been my father's sister. It's not like there was no blood relationship.

"That's about it, Jake," my father said, as he threw up his hands. "Maybe we erred in judgment, but we meant well." I knew they did. There were hugs all around. We were family. A strange amalgam, but family nonetheless. It was all that seemed to matter.

On returning to Boston, my life settled into a dull, predictable, but comfortable regime for the next decade. I got a job at the law firm of Palmer and Dodge, where I had had one of my co-op jobs. I began practicing very boring but very lucrative corporate law. My son Roger was born in March of that year and we bought a house in Wellesley. I had arrived.

The House Assassination Committee of 1977 concluded that there was probably a conspiracy in the murder of John F. Kennedy and that there was also "probably" a gunman who fired one shot, the fatal one, from the grassy knoll. They did this after such soul searching as not allowing the doctors from Parkland Hospital to see the autopsy pictures from Bethesda Naval Hospital. Containment, not truth, was apparently the overall operating principle. I'm sure Corbin was pleased. Somehow my pictures didn't make it into evidence.

Interest in the Kennedy assassination seemed to die down after that as the country slipped into the somnolent Reagan-Bush years. Introspection was out, acquisition was in. From high tech to real estate, Massachusetts was booming and despite my best intentions, I didn't remain an innocent bystander.

As I dreaded the upcoming November 22nd, 1983, a real scare was thrown into our life. My very pregnant wife was due to deliver our second child on or about that date. Sure enough, she went into labor on the evening of the 22nd. We rushed to the hospital and the contractions got closer and closer together. 11:30 P.M. *Keep your legs crossed, Nancy.*

At 12:14 A.M., on November 23rd, a beautiful green eyed baby girl was born. The spell was broken. Katya had arrived.

As Wall Street soared and the Milkens and Boeskys energized the overextended economy, a new spate of assassination theory books, many of them excellent, started coming out. Jackie Kennedy's cousin, John Davis, fingered Carlos Marcello as the source of the original contract in *Mafia Kingfish* and an attorney named Marc North did the same for J. Edgar Hoover as a leader of the cover-up in *Act of Treason.* Another book which rolled together numerous ideas and studies, named *High Treason*, made the New York Times best seller list for many months. I contrasted these books with the unmitigated crap perpetrated on the country in the '60s such as the Warren Report and *The Death of a President.* Maybe the nation was coming to a point where it was ready to face the whole matter, even though it was twenty five years later. Better late than never.

Lucien even made an appearance from a source other than myself in the excellent English series by Nigel Turner called *The Men who Killed Kennedy.* The Europeans, perhaps because of their detachment, had no illusions about the tragedy. If Corbin or the FBI were actually ever seeking a solution to the mystery, boy, could I have given them some corroborating evidence for that documentary series. In fact, now that I think of it, I did. My mistake was not giving it to Nigel Turner first.

But all in all I was content to live out my petty bourgeois existence in a staid Boston suburb and watch my children grow. The seismic decade and a half between 1963 and 1978 had provided me with more than enough excitement and diversion for a lifetime. I was now content to grapple with the more mundane pleasures of little league, girl scouts and growing a sizable adipose layer around my middle.

I was sitting in my den on the night of January 27th, 1992, unwinding from work with my second vodka tonic and listening to the Mozart retrospective on WCRB. The year 1991 was touted as the Mozart bicentennial and indeed the 27th had been his birthday. What the radio failed to mention was that the bicentennial was for his death which had occurred in 1791, December 5th, to be exact, and not his birth, which had taken place some thirty six years earlier.

Be that as it may, the music that poured from the stereo was pure audio orgasm. *The Posthorn Serenade. The Jupiter Symphony. The piano concertos. The Clarinet Quintet.* F. Murray Abraham had been right. It was the voice of God speaking.

I listened to the voice of God celebrating the Mozart 200th something-or-other, sipping my vodka, with little Katya seated on my lap. She was coloring away at some newly day-glo clown and scat singing to him in a low uneven voice. Peace. A few minutes of unmitigated, unabashed, unencumbered peace. It wasn't natural, nor was it lasting, but it sure was nice when it came.

My reverie was broken by a voice from the kitchen. It was Nancy. "Jake, there's an Agent Goslin on the phone for you. Says it's important."

Goslin? I didn't know any Agent Goslin. In fact, I didn't know any agent anything. Fucking Lefkowitz. Today he was Agent Goslin. Fine, I could play along. I ambled to the phone.

"What's happening, you honky mother. What it be?"

"Excuse me?"

"Gerald?"

"Gerald who?"

"Oh my God, I'm sorry, I thought you were an old friend, Gerald Lefkowitz." I felt about two feet tall. I hoped the guy wasn't from Harvard alumni or the Supreme Court or, God forbid, the Civil Rights Commission. "This is Jake. How can I help you?"

"Jake, I don't know if you remember me, we met years ago, very briefly."

I scratched my memory. No Agent Goslin there. "I'm sorry, Sir, I don't recall."

A pause at the other end.

"Agent Quisling, FBI. I think we're ready for you."

The thing wouldn't die. Just when I had resigned myself to its eternal repression, it started steamrollering again. With a spate of books being spawned for the twenty-fifth anniversary, interest in the assassination was starting to pick up. But I had been too frustrated by the resistance I had met and too unnerved from the weird amalgam of connections I had discovered, to pursue it. If it didn't chase me, I wouldn't chase it.

It was chasing me now. I didn't even have to travel. On a warm Sunday in February, I gazed over a hot cup of espresso at the benign presence of Agent Soren Quisling as we sat in a corner booth of the Coffee Connection in Harvard Square. He had put on a few pounds since I had last seen him fourteen years ago, but then again, so had I. The countenance was still pleasant, smiling, not threatening. He could have passed for a little league coach himself, which in fact, he turned out to be. We compared pictures of our children.

The Kennedy assassination was garnering new interest, Agent Quisling began. Yes, I knew, I agreed. I had seen the books, even heard that Oliver Stone was planning a major movie on it. I was happy. I hope they get their man, I informed Quisling.

"No," said Quisling, "that's not what I mean. Interest is up in the government agencies, resistance is down." The FBI was really in a position for the first time to blow the lid off the case. They were recontacting long suppressed witnesses. I would hopefully, be chief among them.

I eyed Quisling skeptically. I asked him to forgive me if I appeared somewhat cynical. Quisling nodded. He understood. But things were really different.

"What about Corbin?"

"Internal Security Chief Maurice Corbin died of a massive coronary this past October."

"My condolences. What about my pictures and tape?"

"Never saw the light of day. Buried with him, no doubt."

Somehow this didn't surprise me. "Sullivan?"

"Retired. Put out to pasture at his farm in Virginia." Quisling went on to explain that Sullivan was just Corbin's mouth piece anyway, did his dirty work for him. I nodded. That had been my impression at the brief meeting with them many years earlier.

"And you?," I nodded at Quisling.

"I inherited the unit and I plan on doing something about it. You wouldn't believe the kind of stuff that's been brought to us that has just been sat on. Yours was only the tip, albeit an important one, of the iceberg." I could imagine.

"So what do you want with me?"

Quisling stared at me with a glance that indicated the answer should be self evident.

"Well of course, Jake, you still have copies of the photos and tape, don't you?" I nodded that I had.

"And you would be willing to allow the Government to have access to them in pursuing the investigation?" I nodded that I would.

"Well then, Jake, that's what we want from you. And to testify in front of any governmental panels that may be set up to reinvestigate the case." Agent Quisling smiled, a blue twinkle emanating from his eyes.

"That one, Agent Quisling, I'm not so sure about. I'm not a kid anymore. I've got my own family and children to worry about. There's a limit to the amount of jeopardy I want to put myself in."

"I understand." Quisling understood everything. I wondered what he knew about Lucien, Katya, and Kennedy himself. I decided to test him.

"The man in the photos I showed you, did you ever track him down?"

"I never saw those photos again, after Corbin bounced me from his office that day."

"And the birth certificate?" Quisling looked at me as if I were nuts.

"Birth certificate? What birth certificate?" Quisling didn't have a clue. He was being straight with me.

"Never mind. Just some things that came up in my little *tête-à-tête* with Maurice the Hun." Quisling laughed.

"Look, Jake, I know you've been through a lot and would probably like to forget the whole thing. But you, we, owe it to the country not to forget. Of all the people in Dealey Plaza that morning, you probably have more first hand knowledge and evidence of what occurred that day than anybody. Never mind probably. Definitely. Sure, you can sit on it, but isn't that what the Corbins and the Sullivans have been doing for the last twenty eight years? Now we don't have to. Now we can move ahead. We owe it to the country. We owe it to our children."

I interrupted. "What I owe to my children is my continued existence until they're old enough to fend for themselves."

"No, Jake, you're wrong. What you owe to your children is the chance to grow up in a country like the one we were starting to grow up in until it was so rudely snatched away from us. A country where the principles of idealism, fairness and opportunity reign supreme again and the Government is for the people, of the people, and by the people, and not some goddamned insidious and hidden plutocracy calling the shots. A country where the Zuckermans and the Quislings and the Smiths and the Joneses can enjoy their dreams and liberties without having them trampled upon and stashed away by the Corbins of the world. A country..."

Quisling stopped. He looked down into his coffee. "Sorry, Jake, if I got carried away. But that's how I feel. I've just seen such much shit go on. It's not right. And I'm not going to let it continue if I have any say in the matter."

Quisling was right. What were my own petty concerns compared to the opportunity to right a wrong, to help restore the faith of a nation so badly shaken from twenty five years of governmental abuse. Didn't I share the idealism that Quisling spoke about until it was brutally shattered by that day in Dallas and then dragged through the mud for the next fifteen years?

Maybe I could make a difference. Maybe I owed this more to my children than any potential risk I might engender. Maybe the time had come to restore, or at least, attempt to restore, the optimism and hope that the long deceased President had instilled in us. I looked over at Quisling. "When do we start?"

He smiled broadly.

"Well it's not that easy, Jake. We're going to require about a three month period where you go undercover."

"You mean like disappear from the face of the earth?"

"Well, not exactly, but essentially...yes."

"And how do you propose I do that, Agent Quisling?"

"It's not that tough, Jake. We do it all the time. We give you a new identity and papers, and hide you away for a specified period. Then when it's safe, you reappear."

"And what if it's never safe?"

"That's not likely Jake, but nothing is guaranteed. The three months, which we call the incubation period, would be that time immediately preceding and following your testifying, along with the presentation of evidence, to any investigative bodies set up by us. During that time, one of two things will happen. Either the evidence will die of its own accord and you will not be a threat to anybody, or it will blossom into such a large affair that anybody connected with it would be safe just by the notoriety. Like Garrison at the New Orleans trial." I nodded. Quisling continued.

"Before news of that trial came out, while he was investigating, that was the danger period. There were parties that didn't want what he was investigating to come to light for obvious reasons. But once the trial started, nobody in their right mind would think about touching him because to do so would be to virtually admit guilt and be subject to the scrutiny of the national media. Once the trial ended and Shaw was acquitted, everybody could heave a sigh of relief. A discredited Garrison was no longer a threat to anybody, so why bother with him? Revenge is less important than the continuing cover-up and why draw attention to yourself, anyway? No, the only danger period is when the wrong party has knowledge of your intention of presenting potentially damaging facts with the subsequent exposure of those facts to the public. Once the facts are out, you sink or swim with the popular verdict, but if there's a way of avoiding them coming out, then the Corbins and the Hoovers will do everything in their power to have that happen, or as the case may be, not happen."

"And if I testify, won't the world know what I'm doing?"

"No, Jake, all testimony would be taken in private."

"So how would any of the wrong parties know?"

"Because wrong parties usually have a way of knowing. That's what makes them wrong parties. A leak here. A dishonest or bought investigator there. It happens. But it can be minimized. And if we can blow through the initial period, I think your evidence will see the light of day. And once it does, I think it will set off a huge domino effect and let us get to the bottom of this whole stinking, massive affair."

I paused to think. What difference would it make? Hoover and Johnson were dead and so were Traficante and Hoffa. Marcello was a geriatric vegetable rotting away at some Federal penitentiary. Lucien was long dead as well as Ruby and Ferrie. Who cared? So Robert and Giancarlo would drink from prison instead of the Mediterenee? What did it matter?

And yet I thought about those brave witnesses who had come forward and paid with their lives. The Lee Bowers and the Rose Cheramis and the Roger Craigs, all long dead for the sin of being in the wrong place at the wrong time, just like me, but having the strength of character to speak up about it. Didn't we owe their memory something, didn't we owe their courage something?

"What about my family?," I queried.

"What about them?"

"Well, how do I go incognito or whatever, and still maintain contact with them?"

"Well, normally, you don't. That's part of the sacrifice."

This part I didn't like at all. I had an idea. "Agent Quisling..."

"Please, call me Soren."

"Soren, would it be possible for me to have this incubation period between Memorial Day and Labor Day?"

Quisling looked at me, seemingly confused. "Why so, Jake?"

"Because if I'm going to disappear, I prefer to take my family with me."

"You might be unnecessarily jeopardizing them, Jake."

"Perhaps so, but as you say, they sink or swim with me. Besides, I couldn't bear being away from them for three months." Nancy had been bugging me to take a Winnebago tour of the country for a while now and both Roger and Katya were at an age where they could enjoy it. So, there would be a little intrigue thrown in as well. I ran the idea past Quisling.

"An unusual request, to say the least. But we've done weirder before. You would need to wear a disguise, have new papers, avoid popular areas. Your wife would have to alter her appearance and I would suggest that for the children as well. And you would have to travel with a minimum of two agents who stay in your constant companionship. You would also have to be on call twenty four hours a day and prepare to abandon your family at a moment's notice. If you agree to those requirements, I think we can arrange it for you. In fact, we would even cover the charges. But you would have to be careful, very discreet."

"What's my alternative?"

"A fish camp in Wyoming."

"I'll take my chances."

I stood up and shook Quisling's hand. I liked this man. I think I almost trusted him. Nancy would have her Winnebago adventure, though probably not on the terms she had imagined. But like the Army, the government was paying us to see the world, or at least America.

Quisling was as good as his word. The arrangements were made. In the last two weeks of May I provided over seventy hours of uninterrupted testimony complete with photos and tape recordings in front of various different Federal agencies. On May 28th, I flew out to meet my family in Dallas where Nancy had the Winnebago gassed and ready. But first I had one small mission.

It was time to return to Dealey Plaza.

Although it took many years, I have finally figured out my identity. I am the Lee Harvey Oswald of the '90s. I am working with a man named Quisling, for my government, or possibly against it. Quisling will use my efforts to advance a governmental agenda, or perhaps to stifle it, under the guise of advancing it. For my efforts, Quisling is providing me with security or perhaps will let me dangle in the wind, as the situation warrants. I am working with the FBI or possibly as their sacrificial lamb. I have my faith in a man named Quisling. You know what happened the last time that occurred.

For our subterranean venture, Quisling has provided two guardian angels, his brother, Olaf, and Special Agent Ted Wilson. *Olaf and Ted's Excellent Adventure* starring the Zuckerman family of Wellesley, Massachusetts. Roger and Katya are excited but aren't sure exactly who Olaf and Ted are, or what their purpose is. I have tried to sell them on the excellent adventure, but they remain skeptical. Nancy is probably the only woman in America who has dyed her hair from blond to brown and I must admit that the new beard tickles and the wire rims pinch, but I am looking very distinguished. Very distinguished, indeed.

Dallas, where I spent my first eighteen years, is a fading memory. Randy is gone. Bruce Cohen and Lois Hymanson are long gone. My parents are the last white family left on the block. I look at my father, who is seventy, and my mother, who is sixty eight. They are older, but not old. I laugh when I think of the mandatory retirement age of sixty five or seventy. These are vibrant people. I wonder when old age sets in. It sure as hell isn't seventy.

Tomorrow we pick up the Winnebago and load it at a secret Dallas location. Olaf and Ted are at the Holiday Inn. We dine with my parents and talk of the past. Of Harvard and Poppa and even of the assassination. It is a somber but joyous meal, a rare meeting of the past and present. The extended family dispersed around the country, sharing a few precious unhurried moments together before the distance of chance and choice scatter them again. How sad the mobility of post World War II America. The suffocating insularity of the first half of the century has been displaced with a pendulum that has swung too far in the other direction. Just because we can be so mobile, should we be? What price do we pay? As I watch the aging patriarch, Emanuel Zuckerman, bounce the little green eyed Katya on his knee, my heart cries out that this is not a weekly or maybe even a daily occurrence, but a stolen bi-annual pleasure, if that. I remember the soft voice of my grandfather and the tales of the U-Kray-een and weep for what has been lost. Everything changes. Poppa's room used to be down the hall. Now it's 1500 miles away.

I am forty-two years old. I have a beautiful wife, two golden children, a semi-successful, if boring, law practice, a sprouting paunch, and a memory of some of the scariest moments of the century. I guess I've done all right. Roger is ready to ramble. Tomorrow we leave on our excellent adventure with new pals Olaf and Ted.

My old bedroom is just about the way I left it. It looks like it has been caught in a time warp from 1963. The baseball cards and the politicians' pictures taped to the bulletin board, the sports trophies on the desk. Different awards I had won, framed on the wall. And a big picture of Poppa, and another of President Kennedy. It is my mother's monument to me.

The old bunk bed is still there, but on this night some thirty years later, my brother and I are replaced by my children, with Katya winning the coin toss and inheriting the top bunk. She climbs into it and is fast asleep in thirty seconds. I kiss her sweet little forehead and gaze at her golden countenance. My father and I are only the first in a long line of men that this little beauty will have at her beck and call.

Roger has settled into the lower bunk and despite his best efforts to the contrary, has soon joined Katya in never never land. I gaze down at his beautiful peaceful face. He is such a mirror image of me, it's frightening. Baseball and history. Roger loves baseball and history. Except that Stan Musial has been replaced by Wade Boggs and John Kennedy by George

Bush. What a sad diminution, I think. Yet everything changes, everything changes.

I look at my watch. It is Wednesday, May 29th, 1992. It would have been John F. Kennedy's 75th birthday. I look down at Roger. He is thirteen years old, the same age I was when it all happened. I have a mission.

I reach down under the bed and grope around in the dark till I feel it. I crunch halfway under the bed and pull it out, the brother-proof safe. I dial the combination, twice to the left, once to the right and a quarter turn back to the left. Every childhood safe in the world must work like that. I hear the click and open the door. There they are, laying still and in peace as they had been for the last eighteen and a half years. Photos and recordings of the Captain and the fragrant cedar box containing Katya. A Katya above and a Katya below. I take the newly copied birth certificate I had demanded from Quisling and slip it inside. I am on my way to Dealey Plaza.

Twenty eight and a half years. I haven't been back for twenty eight and a half years I think, as I ease my car into the parking lot next to the Depository building. Lee Bowers is looking down at me from the railroad tower and so is Lee Oswald from inside the Depository. A council of Lees staring down from the light of a full moon.

It hasn't changed a bit. It looks as if it was frozen in time. I walk up on the overpass and across Elm to the island of grass in the middle. I hear the roar of the crowd, feel the excitement of the moment. The motorcade is approaching. I cross back over Elm and climb up on the abutment where Poppa and Marilyn and I had stood almost thirty years before. I look up at the Depository. I see Lee Oswald laughing from the southeast corner window. The joke's on me, he seems to say, but it's really on you. I look over my right shoulder and there is the Captain pointing his rifle toward the slow moving vehicle coming into his scope. And there in the vehicle, smiling the smile of a god, is the beautiful man. I want to scream, STOP!, but I am powerless to do so.

A few lonely souls wander the Plaza aimlessly. The golden man glides into the Captain's scope and Lucien squeezes the trigger. The safe clicks as I pull the birth certificate out. Roger doesn't need to be burdened with this. I rip it into a hundred pieces. I open the top of the cedar box and mix the torn up document with the ashes of Katya. I hop off the abutment and proceed slowly to the area beneath the sixth floor's sniper's nest. When I am directly below, I reach into the box of Katya and scatter a few ashes. I look up. Robert and Oswald are smiling down at me. I proceed back in front of the Depository and sprinkle a few ashes on the abutment. I move forward, and when there is a break in the uneven traffic, I cross out to the center lane of Elm Street and scatter a few ashes of Katya in the place where the golden man smiled his last smile. I stare at the lights of the oncoming traffic and quickly step up onto the grassy knoll and duck behind the picket fence. I move over to the place where the Captain had stood and I sit there shivering. I pull a little collapsible shovel from my ruck-sack and unfolding it, stare over the fence.

I had written it down in my will. There would be something in Dealey Plaza, if anybody wanted. It would be a choice and not a burden.

I look over the fence post and then at the Depository. Lee Oswald and Robert are grinning at me from the southeast corner. I peer into the distance at the Dallas County Records building and see the somnolent figure of Giancarlo smiling from the barrel of his leveled rifle. The limousine approaches. I glance at the abutment and see Poppa and myself looking left, transfixed in the euphoria of the approaching motorcade. I pull my rifle from over the picket fence and guide it lovingly to the ground where it miraculously transforms again into the shovel it is. I scoop at the soft earth as the President's car approaches and slowly moves by. The wide ivory smile passes by unharmed and quickly disappears below the underpass. They are late for the luncheon at the Trade Mart.

I cradle my safe and place it into the small burrow I have dug at my feet. I bend down and kiss the top and quickly start shoveling dirt atop of it. I look up at the sky. There are Poppa and Katya and the President all looking down at me and clapping. Clapping and laughing and crying as I bury The Secret of the Century.

About the Author

Roger Levine is a 51 year old Boston based attorney. A long time history buff with a comedic flair, his other works include a *Portnoy-esque* novel, *In Search of the Golden Shiksa* and a travelogue featuring a pilgrimage to each American presidential gravesite (*In Search of the Dead Presidents*). He lives in Canton, Massachusetts, with his wife, two sons, and two cats.

CPSIA information can be obtained at www.ICGtesting.com
Printed in the USA
LVOW091941150812

294458LV00001B/4/A